# THE ROCK FROM WHICH YOU WERE HEWN

# THE ROCK FROM WHICH YOU WERE HEWN

## The Lives and Legacy of Holy Irish Men and Women

*Edited by*

*Dr. Patrick Kenny and Father John S. Hogan*

IGNATIUS PRESS    SAN FRANCISCO

Cover photograph:
*Celtic Cross*
© istock/mammoth

Cover design by: Paweł Cetlinski

# CONTENTS

## Part 2: Irish Men and Women with
## a Reputation for Holiness

# FOREWORD

## Archbishop Eamon Martin
### Archbishop of Armagh and Primate of All Ireland

In his reflection on holiness in today's world, *Gaudete et Exsultate*, Pope Francis helpfully points to the "saints next door" whose exemplary witness to Christ accompanies and encourages us along our own pilgrim way through life. Likewise, Pope Emeritus Benedict XVI described such holy people as "lights of hope", "true stars" who point a way through the darkness and shadows to Jesus Christ, the true light (see *Spe Salvi*, no. 49).

Each one of us is searching for God, on earth, and in Heaven. As the *Catechism* (27) puts it: "the desire for God is written in the human heart." In this beautiful and inspiring volume, *The Rock from Which You Were Hewn*, the editors have brought together a unique collection of "stars" to light our way. From each of the short but vivid pen pictures, the light of holiness shines out in the lives of holy men and women of Ireland. Not all of them are yet on the way to beatification and canonization, but every life story told here can provide nourishment and inspiration for prayer and meditation. The overall impact of the book is to remind us that the Church of Christ is fundamentally holy—a truth well worth keeping before us as we walk our synodal pathway.

The editors and contributors trust that this volume will encourage members of the Church in Ireland at this time. They take their cue from Pope Benedict, who, quoting Isaiah in his 2010 pastoral letter to the Catholics of Ireland, asked us to remember "the rock from which you were hewn". The prophet wrote these words to put fresh heart into the beleaguered Jewish people during their exile in Babylon, surrounded at the time by the trappings and temptations of a powerful foreign culture and already beginning to forget the heritage and faith of their fathers:

> Listen to me, you who pursue righteousness,
>> you who seek the LORD;
> look to the rock from which you were hewn,
>> and to the quarry from which you were dug.
> Look to Abraham your father
>> and to Sarah who bore you;
> for when he was but one I called him,
>> and I blessed him and made him many.
> For the LORD will comfort Zion:
>> he will comfort all her waste places,
> and will make her wilderness like Eden,
>> her desert like the garden of the LORD;
> joy and gladness will be found in her,
> thanksgiving and the voice of song.
>
> (Isaiah 51:1–3)

Readers of *The Rock from Which You Were Hewn* should not expect a comfort blanket to help them "huddle up" together against the storms of an alien culture. I find the book personally challenging, shaking me out of any sense of self-pity or spiritual complacency. These holy men and women did not just sit around! They were people of determination and action, driven by the grace and power of the Holy Spirit to give not less than everything in the service of God. What emerges from each of these vignettes of saintliness is their complete openness to doing God's will, nurtured in a loving relationship that naturally flows out into mission, especially among those living in poverty, isolation, and brokenness. In their "apostleship", they were clearly sustained by the Eucharist, the Word of God, and by prayer— including the Rosary and family devotions. It is also unmissable that, in saying their personal "yes" to God, these "heroes" of virtue themselves found resilience by contemplating the lives of the saints and the "*fiat*" of Our Blessed Mother, Mary.

Any one of these generous and courageous men and women could be nominated as "person of the century" or "person of the millennium" for their contribution to Ireland. Heroes such as these, however, are not seeking any earthly accolade; they are "workers for the Kingdom of God".

Therein lies the challenge of this book—that we, in our own time and circumstances, can be like them, champions of faith. None of us are called to be passive bystanders in the Church. We are to be salt and light for the world, using the talents God gives us to help make a difference. We, too, are called to holiness. We are called to be saints.

Pope Saint Paul VI famously said, "The Church needs her eternal Pentecost; she needs fire in her heart, words on her lips, a glance that is prophetic" (General Audience 11/29/72). I am convinced that the Spirit is already actively at work in Ireland, calling, as in past generations, the "saints next door" and inspiring the charisms that will be needed for a new springtime of growth and abundance in faith. If we are to honor the rock from which we were hewn, then like the holy men and women chronicled here, we in our time and place must accept the challenge to get right out of our comfort zones in the service of something much bigger than ourselves.

I hope especially that the young people of Ireland can be introduced to this book and that these stimulating stories will move their hearts to be alert and open to the Holy Spirit, calling and "gifting" them to be part of the "new springtime" for the Faith in Ireland.

For this we can all pray, in the words of the preface used in the Feast of All the Saints of Ireland:

> God our Father ... you are praised in the company of your Saints and, in crowning their merits, you crown your own gifts.
>
> By their way of life you offer us an example, by communion with them you give us companionship, by their intercession, sure support, so that, encouraged by so great a cloud of witnesses, we may run as victors in the race before us and win with them the imperishable crown of glory, through Christ our Lord. Amen.

# INTRODUCTION

Recent decades have been challenging for the Church in Ireland. The confidence of many members of the faithful has been shattered, while the legacy of the sins of some members of the Church continues to horrify. The crimes of the past need to be atoned for, and we must ensure that they are never repeated.

In 2010, Pope Benedict XVI wrote a letter to the Catholics of Ireland addressing the historic scandals, urging the Church in Ireland to take action, while also calling the faithful's attention to a deeper and more positive legacy that may have been forgotten.

In the opening sections of the letter, Pope Benedict wrote:

> As you take up the challenges of this hour, I ask you to remember "the rock from which you were hewn" (Is 51:1). Reflect upon the generous, often heroic, contributions made by past generations of Irish men and women to the Church and to humanity as a whole, and let this provide the impetus for honest self-examination and a committed programme of ecclesial and individual renewal.[1]

This book is a modest response to Pope Benedict's call to remember our local holy men and women and to seek inspiration from the example of their lives and virtues. Ireland was once known as the land of saints and scholars, but this saintly heritage is not a mere relic of the past. Ireland has a vibrant living tradition of holiness and heroism, extending even up to the present day. While most of our saints date from the first millennium of Christian history, holy Irish men and women have continued to emerge in every century. This book aims to offer a picture of this. In fact, over half of the biographies in this book relate to Irish men and women who died in the twentieth

---

[1] Pastoral Letter of the Holy Father Benedict XVI to the Catholics of Ireland, March 19, 2010, § 2.

century, with two young women, Mary Ann O'Driscoll and Sister Clare Crockett, dying as recently as 2015 and 2016 respectively.

We had four specific aims in preparing this book. The first is to encourage and support those Irish causes that have already been opened. The first part of the book contains a short biography of every Irish person with a currently open and active cause. These are written, in most cases, by the promoters or postulators of the cause. We believe that this is unique—we are unaware of any other book published anywhere in the world that gathers together in one place short biographies on every candidate with an active cause for canonization in a particular country. In order to progress, each of these causes needs a miracle, normally a medical cure certified by doctors as scientifically inexplicable. This can only come about when people develop a devotion to a particular candidate for sainthood and they pray through their intercession for that cure. By highlighting the lives of current candidates for sainthood, we hope that devotion to them will grow, that many will pray for their intercession, and that they will soon successfully conclude with canonization.

Secondly, we wish to draw attention to the lives of certain heroic Irish men and women who show great holiness but for one reason or another do not have an active canonization cause. The second part of the book is concerned with the lives of what we might tentatively call "potential causes". In some cases, there is an active process of discernment that will, hopefully, lead in time to the opening of a cause. Some of these individuals are well known globally and seem to have a persistent and growing reputation for holiness in the Church, for example, Ellen Organ (Little Nellie of Holy God). Others were once held in high esteem, but devotion to them seems to have faded; for example, John McGuinness. Others are as yet relatively unknown, but devotion to them may grow as people learn more about their lives. We have tried to provide examples that could appeal to as wide an audience as possible, but our selection is of course incomplete— there are many others who could easily have been included. It is hard for devotion and a cause to develop without at least some publicity— people cannot learn about, and pray to, someone they have never heard of. We hope that this second section of the book will help spread devotion to the individuals who have been included and that at least some of their causes may be opened in due course. At the very least, their lives and virtues have something valuable to say to all of us today. They deserve not to be forgotten.

Our third hope for the book is that it will be a source of good news for a Church sorely in need of it. We are all familiar with bad news within the Church, but bad examples should be abnormal in the Christian life—they are the exception, not the rule. The saints are those who have followed Christ. Theirs is the normal path we should follow; they show us what it truly means to be a Christian. It is those who were faithful to Christ who show us what Christianity means, not those who denied the Gospel by their crimes. Saints are part of our good news, and we need to re-familiarize ourselves with them and what they have done for our country. Each individual profiled in the book made a positive impact in the time and place in which they lived. Some of them have made significant and ongoing contributions to the benefit of the Irish nation. We need to remember this good news and to communicate it to a skeptical population that has forgotten the positive contribution of the Catholic Church.

Finally, and perhaps most importantly, the saints show us that we, too, can be holy. Too often we hear that the teaching of Christ and the Church cannot be lived, that it sets a standard that the ordinary Christian cannot reach. However, the saints not only teach us; they show us that the Gospel can indeed be lived and that God's grace is poured out upon us in abundance to help us live it. Local saints teach us that the Gospel can be lived where we are, in the place and time we find ourselves. Saints from the distant past, or from distant lands, can at times appear exotic, separated from our experience of life. Local saints remind us that holiness is not exotic; the Gospel is not a charter for other people; it is for us, too.

In his homily at the Chrism Mass on Holy Thursday 2012, Pope Benedict commented on the importance of the saints for our lives:

Perhaps at times the figure of Jesus Christ seems too lofty and too great for us to dare to measure ourselves by him. The Lord knows this. So he has provided "translations" on a scale that is more accessible and closer to us. For this same reason, Saint Paul did not hesitate to say to his communities: Be imitators of me, as I am of Christ. For his disciples, he was a "translation" of Christ's manner of life that they could see and identify with. Ever since Paul's time, history has furnished a constant flow of other such "translations" of Jesus' way into historical figures.... The saints show us how renewal works and how we can place ourselves at its service.[2]

The saints are a source of inspiration for us on our journey. Most famously, Saint Ignatius of Loyola had his own life transformed by reading the lives of the saints. He realized that he, too, could do whatever they did—the divine grace that assisted them was available to him. It is also available to us today. Every single person profiled in this book was an ordinary human sinner, with human weaknesses and defects of character just like us. But they were not complacent in their weakness; they strove for holiness, even in the face of setbacks, persecutions, sickness, and their personal limitations. Pope Francis reiterated this in an address to the Dicastery for the Causes of Saints in December 2019,[3] pointing out that saints are not unreachable human beings, but "people who have experienced the daily toil of existence with its successes and failures, finding in the Lord the strength to always get up and continue the journey."[4] Our greatest hope is that this book will inspire us all to follow their example.

---

[2] https://www.vatican.va/content/benedict-xvi/en/homilies/2012/documents/hf_ben-xvi_hom_20120405_messa-crismale.html.

[3] On June 5, 2022, Pope Francis changed the name of the Congregation for the Causes of Saints to the Dicastery for the Causes of Saints; for the sake of clarity and consistency, the new name will be used in this book.

[4] https://www.vatican.va/content/francesco/en/speeches/2019/december/documents/papa-francesco_20191212_cause-deisanti.html.

# A NOTE ON THE PROCESS
## OF CANONIZATION

The act of canonization is an exercise of papal infallibility.[1] The pope declares that the persons in question lived a life of heroic virtue, that they are worthy of imitation and veneration, and that they are in Heaven. Accordingly, the process of having a person canonized involves a thorough investigation of the person's life and virtue.

The first step on the road to being declared a saint is a very informal one. A reputation for sanctity on the part of a deceased person develops among the faithful. They recognize the holiness of the person's life, and they ask him in prayer to intercede for them in Heaven. Reports of alleged favors through that person's intercession may begin to circulate. If this devotion becomes stronger or persists over time, a petitioner or "actor" may emerge to promote the cause. The petitioner takes charge of the cause, finances it, and appoints a postulator to promote it. The entire procedure can take many decades and considerable financial resources, so in most cases the petitioner is the religious order to which the person belonged or the diocese in which he lived. However, any group (congregation, order, parish, association of the faithful) or even an individual can become the formal petitioner or "actor" for a cause. The Church requires at least five years to have passed after the death of an individual before a cause can be introduced. This allows any emotional enthusiasm following the death of the person either to die away or to mature. However, the pope may waive this five-year restriction; this happened in 2005, when Pope Benedict waived this restriction one month after Pope Saint John Paul II's death.

There are three types of causes: heroic virtues—those who are canonized because of a life of great holiness (for example, Blessed Columba

---

[1] Canonization falls into the fourth kind of teaching, which falls into infallibility. See Ludwig Ott, *Fundamentals of Catholic Theology* (St. Louis, MO: Herder, 1954), p. 297.

Marmion or Blessed John Sullivan); martyrdom, in the case of those who were killed in hatred of the Faith (for example, the seventeen beatified Irish Martyrs and potentially Father James Coyle); and a third type, recently introduced by Pope Francis—the "offer of life" in which a candidate willingly laid down his life as a "martyr of charity".

The first formal step is for the actor to petition officially the local bishop of the diocese in which the person died to open the cause. Having satisfied himself that the person has a genuine reputation for holiness, and subject to the approval of the Dicastery for the Causes of Saints, the cause is then formally opened. At this point, the person is given the title Servant of God. This stage of the process is called the Diocesan Inquiry. The actor appoints a Diocesan Postulator to represent its petition at this stage of the cause. Theologians are appointed to examine the candidate's writings for theological orthodoxy, and evidence is sought to verify if the person lived a life of "heroic virtue", or if he died as a martyr for the Faith or a martyr of charity. Historians are appointed to examine the person's life, circumstances, and the time in which he lived. This will involve collecting testimony from those who knew the Servant of God, if those witnesses are still alive.

Following the Diocesan Inquiry, a Roman Postulator is appointed by the actor and all documents are sent to the Dicastery for the Causes of Saints. An in-depth biography, known as the *Positio*, is produced; this includes an analysis of the candidate's practice of heroic virtue or martyrdom. This document is examined by theologians and historians, and if they agree that the candidate lived a life of heroic virtue or that his death was authentic martyrdom, then the candidate is referred, first, to a meeting of the cardinals and bishops who are members of the Dicastery for the Causes of Saints and, then, to the pope, who, if he assents, signs a decree of heroic virtue or martyrdom. At this point, the person is given the title Venerable. He may be beatified immediately if he was a martyr for the Faith. However, those whose causes fall under the category of heroic virtue or of martyr of charity cannot proceed unless a certified miracle is approved by the Church. The miracle must be found to be physical, instantaneous, lasting, and beyond natural explanation. In the case of healings, the evidence is submitted to a medical board; if the miracle is not a healing but another form of physical intervention, experts in the appropriate area are assembled to examine it. If, having reviewed the evidence, the experts and theologians agree to its supernatural nature, the miracle is referred to the pope. If he recognizes the intervention as a miracle, the candidate can be beatified and is granted the title Blessed. The pope designates a feast day, and liturgical texts are composed. The *memoria* of this new Blessed is usually confined to his local area (diocese or country) and, if a religious, to his congregation.

One further miracle, granted post-beatification, is required before a Blessed can be canonized. Once this second miracle is approved, the candidate can be canonized, being enrolled in the Church's official canon of saints, and public veneration of the new saint is permitted throughout the Church. While many saints from other countries have been formally canonized, only one Irish person (Saint Oliver Plunkett) and one "adopted" Irish person (the Dutch Passionist priest, Saint Charles of Mount Argus) have been canonized in the last 500 years.

Part I

# Causes in Progress

# Blessed Thaddeus McCarthy

## *(1455–1492)*

### *Father John S. Hogan*

On October 24, 1492, an unknown man staggered into a pilgrim's hostel at Borgo Sant'Antonio, outside the Italian alpine town of Ivrea, seeking refuge for the night. The young man, he was only thirty-seven, was dressed in a poor habit, his head covered with a hood; he wore an oyster shell on his clothing, the symbol of the pilgrim and an emblem that guaranteed safe passage. The rector, Father Chabaud, received him with great kindness, but noting the poor man's state, he was concerned for him. Supper was offered, but the man declined and wearily went to his room. The next morning the rector was alerted by servants to a light emanating from under the door of one of the rooms: it was where the pilgrim had spent the night. Entering the room, it was revealed that the light was radiating from the pilgrim who, it was discovered, was now dead.

The rector was distressed. Though the young man wore a peaceful expression on his face, he had died without the sacraments; the bishop was informed, and he came at once. The bishop, Nicolò Garigliati, had had a sleepless night; he had been tormented for hours by a recurring dream in which he saw a bishop he did not know ascending to Heaven. When he arrived to tend to the recently deceased, he was surprised to see the very man he had been dreaming of all night. The man's few possessions were examined—he possessed only a satchel, a pilgrim staff, and a water bottle. When opened, the contents of the satchel revealed who he was. It contained official Church documents attesting that he was Thaddeus McCarthy, an Irish bishop—the Bishop of Cork and Cloyne. Also found in the satchel were an episcopal ring and a pectoral cross.

Bishop Garigliati had Thaddeus' body removed from the inn to be prepared for burial. Dressed in full episcopal regalia, he was laid out in the cathedral of Ivrea for a solemn Requiem Mass, after which he was interred in a tomb befitting a bishop, under the altar of Saint Eusebius. By now the story of the miraculous light had become widely known, and locals were making their way to the tomb of the Irishman to seek his intercession. He had found the door opened to Heaven at Ivrea, they had given him a tomb in their cathedral, now they asked him to help them, and he did; the miracles began. Bishop Garigliati wrote to inform the people of Cork and Cloyne that their bishop had died; as he enquired into the life of Bishop Thaddeus, he discovered a sorry tale.

Thaddeus McCarthy (Tadhg Mac Cárthaigh) was born in 1455 into a noble and powerful family during a time of great unrest in Ireland. Born in Innishannon, Co. Cork, his father was the Lord of Muskerry, and his mother was a Fitzmaurice, the daughter of the Lord of Kerry. The McCarthys had once been kings, but following the Norman invasion, after having held the title for as long as they could, they had been dispossessed in 1395. Despite their deprivation, the McCarthys still stood on their honor, and Thaddeus was accorded a good education, most likely with the Franciscan friars. Not inclined to politics, he heard the call to priesthood and with his family's permission began studies under his uncle Canon Thady McCarthy. He would later travel to Paris, where he continued his preparation for ordination under another relative, Don Raymond, who was a professor at the university. Returning to Cork, he was ordained priest by Bishop William Roche, Bishop of Cork and Cloyne. Sometime afterward, he was sent to Rome.

Thaddeus flourished in Rome; it seems he was working within the papal curia. His qualities soon became apparent to those around him: diligent and capable, with no interest in politics or intrigue, he was recognized as a man of integrity and honor. Prayerful and humble, these qualities could be used to serve the Church and her mission. Among those who took note of this was Pope Sixtus IV, who realized that he would make a good bishop. The opportunity came in 1482, when the pope was informed that the Bishop of Ross, Domhnall Ó Donnobháin, had died. Thaddeus was chosen for the office and was consecrated bishop in the Church of Santo Stefano de Cacco in Rome, on May 3, 1482; though he was only twenty-seven and under the age for episcopal appointment, the pope issued a dispensation to facilitate the consecration.

Within weeks Thaddeus was making his way back to Ireland to be installed. However, when he arrived, he discovered that the Diocese of Ross was not vacant: it had been occupied by Hugh O'Driscoll, who claimed he was the rightful successor of Domhnall, elected and allegedly confirmed by the pope himself. It seemed there had been confusion somewhere, and now there were two bishops of Ross; both, it seems, legitimately appointed. As both men understood themselves to be the true bishop, a serious dispute was about to break out; the McCarthys and O'Driscolls, already old enemies, were lining up for what could be a long and hard battle. In the meantime, Pope Sixtus IV died, and his successor, Innocent VIII, knew nothing about the controversy or either of the disputants; it would fall to him to sort out the mess, and he would have to rely on confused and highly partisan reports to make his decision.

As families and influential figures took sides, and as recriminations were made by both sides, it was Thaddeus who bore the brunt of the dispute. Slanderous and erroneous accusations were hurled against him, and his reputation was destroyed. The young bishop refused to respond in kind and urged his supporters not to engage in violence but to uphold his claim by peaceful means; he himself preferred to turn to God and prayer to find solace and guidance. He took refuge in the Cistercian Abbey at Carrigillihy, under the protection of Bishop Edmund de Courcy of Clogher, and while this brought him some relief, it fueled the row as the Anglo-Normans, who had their own dispute with Bishop de Courcy, entered the fray. Supported by the O'Driscolls, they denounced Thaddeus to Rome. The pope, receiving biased and damaging reports about the young bishop and his "intrusion" into the See of Ross, was led to believe that the accounts were true. In August 1488, Innocent promulgated a papal bull excommunicating Thaddeus and declaring him to be "a son of iniquity".

Thaddeus immediately lodged an appeal, asking the pope to institute a formal enquiry and indicating that he would unreservedly accept the outcome, whatever it would be. Innocent agreed and two years later, on April 21, 1490, he promulgated bulls that revealed the outcome of the investigation. Thaddeus was found to be innocent of the charges made against him, and the excommunication was declared null. It was discovered that Bishop Domhnall had resigned in favor of Hugh O'Driscoll but had died before Hugh's election had been formally approved. However, Hugh was judged to be the rightful Bishop of Ross. As Thaddeus was innocent of seizing the office of bishop and possessed qualities that would be of great service to the Church, he would be appointed to another diocese: that of Cork and Cloyne, upon the death or resignation of the then incumbent, Bishop William Roche. Pope Innocent was prudent enough to issue a bull officially declaring that when the See of Cork and Cloyne was vacated, Thaddeus would be the lawful bishop.

As Hugh O'Driscoll settled down to govern his diocese in peace, Thaddeus left to take possession of Cork and Cloyne armed with the papal bulls; Bishop Roche had freely retired to allow the young bishop to succeed. However, peace would elude him. His enemies, the Anglo-Normans, had already seized the episcopal office with the support of local clans. Taking possession of the cathedral, they refused Thaddeus entry to be installed, and as they controlled the properties and assets of the diocese, the new bishop was homeless and destitute. Though he had the papal bulls to prove his validity, to those who now controlled the diocese not even the pope could decide who would be their bishop. For two years, Thaddeus wandered throughout his diocese trying to gain support for his claim, presenting the papal bulls to convince anyone who would listen. By this time even his own family had abandoned him. He had forbidden them to engage with the O'Driscolls in the last controversy; they now decided he was a lost cause and he could fight for himself. The bishop bore his trials and hardships with serenity and patience.

In the end, Thaddeus realized he would have to go back to the pope. Arriving in Rome in early 1492, he appealed to Innocent for help. The pope was quick to respond; he issued another bull not only recognizing Thaddeus as the legitimate Bishop of Cork and Cloyne, rejecting all other claims, but commanding the most powerful man in Ireland, Gerald, the Earl of Kildare, the premier peer and Lord Deputy of Ireland, to restore what he had taken from the bishop, to protect him and defend his claim, his rights and assets; indeed, Gerald was ordered by the pope to use his army to do so if necessary.

Vindicated, Thaddeus left the city and began his journey back to Ireland. For reasons of security, he dressed as a simple pilgrim and took nothing with him save his satchel with the bulls, his ring, and pectoral cross. It took him fourteen weeks to walk from Rome to Ivrea, north of Turin, and to the hostel at Borgo Sant'Antonio. Already worn down by ten years of controversy—only prayer had sustained him. By the time he arrived at the door of the hostel, his health was broken; his death seemed a natural consequence of his hardships and suffering.

While news of his death was noted, it made no impact on the Irish, though the people of Ivrea, and many others in the years to come, responded with awe and devotion. His tomb became a place of pilgrimage as the example of his holiness and godly serenity and patience touched hearts, and miracles brought healing and hope to the afflicted. In 1742, the tomb was opened and Thaddeus' body was moved to a finer place of rest in the Blessed Sacrament Chapel of the cathedral. The body was moved again later to rest under the High Altar.

Those who came to learn of Thaddeus were touched by the heroic patience that marked his life. Living in an extraordinarily charged political climate, where clans and nobles, whose rights and honor were easily offended, sought any excuse to initiate conflict, he drew back, urging peace and enduring calumny and hardship for the sake of reconciliation and resolution. He still maintained his claim—he believed he was the rightful Bishop of Ross and, in turn, Bishop of Cork and Cloyne, but he would not allow the values of the world or ambition influence how he conducted his case; he put his trust in God. His option for peace and Christian endurance lost him the support of his family and the respect of many in Ireland who saw honor and family rights as paramount values in their society. Such qualities single out this man of God today where honor, pride, and status are as important for many now as in the fifteenth century. Like Jesus, Thaddeus preferred the cross.

In the nineteenth century, Irish Catholics were becoming more aware of Thaddeus McCarthy; this was helped by charitable donations from Ivrea to Ireland during the Famine. Negotiations between the Bishop of Cork and Ross and the Bishop of Ivrea led to the submission of a petition to the Holy See formally requesting his beatification. The Holy See initiated an investigation that lasted two years. On September 14, 1896, Pope Leo XIII enrolled Thaddeus among the *Beati* with his feast to be celebrated on October 25. To date, the cause for his canonization has not yet resumed, though devotion to the one they call "the White Martyr of Munster" continues to this day.

## 2

# The Martyrs of Ireland

## Bishops, Priests, Religious, and Laypeople Who Died for the Catholic Faith

### (1537–1714)

### *Father John S. Hogan*

In March 1915, Pope Benedict XV signed a Commission of Introduction, opening the Cause of Beatification and Canonization for 257 Irish men and women who, it was said, had given their lives for the Catholic Faith between the years 1537 and 1714. This group included people from all walks of life united in their fidelity to the Catholic Faith in a tragic time of great persecution. Leading the group was Archbishop Primate Richard Creagh—Saint Oliver Plunkett's cause had been opened separately in 1886. Archbishops Creagh and Plunkett, and the other shepherds in the group, had urged their brother bishops and priests, religious, and people, to remain true to the Faith, to love those who persecuted them, to forgive, as they died in witness to the sacrifice of Jesus Christ.

Martyrdom is the supreme act of witness a Christian can make to Christ and the Faith. The story of Christianity is, for a great part, the story of martyrdom as men and women, enlivened by their faith, unite themselves with Christ in his sacrifice. A martyr is one who has been objectively judged to have been killed *in odium fidei*—in hatred of the Faith. Saint Augustine teaches "It is not the torture, but the cause that makes the martyr"; the form of death, then, is secondary in the investigation into the cause of a possible martyr. This means that included among martyrs are not only those who have been actively killed, but those who have died as a direct result of sufferings that had been inflicted upon them for their faith; for example, dying in prison from hardship or neglect. Augustine also notes, "where there is no true faith or charity, there is no true and perfect righteousness"— authentic martyrdom must be accompanied by charity, manifested most potently in forgiveness. The Church sees the martyr as another Christ, and so, if they are to reflect the sacrifice of Christ in their death, they must also reflect his oblation and pardon.

The history of Ireland has been a vexed one. Over the centuries, numerous conflicts have claimed innocent lives. Despite this, it has been noted many times that from the time of Saint Patrick to the Reformation, few Irish had been forced to shed their blood for the Christian Faith, and none on Irish soil. That would change in 1533, when Henry VIII broke with Rome so he could annul his valid marriage to Katherine of Aragon to marry Anne Boleyn; as England and Wales had to conform to a new religious entity, so too Ireland. Political matters aside, however, the Catholic Faith meant too much to the men and women of Ireland; they were not inclined to abandon it to appease Henry.

In the centuries that followed, as Irish men and women refused to conform and the clergy continued their ministry, often at the risk of their lives, the question of religious reform was merged with that of loyalty to the Crown. While there were those in Ireland who wanted freedom from the English Crown and their Catholic Faith was an issue, there were those who preferred not to mix politics with their deeply held faith, as there were others who were prepared to accept an English Crown while remaining faithful to their Catholic religion. The authorities did not see it that way, nor could they see that those who rebelled against the Crown should not also be made to answer for their religion. Many times, those captured in rebellions were interrogated with regard to their Catholic Faith, and it was their refusal to adhere to the new religion that was often the greater cause for concern for the authorities and led to their condemnation and execution. This has created a problem that has to be overcome when examining the cause of Irish martyrs—politics and faith have to be separated.

The first martyr of the Reformation in Ireland is believed to be the Venerable John Travers, priest and Chancellor of Saint Patrick's

Cathedral in Dublin. An Englishman, he was appointed to the office in 1533/4 and had written a book in support of the supremacy of the pope. Captured following Silken Thomas' revolt, he was hanged, drawn, and quartered in Dublin perhaps at the end of July 1535. His cause was introduced with the English martyrs and declared Venerable. In the following years, two communities of Trinitarians, in Adare and Dublin, were put to death in 1539 for their faith, as were members of communities of Franciscans in Monaghan in 1540 and Cistercians in Dublin in 1541. With these atrocities the official persecution of Irish Catholics was underway.

At first, persecution was sporadic—with Catholics being the majority on the island, they did not suffer as much as their English and Welsh confreres. However, in the 1570s the situation intensified, and over the next century numerous Catholics were martyred in various circumstances. Bishops, priests, and religious were put on trial and executed either by hanging or by the more dreadful hanging, drawing, and quartering—the sentence for treason. Laymen were most often hanged or perished in prison, as were some women. Others were killed during sectarian massacres, as in the case of those martyred by Oliver Cromwell.

Given the limited scope of this chapter, it is not possible to offer an in-depth examination of all the martyrs. In reality, the exact number of those who died for their Catholic Faith in Ireland is unknown. The cause introduced in 1915 concerned individuals who could be verified as having died for the Faith. This list had taken centuries to compile as various difficulties had prevented the collation of materials required to establish names and accounts of alleged martyrdom. An initial list of candidates drawn up consisted of 460 reputed cases; that number was reduced to 292 that could be verified and relied upon. By 1915, 257 alleged martyrs were chosen to be put forward, but three more were added by the time the Apostolic Process opened in Dublin in 1917. Various factors, however, would delay the cause, though Archbishop Oliver Plunkett proceeded as an individual cause to canonization in 1975. Examining the difficulties with such a large group, it was decided to select a number of the most verifiable candidates to form a group representing all states of life. This cause, consisting of seventeen individuals, proceeded and advanced to beatification in 1992. A further forty-two, headed by Archbishop Richard

Creagh, were also selected, and this cause is now being investigated. This chapter will confine itself to presenting the martyrs from these two causes.

Most prominent among these martyrs are Richard Creagh of Armagh and Blessed Dermot O'Hurley of Cashel. Archbishop Creagh was an early casualty of the Reformation, spending almost twenty years imprisoned in the Tower of London and dying from his sufferings in 1585. He had earned the ire of the Irish chieftain, Shane O'Neill, for his loyalty to the English Crown: O'Neill burned down the Armagh cathedral in anger at the archbishop's refusal to engage in rebellion. When Richard was arrested and interrogated, it was obvious that he was being persecuted for his faith. His death may have been due to hardship, or he may have been poisoned. Richard was an extraordinary noble man, and, as primate, his refusal to conform to Queen Elizabeth's religious settlement presented serious problems to the reformers, and though he had to be dealt with, they feared the outcome of a public execution.

Blessed Dermot O'Hurley, Archbishop of Cashel, a Tipperary man, never thought he would be destined for holy orders. He worked as a lay academic in universities in Louvain, Reims, and Rome as a professor of law. Though a layman, in 1581 Pope Gregory XIII asked him to accept the office of Archbishop of Cashel. Dermot was known as a fine scholar and as a man of profound faith, but he was in middle age and the idea of leaving his settled life to return to Ireland to live as a fugitive in the midst of persecution would be difficult. However, he consented and was ordained deacon, priest, and archbishop in Rome. He arrived in Ireland in 1583, made his way to his diocese, and started to minister with great ability in difficult circumstances; but by now he was a wanted man. Thomas Fleming, Baron Slane, had been arrested for harboring the archbishop during a visit in 1583; he had called on Dermot to help him, and he responded, knowing it might cost him his freedom. He was immediately imprisoned in Dublin Castle and subjected to the most horrendous torture. He was hanged on Hoggen Green, now College Green, on June 20, 1584.

The sufferings of these two archbishops were repeated in the bishops, priests, and religious who are among the candidates in these causes. The earliest of the martyrs in these groups is Edmund Daniel, a Jesuit cleric, who was hanged, drawn, and quartered in Cork in 1572; he had dedicated his ministry to providing education for Catholic children. Of the other Jesuits, most notable is Blessed Dominic Collins, a Jesuit lay brother, martyred in Youghal in 1602; he had been catering to the spiritual needs of Irish soldiers during the Battle of Kinsale. The Jesuit priests in the groups are William Boyton, killed for his faith during the massacre at Cashel in 1674, and John Bathe, martyred during Cromwell's massacre at Drogheda in 1649.

A number of Franciscans are included in the two causes. Prominent among them are two Franciscan bishops: Blessed Patrick Healy, Bishop of Mayo, hanged in 1579, and Blessed Conor O'Devany, Bishop of Down and Connor, hanged, drawn, and quartered in Dublin in 1612. Friars Blesseds Conn O'Rourke and John Kearney, martyred by hanging in 1579 and 1653 respectively, are included in the seventeen; and among the forty-two, there are six friars. Dominicans are also present. Blessed Terence Albert O'Brien, Bishop of Emly, hanged and beheaded in Limerick in 1651, leads a group of eight Dominicans among whom is the prior of Naas, Blessed Peter O'Higgins, hanged in 1642. There are two Augustinians: Blessed William Tirry, martyred in Cork in 1654, and Peter Taaffe, who perished in Drogheda in 1649. One Carmelite completes the band of mendicants, professed cleric Angelus of Saint Joseph. Born George Halley in Herefordshire in England, he joined the Discalced Carmelites in Ireland and was living in Drogheda when persecution broke out. He was shot and beheaded at Syddan Castle, near Lobinstown, Co. Meath, in 1642.

As in England and Wales, the monasteries in Ireland were targeted by the authorities, not only for their assets, but, given their reputation for holiness, either to force conformity or to destroy them. Three monks from these abbeys are numbered among the forty-two. Gelasius O'Cullinan, Cistercian Abbot of Boyle, leads this little group. When the abbey of Boyle was seized, he was in France but came back to Ireland to restore it and was created Abbot. However, his determination to renew religious life led to his arrest and execution in 1580. His fellow Cistercian in the group is Luke Bergin, a priest martyred in Wexford in 1655. Martyred with Gelasius was the third monk, Eoin O'Mulkern, the Norbertine Abbot of Holy Trinity Abbey at Lough Key.

Twelve secular priests are among the martyrs, two have been beatified: Blessed Maurice MacKenraghty, who was chaplain to the Earl
of Desmond and captured following the revolt; he was hanged and
beheaded at Clonmel in 1585; and Blessed Patrick O'Loughran, a
priest from County Tyrone; he died with Blessed Conor O'Devany
in 1612. Among the forty-two are: Maurice Eustace, martyred following the unsuccessful Baltinglass rebellion in 1581—he was betrayed
for renouncing his father's ambitions for him and being secretly
ordained a priest; Brian O'Carolan, a priest of the Diocese of Meath,
hanged in Trim in 1606; Donough O'Cready, a priest of Down and
Connor, martyred in Coleraine in 1608; Thomas Bathe, of the Archdiocese of Armagh and Conor McCarthy of Kerry, hanged together
in Killarney in 1653; and Wexford martyrs Donal Breen and James
Murphy, priests of the Diocese of Ferns, hanged in 1655. Three of
these twelve were priests of the Archdiocese of Cashel who were
killed in the assault on Cashel in September 1647. Edward Stapleton
and Thomas Morrissey perished in the massacre, while Theobald Stapleton, a renowned scholar of the Irish language, was martyred in the
cathedral in Cashel. As he was offering Mass and distributing Holy
Communion, the forces of Lord Inchiquin breached the building,
and he was stabbed to death in the sanctuary.

These two causes of Irish martyrs include a number of laypeople,
testifying to the fact that many ordinary Irish men and women gave
their lives for the Faith in those years. Six individuals have already
been beatified: Blessed Margaret Ball, Blessed Francis Taylor, Blessed
Matthew Lambert, and the three Blessed Sailors of Wexford. A further twelve are being proposed among the forty-two.

The most renowned of these lay martyrs, indeed of all the martyrs,
given the history of veneration, is Blessed Margaret Ball. Born in
Meath in 1515, she married Bartholomew Ball, a Dublin merchant,
in 1530. As the wife of a wealthy merchant who was also elected
Lord Mayor of Dublin, Margaret was a prominent citizen; she was
also a devout Catholic. As soon as persecution began, she set up a
center for Mass in her home, protected and provided for bishops
and priests, and became an evangelical force within the city. This
brought her to the attention of the authorities, and though she was
arrested several times, she was feared because of her reputation for
charity and goodness. It was her son, Walter, a convinced Protestant,

who would be the cause of her downfall. When he was elected Lord Mayor in 1581, he had his mother arrested and imprisoned in a dank cell in Dublin Castle: only when she adhered to the new religion would she be set free. She refused to conform and died about three years later from her sufferings. The merchant Blessed Francis Taylor shared a similar fate. A former Lord Mayor of Dublin himself, and married to Blessed Margaret's granddaughter, Francis refused to embrace the new religion. In 1613, he too was imprisoned in Dublin Castle. It took seven years for the deprivations and sufferings to kill him; he died in January 1621.

The Wexford martyrs share Blessed Margaret's fame. These four men—a baker, Blessed Matthew Lambert, and three sailors—are acknowledged to have been pious men—not an appellation usually applied to sailors, Blesseds Patrick Cavanagh, Edward Cheevers, and Robert Myler appear to have been extraordinary. These four worked with others to help persecuted priests escape from Ireland. When they were caught, their simple faith and goodness became all too obvious at their trial, and they were condemned to hang on July 5, 1581.

A similar group of laymen was martyred in Dublin in November 1581 and June 1583; these had been captured following the rebellion of Viscount Baltinglass. That rebellion had been religious in nature, and upon capture these men were condemned for their Faith as much as for their part in the rebellion. They were David Sutton and his brother John; Thomas Eustace and his son, Christopher; William Wogan, the Esquire of Rathcoffey; Robert Scurlock and Robert Fitzgerald; the priest Maurice Eustace shared the gallows with them in 1581. Walter Eustace would later join them in martyrdom in 1583.

A prominent nobleman among the forty-two martyrs is Sir John Bourke of Brittas. He was a devout man, a member of the Dominican Confraternity of the Holy Rosary, and while no rebel, he refused to submit to the new religion. He was betrayed by his relations, who alerted the authorities to a Mass being offered in Brittas Castle. Sir John sealed the building and refused to surrender the priest. The castle was put under siege, but he escaped to Waterford to find a boat to Spain. Captured before he could flee, he remained steadfast in his faith and was hanged in Limerick in 1607.

Two women are included in the forty-two, Elizabeth Kearney and a woman known only as Margaret of Cashel. They were massacred in

Cashel on September 13, 1647. These pious women were slaughtered with about a thousand others, but their names have been preserved as having shed their blood for their Catholic Faith. Elizabeth is the mother of the Franciscan martyr Blessed John Kearney in the group of seventeen. Margaret was particularly heroic. A Dominican tertiary, she had escaped the massacre but came back to the scene to look for survivors and to see if she could find her spiritual director, Father Richard Barry, O.P. She was discovered by Inchiquin's men and put to death.

Given that emigration is an important part of Ireland's history, it too is reflected in the martyrdom of Ireland following the Reformation. Among the beatified English and Welsh martyrs are six individuals of Irish birth or descent. Three are Irishmen who emigrated to find work in England. Blessed John Roche, a Dubliner, worked as a boatman on the Thames in London. He was a friend and ally of Saint Margaret Ward in her work of helping priests. The two were captured following their successful attempt to help a priest escape from the Bridewell. The two were hanged with several others in 1588. Blessed John was beatified in 1929 and with him two other Dubliners, Blesseds John Terence Carey and Patrick Salmon; they had also emigrated to England and found work as servants in the household of Catholic nobleman Blessed Thomas Bosgrave. Their employer was arrested for protecting a priest, and as he was condemned to be hanged in Dorchester in 1594, as devout Catholics they shared his fate.

Two priests, Blesseds John Cornelius and Ralph Corby have connections with Ireland. Blessed John was born in Cornwall of Irish parents. Ordained priest, he served as chaplain to the noble Arundell family. He was the priest Blessed Thomas Borgrave tried to protect; he was martyred for his priesthood with the nobleman and his servants in Dorchester. Blessed Ralph Corby was born in Dublin of English parents who returned to the north of England while he was still a child. He joined the Jesuits, was ordained, and served on the English mission for twelve years before capture and execution in 1644. Perhaps one of the most tragic cases was Blessed Charles Meehan. Born in Ireland, he joined the Franciscans and was ordained in Rome. He was on his way back to Ireland when he was shipwrecked off the coast of Wales. He was arrested and put on trial for priesthood;

he was hanged in Ruthin in 1679. He was beatified among the eighty-five martyrs of England and Wales in 1987.

Following their beatification in 1992, the cause of the seventeen has not advanced as of yet; the cause of the forty-two is proceeding. It had been suggested by an earlier postulator of the cause, Monsignor John Hanley, that when the latter group is beatified, the two could be combined into one group and a miracle through their joint intercession sought to advance them to canonization. The remaining martyrs may be investigated in the future and new processes opened. In the meantime, the heroism of these ordinary Irish men and women serves as an example of fidelity and reconciliation to the Church in Ireland.

## The Lists of Martyrs

Blessed Dermot O'Hurley and Sixteen Companions
(The Seventeen Irish Martyrs)
Beatified 1992

Blessed Patrick O'Healy, Franciscan Bishop of Mayo,
Blessed Conn O'Rourke, Franciscan priest,
    Both hanged on August 31, 1579, in Killmallock, Co. Limerick.

Blessed Matthew Lambert, Layman and Baker,
Blessed Patrick Cavanagh, Layman and Sailor,
Blessed Edward Cheevers, Layman and Sailor,
Blessed Robert Myler, Layman and Sailor,
    All four hanged with unknown companions on July 5, 1581, in Wexford.
Blessed Margaret Bermingham Ball, Laywoman,
    Died of her sufferings in Dublin Castle in 1584 after three years of imprisonment.
Blessed Dermot O'Hurley, Bishop of Cashel,
    Hanged after torture on Hoggen Green (Saint Stephen's Green), Dublin, June 20, 1584.
Blessed Maurice MacKenraghty, Priest and Chaplain to the Earl of Desmond,
    Hanged and beheaded at Clonmel, April 20, 1585.

Blessed Dominic Collins, Jesuit Lay Brother, Youghal, Co. Cork,
  Hanged in Youghal, Co. Cork, October 31, 1602.
Blessed Conor O'Devany, Franciscan Bishop of Down & Connor,
Blessed Patrick O'Loughran, Priest from County Tyrone,
  Both hanged, drawn, and quartered in Dublin, February 11,
    1612.
Blessed Francis Taylor, Layman and former Mayor of Dublin,
  Died of his sufferings in Dublin Castle in 1621 after seven years
    of imprisonment.
Blessed Peter O'Higgins, O.P., Prior of Naas,
  Hanged in Dublin, March 23, 1642.
Blessed Terence Albert O'Brien, O.P., Bishop of Emly,
  Hanged and beheaded in Limerick, October 30, 1651.
Blessed John Kearney, Franciscan Prior of Cashel,
  Hanged in Clonmel, March 11, 1653.
Blessed William Tirry, Augustinian Priest,
  Hanged in Clonmel, May 12, 1654.


### The Servants of God
### Archbishop Richard Creagh and Forty-One Companions
### (The Forty-Two Irish Martyrs)

Cause advancing.

Edmund Daniel, Professed Jesuit Cleric,
  Hanged, drawn, and quartered in Cork, October 25, 1572.
Teige O'Daly, Franciscan Priest,
  Hanged, drawn, and quartered in Limerick, in March 1578.
Donal O'Neylon, Franciscan Priest,
  Thrown from the town gate and torn to pieces in Youghal, March
    28, 1580.
Gelasius O'Cullinan, Cistercian Abbot of Boyle,
Eoin O'Mulkern, Norbertine Abbot of Holy Trinity, Lough Key,
  Both hanged in Dublin, November 21, 1580.
Maurice Eustace, Priest,
David Sutton, Layman,
John Sutton, Layman,
Thomas Eustace, Layman,
Christopher Eustace, Layman,

William Wogan, Layman,
Robert Scurlock, Layman,
Robert Fitzgerald, Layman,
  Hanged in Dublin, November 13, 1581.
Felim O'Hara, Franciscan Lay Brother,
  Strangled at the altar at the Franciscan friary church in Moyne, Cork, May 1, 1582.
Walter Eustace, Layman,
  Hanged in Dublin, June 14, 1583.
Richard Creagh, Archbishop of Armagh,
  Died of his sufferings in the Tower of London after nineteen years of imprisonment, late 1586.
Brian O'Carolan, Priest of the Diocese of Meath,
  Hanged at Trim, March 24, 1606.
Sir John Bourke of Brittas, Layman,
  Hanged in Limerick, December 20, 1606.
Donough McCready, Priest of the Diocese of Down and Connor,
  Hanged at Coleraine around August 5, 1608.
Angelus of Saint Joseph (George Halley), Discalced Carmelite cleric,
  Shot and beheaded at Syddan Castle, near Lobinstown, Co. Meath, August 15, 1642.
Theobald Stapleton, Priest of the Diocese of Cashel, Chancellor of the Diocese,
  Stabbed while administering Holy Communion at Mass in the cathedral in Cashel, September 13, 1647.
Edward Stapleton, Priest of the Diocese of Cashel,
Thomas Morrissey, Priest of the Diocese of Cashel,
Richard Barry, Dominican Priest,
Richard Butler, Franciscan Priest,
James Saul, Franciscan Brother,
William Boyton, Jesuit Priest,
Elizabeth Kearney, Laywoman,
Margaret "of Cashel", Laywoman,
  All eight massacred among a thousand people at Cashel, September 13, 1647.
Laurence O'Ferrall, Dominican Priest,
Bernard O'Ferrall, Dominican Priest,
  Hanged in Longford, February/March 1649.
John Bathe, Jesuit Priest,

Thomas Bathe, Priest of the Archdiocese of Armagh,
Peter Taaffe, Augustinian Priest,
Dominic Dillon, Dominican Priest,
Richard Oveton, Dominican Priest,
    Massacred in Drogheda, September 11, 1649.
Conor McCarthy, Priest of the Diocese of Kerry,
    Hanged in Killarney, June 5, 1653.
Francis O'Sullivan, Franciscan Priest,
    Beheaded by the sword on Scariff Island, Kerry, June 23, 1653.
Thaddeus Moriarty, Dominican Priest,
    Hanged in Killarney, October 15, 1653.
Donal Breen, Priest of the Diocese of Ferns,
James Murphy, Priest of the Diocese of Ferns,
Luke Bergin, Cistercian Priest,
    Hanged in Wexford, April 14, 1655.

### Irish Martyrs among the English and Welsh Causes

Blessed John Roche, Layman,
    Hanged at Tyburn, London, August 30, 1588. Beatified in 1929.
Blessed John Cornelius, Priest,
    Hanged, drawn, and quartered at Dorchester, Dorset, July 4, 1594.
    Beatified in 1929.
Blessed John Terence Carey, Layman,
Blessed Patrick Salmon, Layman,
    Both hanged at Dorchester, Dorset, July 4, 1594. Beatified in 1929.
Blessed Ralph Corby, Jesuit Priest,
    Hanged, drawn, and quartered at Tyburn, London, September 7,
    1644. Beatified in 1929.
Blessed Charles Meehan, Franciscan Priest,
    Hanged in Ruthin, Denbighshire in Wales, August 12, 1679.
    Beatified in 1987.

3

# The Servant of God
# Father John Meagh

## (1598/1600–1639)

### Priest and Martyr, *uti fertur*[1]

### *Patrick Corkery, S.J.*

In the midst of a war zone, an old Jesuit priest lived among a war-torn population, most of whom did not share his faith. This did not deter the old man, who remained present and available to assist all who called on him. He provided food and medical help to those who needed it and was a symbol of peace in a country torn by war. When a group of fundamentalists came to his town and demanded that he leave, the priest refused. The fundamentalists decided that his disobedience demanded a challenge. They had warned him once and saw no reason for further negotiation; the old man was beheaded. His crime, remaining with the people he had served for over thirty years.

The priest was Father Frans van der Lugt, and his martyrdom occurred in 2014, relatively recently.[2] Why mention this story in a chapter about an Irish martyr? It is important to realize that even though many of those we read about in this book existed outside of our lifetimes, those who hold to the Catholic Faith will face opponents in every generation. In some cases, they may even pay the

---

[1] "*Uti fertur*", from Latin, "as it is reported": a designation given to those who are reputed to have been martyred, but, as yet, the Church has not formally declared it.

[2] The cause for Father van der Lugt's beatification has been opened.

ultimate price for their fidelity. Father van der Lugt's story has existed throughout the history of Christianity from the early Church. Since its foundation in 1540, the Society of Jesus has offered numerous martyrs for the Faith, many of whom, like Father van der Lugt, were missionaries in foreign lands.

One of those who share in this long history of Jesuit martyrs was Father John Meagh, an Irish Jesuit. Father Meagh was born in Cork in either 1598 or 1600. Little is known of his childhood, but at some point in his late teens or early adulthood he and his father were forced to flee to the continent due to disagreements with Ireland's English authorities. Arriving first in France, they made their way to Naples. When his father died, he entered the service of the Duke of Osuna, Viceroy of Naples. Mercenary life was not uncommon among Irish Catholics in exile during this period. He never settled into court life; he had begun to examine his life seriously and became dissatisfied with the frivolity of a courtier's existence. In some ways, his experience paralleled that of Saint Ignatius of Loyola. Like Saint Ignatius, Father Meagh began his life in the worldly service of a nobleman. Also, like Saint Ignatius, he turned to spiritual reading, and he drew great fruit from a book on the life and martyrdom of Saint Dymphna.

At this time, Father Meagh felt destined to enter religious life and decided to leave the courtly world behind. James B. Stephenson tells us in a document in the Jesuit archives:

> During his preparations to enter religious life, he was wrongly accused and cast into prison. Observing therein a statue of Saint Ignatius, he recalled how that saint had also been wrongfully imprisoned. He invoked him and soon after was set free. His devotion led him to visit Rome during the Jubilee, and there he met with an accident, seriously injuring his leg. The Jesuit Fathers kindly received him into their house, and recalling that Saint Ignatius had also been injured in the leg, he came to the conclusion that he was called to the Society.[3]

Again, there are interesting parallels between Father Meagh and Saint Ignatius. Both experienced wrongful imprisonment and leg injuries that changed the course of their lives. While we have limited

---

[3] James B. Stephenson, S.J., *Irish Province Menologies* (Dublin: Jesuit Archives, 1973).

information on Meagh's incarceration, we know Ignatius was imprisoned for suspected heresy, charges that were investigated and found to be baseless. Saint Ignatius suffered a severe leg wound at the Battle of Pamplona in 1521; he was struck by a cannonball, which left him bedridden for nine months. He used his time in bed to study the life of Christ and the saints. His reading inspired him to abandon his career as a courtier and embark on a spiritual journey. Father Meagh's leg injury was similarly transformative, leading him to join the Society of Jesus. He applied and was admitted in Naples in 1625.

Entering the novitiate would have been a dramatic change for Father Meagh. The life of the former courtier would have been reduced to a slower pace. Manual labor and prayer became part of his daily routine. He could have found himself spending time in a hospital working with the sick and dying, a practice encouraged by Saint Ignatius for Jesuits. The mainstay of his novitiate experience would have been undertaking the *Spiritual Exercises*. These were meditations composed by Saint Ignatius during his time in Manresa and were most commonly undertaken over thirty days. It is likely Meagh would have received the *Exercises* via a series of lectures by the novice master, who would deliver the relevant points of prayer for each session. The novice, operating in silence, was required to pray with these points and draw himself more intentionally into the life, death, and Resurrection of Jesus. Saint Ignatius' intention with the *Spiritual Exercises* was not just to familiarize retreatants with the person of Christ but to discern concretely how they were being called to serve Christ in the world. No notes exist from Father Meagh's experience of the *Spiritual Exercises*; one can only imagine how formative they were in preparing him for life as a Jesuit. After First Vows, he embarked on priestly studies that took him to various locations including the Gregorian College in Rome. It is likely that he was ordained around 1628 in Naples, and from there he went to Austria.

Life was not completely without turmoil, though; Father Meagh encountered some problems within his family at this point in his life. His niece's marriage had collapsed due to her husband's mental illness. Father Meagh managed to assist her as she sought to enter a convent. This did not sit well with the woman's husband, who tried to slander and attack Father Meagh's character. These attempts failed, and with the Queen of Hungary's help, his niece found some security. The fact that his niece was being aided by royalty gives us some idea of how influential his family must have been in European circles. We are also told he inherited some money that he put toward founding an Irish Jesuit house in Austria.

The plan for an Irish Jesuit House in Austria would have been common in this period due to the persecution of Catholics and Jesuits. An edict issued by English authorities in Ireland in 1604 railed against the Society, which had begun to make incursions into the country's faith life since Father David Woulfe, S.J., began his mission in 1560. High levels of suspicion among the authorities led to the Jesuits having large bounties placed on them compared to other clergy and religious orders. A captured Jesuit was worth £10 ($13); other priests captured were priced at £5 ($6). As a result of this persecution, the Irish Jesuit mission remained relatively small and existed mostly underground. Protection by some of the Norman lords in Munster allowed them to have relatively fruitful apostolates in Tipperary, Limerick, and Waterford. As Jesuits were educated and formed on the continent, the more academically gifted students were retained for staff schools in continental Europe rather than being returned to serve the Irish mission.

Father Meagh was among those destined to return to Ireland to assist the apostolates that the Jesuits were undertaking at the time. These included preaching, the administration of the sacraments, arranging marriages—obtaining dispensations where necessary, and mediating in private disputes. The work involved was bread and butter ministerial work. Given the obstacles faced by Catholicism in Ireland, the academic work that was common among Jesuits was not possible. This meant Father Meagh would have returned to the busy pastoral work of a priest. These plans, however, were cut short by violent events that engulfed continental Europe.

From 1618 to 1648, the Thirty Years' War devastated central Europe. It is estimated that eight million people died in what is now Germany due to the war. The war was fought mainly between Lutheran German princes disputing the authority of the Catholic Holy Roman Emperor. The intrusion of other powers like France and Sweden helped spread the war to other parts of Europe. During this period, Father Meagh found himself in Bohemia (the modern-day Czech Republic). Bohemia had a long history of being open to ideas of church reform. The reformer, Jan Hus, even had some success before Martin Luther issued his protest, so this territory was ripe for Protestantism. It was in this hostile climate that Father Meagh found himself in 1639. Information on his ministerial life is limited; what we do know is recorded with limited detail by Father Francis Finegan: "While in Vienna he was allowed by the General to serve as a Military Chaplain in the Imperial Army until he could go to Ireland. When he was asked to go, his Colonel refused to part with him, and over the next four years he was stationed mostly at Prague, but he saw service also in Pomerania and Saxony."[4]

The year 1639 also marked a change in the Irish Mission. There was a growing demand for an Irish novitiate, and the Mission Superior wanted Irish Jesuits on the continent to return and minister in Ireland. Permission was given for Father Meagh to return to Ireland, and plans were well underway for him to go home when he met his martyrdom. The Swedish incursion into Bohemia had alarmed the Jesuits, so a decision was made to move to the relative safety of their college in Guttenberg. On May 31, 1639, as he was traveling from Bohemia to Ireland via Guttenburg, Father Meagh was captured by Swedish troops. His captors were hostile to Catholicism and had a great disdain for Jesuits in particular. While we do not know the circumstances that led to his death, we know that the Swedish soldiers killed Father Meagh by shooting him in the chest.

While the manner of his death merits notice, it would seem Father Meagh led an exemplary life as a Jesuit and in his priestly ministry. One account suggests that he had even foreseen his eventual martyrdom. Notes in Jesuit archives of the Irish province preserve what his colleagues thought of him:

A man of very great zeal, and some with pious curiosity took notice of him while celebrating the sacred mysteries, and because they had observed his devotion, they assisted attentively at his Mass. With externs his conversation was of God, and he spoke with such unction and if permissible they would enjoy his conversation a whole day without weariness. He was much grieved when required to speak of common subjects. Known for his integrity of life and spirit of prayer.[5]

---

[4] Francis Finegan, S.J., General Notes, Jesuit Archives, Dublin.
[5] *Jesuit Irish Province Notes*, Jesuit Archives, Dublin.

While no major work of Father Meagh's life exists, his public life and ministry mirrored that of many Jesuits in the sixteenth and seventeenth centuries. A strong love of the Church marked them, and, like Saint Ignatius, they were motivated with a zeal to "help souls". This desire took them to places that were often hostile to them or their message. Whether it was to Elizabethan England or Feudal Japan, Jesuits went knowing that their lives were at risk. They did so because the God they had come to know through Saint Ignatius' *Spiritual Exercises* was worth preaching about, and they sought to bring a greater knowledge of this God to others. Whether it was Father Frans van der Lugt in Syria or Father John Meagh in Bohemia, the fire at the heart of the mission remained the same. It is a fire that continues to call young men to join the Society of Jesus to serve the Church in places where others may not go to be visible witnesses of Christ in the world.

Father John Meagh was one of many Catholics who gave their lives for the Catholic Faith in Bohemia in troubled times. His cause for beatification has been introduced with a number of companions, designated the Martyrs of Bohemia. While the cause is being examined by the Holy See, to date no progress appears to have been made.

# 4

# Venerable Nano Nagle

## (1718–1784)

## Founder

### Sister Elizabeth Maxwell, P.B.V.M.

Nano Nagle was born in Ballygriffin, Co. Cork, the eldest child of Garret and Anne Nagle, in 1718. She had a comfortable upbringing in a Catholic gentry family whose land bordered on the River Blackwater facing the Nagle Mountains. By all accounts, she was a spirited girl who enjoyed riding her pony when she was not attending classes in the nearby hedge school with some of her six siblings. The Penal Laws of the period meant that Catholic schools were not available to Catholic families wishing to educate their children in a faith-filled environment. She was eventually smuggled out of Ireland and sent to join cousins in France, members of the extended Nagle family. Records show that she was most likely educated in the Benedictine Convent in Ypres, which was then a French city. From there she joined her many Nagle cousins in Paris and mingled with the society of the French Court of King Louis XV.

Returning from a ball at the court in her carriage early one morning, she noted a group of people waiting for a church to open to allow them to attend Mass. The contrast between her life of gaiety and the devotion of these people began a period of reflection for Nano that led her to seek to enter a convent where she could pray for the impoverished Irish at home. However, her Jesuit confessor guided her to return home to Ireland and seek to address the lack of educational facilities among her own Catholic people due to the injustice of the Penal Laws.

Nano returned to live in Dublin with her mother and her sister Anne after the death of her father, Garret, in 1746. As most ladies of their station at the time, they were involved in philanthropic work while enjoying the benefits of the cultured society of the capital city. When Nano inquired of her sister Anne where she had placed the bolt of silk that they had brought from France to make some evening gowns, she was dismayed to hear that Anne had sold the silk to alleviate the suffering of some poor people she visited in Dublin. Anne's example was the catalyst for yet another reflective period in Nano's life.

She returned to Cork to live with her brother Joseph and his wife in the city. Appalled by the conditions of the poor children playing on the streets—vulnerable to opportunities to become involved in crime, illiterate and ignorant of their religion, with no prospects whatever of improving their living conditions—she began her work. Surreptiously, without telling her brother or his wife, she rented a little cottage in Cove Lane in Cork City and opened the door to her first school.

Nano was a pioneer in her day. She was creative in circumventing restrictions but discreet in not drawing unwanted attention from the authorities. The Penal Laws were still in force, and penalties for those who flouted them were severe. Her brother Joseph stood to lose his property if her activities were exposed. When he heard about her school through a parent approaching him to have his daughter admitted, he was furious. Luckily, in time, and with the support of his wife, Frances, he came to appreciate the value of what Nano had begun. Eventually she had seven schools across the city; five for girls, two for boys. She employed young women to teach subjects such as reading, writing, arithmetic, and sewing but reserved to herself the instruction in the Catholic Faith. She visited each school daily. School ended at 5 P.M., so she needed a lantern to light her path through the streets in the dark winter months, hence her title "Lady of the Lantern".

As time went on, Nano was faced with the need for "succession planning". She reached out to the Ursuline Sisters in Paris, and a conversation began about making a foundation in Ireland. Eleanor Fitzsimons, an Irish woman, was accepted as a member of the Paris community with that purpose in mind. Nano succeeded in persuading four of the community to come to Cork, and she built a convent for them. She was quietly confident that her enterprise was in good hands because the Ursulines were acknowledged as excellent educators. But it was with great dismay that she learned that the Ursuline nuns, bound by the rule of enclosure, required the students to come to their place of residence for instruction. There was no question that they would be allowed to visit the seven schools across the city.

Nano did not give up. She approached her friend, Bishop Moylan, with a plan to establish a "pious society" of women to continue the work she had begun. He opposed the idea. Undaunted, Nano threatened to go to some other diocese. Seeing her determination, the bishop relented. On Christmas Eve, 1775, Nano and three companions founded the Congregation of Charitable Instruction of the Sacred Heart, later known as the Presentation Sisters. This was the first new congregation to be established in Ireland in over a millennium. The early years of the foundation were difficult due to small numbers of personnel, but news of her work developed and spread. Teresa Mulally, a Dublin woman, became acquainted with Nano and eventually undertook the establishment of the first convent in Dublin in George's Hill, Dublin 7.

Nano's family motto was "Not words but deeds", and she lived it to the full. She was convinced that the alleviation of spiritual and economic poverty would give dignity to the lives of her students. Her primary focus was the formation of the children in the Catholic Faith, as well as the acquisition of knowledge and the development of useful skills that would enhance the ability of the students to make a living later in life.

Nano was a visionary. She laid the foundation for the Irish educational system. In all of this, she was driven by her religious conviction and nourished by her life of prayer. Her vision was global, and her generosity enormous. Her missionary impulse is expressed in her claim that "if I could be of any service in saving souls in any part of the globe, I would willingly do all in my power." By 1800, there were four foundations in Killarney, George's Hill (Dublin), Waterford, and North Presentation, Cork. Over the next fifty years, thirty-five foundations were made in the towns of Ireland, and throughout the nineteenth century her sisters realized her dream of offering "service ... in any part of the globe" by establishing schools in England, Newfoundland, India, Australia, and North America.

Nano's generosity was inspired by her profound faith in Divine Providence, claiming in her letters that "the Almighty is all-sufficient." The practical proof of this was that she was still a laywoman, not yet a nun, when she gave all her inherited wealth to the realization of her dream to help the poor children and deprived families of her time. But her charitable works were multifaceted. She visited the sick and the housebound, built an alms-house for destitute elderly women, and equipped some of her boy pupils bound for the West Indies with religious pictures and material, to serve as missionaries to the Irish seafarers in that part of the world. Her example inspired Edmund Rice, Catherine McAuley, and others to found religious congregations and schools as the political landscape in Ireland improved with Catholic Emancipation in 1829.

Worn out by ill health and exhaustion, Nano died on April 26, 1784. The newspapers of that time paid tribute to her and her contribution to the city and people of Cork. The *Hibernian Chronicle* recorded her death as follows:

> Last Wednesday the indisposition of Miss Nagle was announced in the sorrowing countenances of the poor of this city to whom she was the best of benefactors and patronesses. She died this day about noon and truly indescribable is the extreme of universal lamentation for the departure of a lady possessed of all that merit which for many years rendered her the object of unexampled admiration and acquired her the most unlimited esteem of all ranks of people.

Nano's legacy lived on among the Irish diaspora as convents were founded in Newfoundland, England, the U.S., India, Australia, and Tasmania. Her sisters abroad, faithful to her global vision, longed for her sanctity to be recognized. In 1939, Pope Pius XII referred Nano's cause to the Sacred Congregation for Rites, but World War II prevented further developments in the cause.

In 1979, the Union of Presentation Sisters decided to recommence work on the cause of Nano Nagle, and the *Positio* on her life and virtues was completed in 1994. In 2013, Nano's heroic virtues were officially recognized by the Church, and she was declared Venerable.

If a miracle through her intercession is confirmed by the Dicastery for the Causes of Saints, she will proceed to beatification, the next step in the process of being declared a saint.

But admiration for Nano's legacy is not confined to the Church. In 2005, an RTÉ radio show voted her Ireland's "greatest woman", and G. O'Brien and J. Castle, writing in *History Ireland*, describe Nano as: "An indomitable woman who transcended the narrowly prescribed boundaries of her time, challenging all obstacles in her way (including, at times, Catholic clergy) to ensure that her vision became a reality."[1]

Today, when it is neither socially or politically prudent to question the prevailing culture, Nano's refusal to align herself with the values of the consumer society of her day is inspiring. Long before *Gaudium et Spes* of Vatican II, it could have been written of Nano that "The joys and hopes, the griefs and anxieties of the men and women of this age, especially those who are poor ... (were) the joys and hopes, the griefs and anxieties" of Nano Nagle and the thousands of women across the globe who were inspired by her example.

## Further reading:

Flanagan, B., M. T. O'Brien, and A. M. O'Leary, eds. *Nano Nagle and an Evolving Charism, A Guide for Educators, Leaders and Care Providers.* Dublin: Veritas, 2017.

O'Farrell, Sister Mary Pius. *Nano Nagle, Woman of the Gospel.* Cork: Cork Publishing Company, 1996.

Raftery, D., C. Delaney, and C. Nowlan-Roebuck, eds. *Nano Nagle: The Life and the Legacy.* Dublin: Irish Academic Press, 2018.

Walsh, T. J. *Nano Nagle and the Presentation Sisters.* Dublin: Gill, 1959.

## Further information:

Devotional material, information, biographies, relics, and prayer cards are available from South Presentation Convent, Cork, and Presentation Convents in Ireland and elsewhere. Visitor Centers presenting aspects of her life and times are in the Nano Nagle Center, Ballygriffen, Cork (her birthplace); Nano Nagle Place, Cork City (her first Convent), and "Heart Aflame" Visitor Center, Mt. Saint Anne's, Killenard, Portarlington, Laois.

---

[1] *History Ireland*, vol. 26, no. 4 (July/August 2018): 25.

# 5

# Venerable Catherine McAuley

## (1778–1841)

### Founder

## Sister Brenda Dolphin, R.S.M.

Family was the center of Catherine McAuley's life. Her father, James McAuley, a Dubliner by birth, was about thirty years older than her mother, Elinor Conway, when they married in 1777. Catherine was born on September 29 the following year. The couple had three children: two girls, Catherine and Mary, and a boy, James. While her father was alive, the family was comfortably off, unusual for a Catholic family in Ireland at the time because of the Penal Laws. James McAuley was an astute businessman who was also known to be an excellent carpenter and wood carver, and a timber merchant with property holdings, who identified himself as a "grazier" when he leased land in the Stormanstown area of Dublin in 1770. He had houses in the inner city in Dublin on Fishamble Street and a business in Copper Alley, off Lord Edward Street in the direct shadow of Dublin Castle.

Catherine was only five years old when her father died. As the years passed, her childhood memories of her father, though faint, are said to have clustered around his kindness to the poor children in the Stormanstown and Fishamble neighborhoods. While her memories may have been vague, her father's influence seems to have penetrated deep into the recesses of her heart. She held onto her Catholic Faith even though the other members of her family converted to Protestantism. She also grew up to be a woman who had a deep and abiding respect and love for those less fortunate than she was.

In 1784, a year after her husband's death, Elinor McAuley, with three small children to rear on her own, moved the family to a house in Glasnevin on the north side of Dublin. Three years later, they moved again, to 52 Queen Street, where they shared a house with Mrs. Saint George, a Protestant and a very close friend of Elinor. For the fifteen years between her father's death and that of her mother, Catherine lived in the inner city of Dublin. As the years went by, their financial situation deteriorated: Elinor was unable to manage the family finances and the business interests left to her by her husband. Mother and daughter also differed with regard to the practice of religion, although her mother did not force her to change her faith.

Two years before Elinor's death in October 1798, the family was in very difficult financial circumstances and had to break up. Catherine stayed with her mother, and they moved in with her uncle Owen Conway and his family on East Arran Street. Catherine nursed her mother through her long illness. Elinor seemingly had a difficult death, and this had a strong influence on Catherine herself. She was always frightened of death until she came to her own deathbed, by which time she had reached an extraordinarily calm acceptance that was a long way from the terror that gripped her in the face of death as a young twenty-year-old. Following Elinor's death, Catherine, her sister, and brother were orphans without much money, dependent on the goodwill of family and friends for their bed and board; a very precarious position, especially for girls at the time.

In 1803, Catherine accepted the invitation of William and Catherine Callaghan, friends of her relative William Armstrong, to live with them as a companion to Catherine in their home in Mary Street. Later that year, she moved with them to Coolock House on the outskirts of the north side of Dublin, not very far from Stormanstown where she was born. William was a prominent pharmacist in Dublin at the time. He was a Protestant, his wife a Quaker. They were a childless couple who had spent a number of years in India. Coolock offered Catherine the security of a comfortable home. More importantly, the Callaghans loved her from the start. For them she was the daughter that they had never had.

For a long time after she moved in, something she treasured was missing; her unease came from the fact that she felt she could not express her Catholic faith openly. Despite this, Catherine grew deeply fond of her adoptive parents. She spent hours with Catherine Callaghan reading to her. She nursed her constantly until her death in 1819. She was instrumental in enabling Catherine Callaghan to become a Catholic. In time she began, unobtrusively but steadfastly, to teach the children of Catholic parents on the estate the basics of their Catholic Faith. She would share food from the house with them and used a large part of her own allowance to feed and help their families. She often visited the children's homes and spent time with their parents, especially their mothers, sisters, and grandmothers. As she did regularly on a Sunday afternoon, Catherine worked tirelessly with the children who had not yet made their First Communion, teaching them the Apostles' Creed, as there was nowhere else for them to learn about their faith at that time. The Callaghans were aware of this and were happy to be associated, even indirectly, with Catherine's kindness.

After his wife's death, William Callaghan lived for another three years. Catherine devoted herself to his care and was as devastated by his death as she had been by Catherine's. He was not outraged by his wife's conversion to Catholicism as Catherine had feared; in fact, toward the end of his life, he began to move in that direction himself but died before it came about. Before he died, he protected Catherine's future and secured it for her, galvanized into action after overhearing relatives discuss what they would do to Catherine when they had control of his house and estate. The fact that he left her the sole, residual legatee of his entire estate came as a surprise to her. It was not something that she had expected. She had to endure the contesting of the will by William's relatives, but their challenge was to no avail. Catherine finally became his rightful and legally recognized heir in 1823–1824.

After William Callaghan's death, Catherine continued to live in Coolock and to teach in the poor school in Middle Abbey Street. Ever practical, she also opened an outlet for the sale of plain and fancy needlework done by the pupils under her tuition. With the Callaghan fortune at her disposal, she had a threefold plan for using her inheritance: to provide a solid religious education for young girls roaming the Dublin streets; to provide protection, temporary shelter, and training for young women who thronged the city streets at the time looking for work; to assist the sick and dying poor both physically and spiritually in their homes and in hospitals.

This plan had matured in Catherine over the years, and when the time came to put it into practice, she was clear about what she wanted to do. She consulted another good friend, Daniel Murray, Archbishop of Dublin, and a site was leased on Baggot Street in Dublin 2. Building a house for the purpose for which Catherine intended it at the historical time in Ireland was a daring and courageous act, all the more remarkable since it was done by a single woman who was also a Catholic. In the house under construction, Catherine had schoolrooms, dormitories for young women, simple apartments, and a small oratory for herself and the volunteers she hoped to attract to the work. She poured every penny of her inheritance into the project.

On September 24, 1827, feast of Our Lady of Mercy, the house was formally opened to the poor, the uneducated, and those who needed shelter. At that time in Dublin, the majority of the people were hungry for food, education, and justice. Among her first helpers on that day in September 1827 were Catherine Bryn, her cousin, and Anna Maria Doyle, a young Dublin woman and ancestor of Arthur Conan Doyle; they administered the house until Catherine was free to join the group—at this time she was nursing her sister Mary, who was dying of tuberculosis.

Catherine always imagined this enterprise would be run by a group of laywomen volunteers who would do the very best they could, within their circumstances, for those who were less fortunate than themselves. She was very single-minded in terms of using every resource she had at her disposal for the poor. Her own wants and those of her young helpers were very modest; they had a simple life in common, wore very simple clothes, and actually attracted attention by their utter simplicity to the extent that voices began to murmur that another Catholic community of religious women was being brought into being surreptitiously in the Dublin diocese. The Archbishop of Dublin, as her mentor, was forced to tell her that she would have to regularize her undertaking canonically, meaning she would have to establish publicly a congregation of women religious under his patronage, or else the whole enterprise would have to be given over to an already established congregation that had the same vision and orientation.

For Catherine, this turn of events was most unexpected. She was now fifty years old. She could be forgiven for thinking that she had given her all; she had invested every penny she had in the building on Baggot Street, she had spent the greater part of her life nursing sick relatives and friends, taking responsibility for the next generation in her family, teaching and caring for the poor whom she knew. Now she was being asked to found a congregation of women religious! The immediate and most demanding aspect of this new turn of events was that Catherine and two others, Anna Maria Doyle and Elizabeth Hartnett, set out for the novitiate of the Presentation Sisters in Dublin's North Inner City. When Catherine, Anna Maria, and Elizabeth made their profession of vows on December 12, 1831, a new congregation was born—the Congregation of the Sisters of Mercy.

Catherine lived for ten years after the congregation was founded. She herself founded fourteen convents, twelve in Ireland and two in England, and had plans to move farther afield to Canada. The congregation thrived under her direction. Her vision and ability to organize, her sound common sense in her way of leading others, her warmth and good humor, and above all her unshakeable trust in the Providence of God and in the importance of the Cross in life, all contributed to setting the congregation on a sound foundation that enabled it to spread far and wide in the years since her death right up to the present day.

Catherine died peacefully on November 11, 1841, surrounded by her family, friends, and members of the congregation. She had been suffering from tuberculosis for some time but managed to hide it from those around her until it reached its last stages. Even on her deathbed, she was thinking of others and asked that those who came to her funeral might enjoy "a comfortable cup of tea".

Those who knew her declared her to be holy and called for her canonization. Her fame for holiness spread right around the world due to the depth and simplicity with which she lived the charism of mercy and the extraordinary expansion of the congregation she founded. The process for beatification and canonization began in 1903, sixty years after her death, which was the length of time required to elapse at that time before a canonization process could begin. Catherine was declared Venerable by Pope Saint John Paul II on April 9, 1990.

Catherine was an ordinary Irish woman, a city girl, who used the hand that life dealt her to live a life of deep trust in God and extraordinary openness and generosity toward other people. She truly deserves the title of saint.

# 6

# Blessed Edmund Ignatius Rice

## *(1762–1844)*

## Founder

## *Brother Donal Blake, C.F.C.*

Let us do ever so little for God, we will be sure he will never forget it, nor let it pass unrewarded. How many of our actions are lost for want of applying them to this end. Were we to know the merit of only going from one street to another to serve a neighbor for the love of God, we should prize it more than Gold or Silver.... One thing you may be sure of, that whilst you work for God, whether you succeed or not, he will amply reward you.

In these words, from a letter to his friend, the architect Bryan Bolger, in 1810, Blessed Edmund Ignatius Rice summed up the direction of his life; a life dedicated to the service of the young and the poor. Facing the most extraordinary difficulties, at times with only God to turn to, his life was marked by fidelity to Christ and an ardent love for the poor. Founding two congregations, the Christian Brothers and Presentation Brothers, to continue this work, he urged the disciples of Christ to reach out to those most in need, to see the face of Jesus in the poor, and to make a home for the destitute, not just in physical buildings and charitable projects, but also in the heart so one's life is marked by a sacrifice of love for others.

Blessed Edmund was born to Robert and Margaret Rice, prosperous tenant farmers, at Westcourt, Callan, Co. Kilkenny, on June 1, 1762.

He was the fourth of seven brothers; he had two stepsisters, Joan and Jane Murphy, from his mother's first marriage. While the Penal Laws against Catholics were still in force in Ireland, Kilkenny fared better than many places because of the tolerance of John Butler, the Protestant Duke of Ormonde, who resided in Kilkenny Castle. As a result, enterprising Catholics such as Robert Rice were enabled to rent farmland from tolerant Protestant landlords at reasonable rates. Edmund was fortunate in a land where the majority of Catholics were "hewers of wood and drawers of water".

After education at a hedge school, an unlicensed pay school, and at a commercial academy in Kilkenny, he was apprenticed at the age of seventeen to his uncle Michael, who was involved in the provisioning and ship-chandling business in Waterford; Michael's own two sons showed no interest in commercial enterprise. A born entrepreneur, Edmund quickly mastered the importing and exporting trade and expanded his uncle's business. He signed a lucrative contract to supply meat to the Royal Navy and initiated trading connections with Bristol, Newfoundland, and Boulogne-sur-Mer in France.

A personable young man, Edmund soon became well known among the merchant class in Waterford and became quite wealthy in a short time. Success led to further success. He married at the age of twenty-three, and the future looked rosy. Then, in 1789, his pregnant wife died, tragically leaving him with a baby daughter with a disability, Mary. Edmund's world was turned upside down. So, too, was the political world in that same year by the egalitarian ambition of the French Revolution. His uncle had appointed him his heir, but his recent tragedy caused Edmund to look for a deeper meaning to his life. He looked to God for guidance, and, unusual for a lay Catholic at the time, he turned to the Scriptures for inspiration. He became a daily Mass-goer and a reader of the mystic Saint Teresa of Ávila. His commercial career still prospered. The forward-looking principles of the French Revolution, if not its crude methods, appealed to his generous heart. "Liberty, fraternity, equality", but with a more Christian overlay, were ideals that Edmund dearly wished for his benighted fellow-Catholics.

He became a frequent visitor to the other Waterford that existed behind the façade of commercial prosperity and merry social life—the Waterford of narrow lanes and dark alleyways where the miserable hovels of the poor were crowded together. Scope for helping the poor seemed endless. He was encouraged by a woman friend to turn his attention to the plight of poor destitute boys. He soon realized that education, and not mere handouts, was the key to their emancipation. He looked around for a template for the way forward. Inspired by what Nano Nagle had achieved by her Presentation Sisters for the plight of poor girls, Edmund, at the age of forty, turned his back on his business career in 1802 and opened a temporary school for poor boys in New Street. Having made provision with his relatives for his daughter's special needs, he deployed all his energies and wealth in this new undertaking.

Edmund sank most of his assets into the building of a permanent school and residence at Mount Sion. There was to be no turning back. He employed two paid assistants, but they eventually left him. He quickly realized that temporary commitment to a full-time problem was no solution, and so he invited young men to join him permanently in his work and prayer. In 1808, Edmund and his early companions gave total commitment to their new way of life by taking vows before the local bishop, thus forming the Society of the Presentation. Edmund became Brother Ignatius, named after the founder of the Jesuits.

The work soon spread to other towns, in the Diocese of Waterford first, and then to larger centers of population, such as Cork, Limerick, and Dublin, where the local bishops, impressed by what they saw in Waterford, hoped to spread the benefits of Catholic education to their own dioceses. For Edmund, education was not confined to the "Four Rs"—Reading, Writing, 'Rithmetic, Religion; with his background in business, it included subjects such as accountancy for the business houses, mensuration for the measurement of land, and navigation for the sailing of ships, in order to give these young people useful skills for work and to prepare them for life.

In 1820, with the blessing of Pope Pius VII, the majority of the brothers, with Edmund as Superior General, were organized into a pontifical congregation—the Congregation of Christian Brothers, to make it more available not only in Ireland but wherever the need for education was greatest. A minority retained the Presentation name and, in 1826, as a diocesan group loyal to the Bishop of Cork, evolved into today's Presentation Brothers. During Edmund's lifetime, day and evening schools to meet the educational needs of the poor were opened by his followers in Ireland and England, and a beginning was made in overseas missions that were to blossom after his death, in Gibraltar, India, America, and Australia.

Edmund and his brothers did not confine their work to the classroom; they were to be found visiting the hospital wards, the debtors' prisons, and even accompanying poor wretches to the gallows. Fighting for the legal rights of widows and orphans occupied much of his time as he brought his knowledge of the law, learned during his business career, to the defense of those in danger of being deprived of their rights. Being the prototype of the teaching brother in the English-speaking world, he endured much hardship, misunderstanding, and opposition, even from some bishops and, more hurtful, from some of his own confreres. Nurturing his vision through prayer and a wonderful trust in Divine Providence, he persevered with his extraordinary mission until his death on August 29, 1844.

After initial neglect due to the Great Famine and division among his followers, Edmund's reputation for holiness and care for the poor and ignorant grew over the years. Admiration for his life's achievements, for his vision and legacy, led to a growing number of people on all five continents who were touched by his charism and devoted to his memory. Prayer and apostolic groups—the Edmund Rice Network—sprang up wherever there was a Christian Brother or Presentation Brother presence. There were repeated requests to Rome for Edmund's canonization. On October 6, 1996, at the end of a long process and after a miracle worked through his intercession was recognized, Edmund was declared Blessed by Pope Saint John Paul II at a memorable ceremony in Rome. His feast day is celebrated on May 5 each year.

In more recent years, Edmund's brothers, despite being fewer in number, have concentrated on the developing-world countries of Africa, South America, India, and the West Indies, and on the inner cities of Dublin, Cork, Waterford, Limerick, Belfast, Liverpool, Manchester, New York, Chicago, Calcutta, Goa, Melbourne, and Sydney. Their lay collaborators staff hundreds of schools imbued by the spirit of Blessed Edmund on all five continents.

His birthplace at Westcourt, Callan; the O'Connell School, North Richmond Street, where he lived when in Dublin; Mardyke House in Cork, where the founding Presentation ethos lives on; and Mount

Sion, Waterford, where he began his educational project and where he died, are now centers of prayer for his devotees. The appeal of Edmund Ignatius Rice reaches beyond the members of his own brothers. He is now invoked by a growing number of teachers, priests, and religious, parents, students, business people, the unemployed, members of voluntary groups (such as Edmund Rice Camps and Edmund Rice Young Adults), former brothers and new devotees as Edmund the family man, widower, father of a child with a disability, businessman of integrity, humane teacher, lay Catholic activist, lay religious, advocate for the deprived, and patron of the ordinary in daily life.

7

# Venerable Mary Aikenhead

## *(1787–1858)*

### Founder

*Sister Phyllis Behan, R.S.C.*

The cause for the beatification of Mary Aikenhead began in 1908 following a request from the Sisters of Charity of Australia. The cause was then taken up in Ireland in 1910. Like many beatification processes, it had stops and starts along the way, but it took a giant leap forward on March 18, 2015, when Mary Aikenhead was declared Venerable by Pope Francis. This was largely due to the dedication and determination of the Sisters, postulators, and vice postulators who worked on the cause from the beginning. Being declared Venerable means that the Church recognizes that Mary lived the life of a saint and practiced heroic virtue.

So, who was Mary Aikenhead? Mary was born in Daunt's Square, Cork City, on January 19, 1787. She was the eldest child of Mary Stacpole, a Catholic, and David Aikenhead, a doctor and chemist who was a Scottish Presbyterian. Mary was frail as a child and was fostered to a Catholic couple, John and Mary Rorke. From her earliest years, Mary moved easily between the Catholic Faith of her mother and the Anglican tradition in which she was baptized. She also moved easily between the two levels of Cork society at that time—the poor and the wealthy—and like her father had a great compassion for those less well off than herself.

Mary's father died in 1801, converting to Catholicism on his deathbed. Mary had delayed embracing the Catholic Faith up to this time, thinking it would upset her father. She was known to slip out of the house early in the morning to attend Mass and to stay up late at night praying. But it was the occasion of a sermon preached by Florence MacCarthy, Coadjutor Bishop of Cork, on the Gospel story of the Rich Man and Lazarus (Lk 16:19–31) that seems to have had a major impact on her. Ever afterward she had a burning love for "God's nobility, the suffering poor", as she called them. She began to receive instruction in the Catholic Faith and was solemnly received into the Church in June 1802.

For some years, Mary ran the family home, becoming head of the family on her mother's death in 1809. Around this time, Daniel Murray, Coadjutor Bishop of Dublin, and Mary's former spiritual director, was becoming increasingly convinced of the need for an active congregation of religious Sisters—at that time, every convent of nuns in the country observed a strict enclosure. The seed of Bishop Murray's desire took root in Mary's heart, and she eventually, reluctantly, agreed to lead the congregation, later to be known as the Religious Sisters of Charity. She and her first companion, Alicia Walsh, entered the novitiate of the Institute of the Blessed Virgin Mary in Micklegate, York, England, in order to learn the fundamentals of religious life. Mary liked their spirituality, which was based on that of Saint Ignatius of Loyola, and the fact that the Sisters there were not enclosed. Mary and Alicia returned to Dublin in 1815, at which point Mary founded the Congregation of the Religious Sisters of Charity in North William Street. The Sisters became known as the "walking nuns" as they traversed the streets of Dublin visiting the poor and the sick.

In 1821, the Sisters were asked to visit two girls awaiting trial for murder in Kilmainham Jail. Mary and another Sister visited the two girls almost every day. Their loving attention and care touched the once-hostile hearts of the two girls, whose faith in God was restored. Being found guilty of murder, the two girls were hanged in front of a crowd of onlookers, and the Sisters stayed inside Kilmainham Gaol chapel praying for the girls for two hours after their execution. This experience ensured that the care of prisoners became an important work of the congregation in the years that followed.

The year 1832 was a dark time in Ireland—a major cholera epidemic claimed the lives of over 50,000 people. Their suffering was great. Mary Aikenhead was asked to send Sisters to Grangegorman temporary hospital to assist the patients. Her Sisters spent themselves tirelessly to serve the sick and dying, often at great risk to themselves; remarkably only one Sister caught the disease, but she recovered quickly. At the height of the plague, between fifty and eighty patients died each night in the hospital, but Mary urged her Sisters to work with "perfect composure" and "great simplicity" in order to "tranquilize minds suffering from the effects of agonizing disease and false terror". When cholera broke out again the following year, Mary bought an old store for £50 ($63) and opened a hospital in Ringsend. She sent three Sisters to Paris to train as nurses and opened Saint Vincent's hospital in Saint Stephen's Green, Dublin, in 1834, which would go on to become one of the most important hospitals in Dublin in the twentieth and twenty-first centuries.

Many others were attracted by Mary's vision, and the congregation spread rapidly with fourteen houses established while she was still alive, including houses in England and Australia. She had a pioneering spirit and felt called to address needs that weren't being addressed by others—the opening of the congregation's convent in Australia was occasioned by the needs of the convict women being deported there in the 1830s. Against all kinds of odds, her courage and determination established within the Church a mission that would become the foundation for hospitals, schools, welfare services, and centers of spirituality.

Mary saw at firsthand the poverty, destitution, and distress of the people, particularly during the hard years of epidemic and famine in the 1830s and 1840s. While her Sisters struggled to help the poor in whatever way their meager means could allow, Mary maintained a constant concern for the Sisters, encouraging them to avail "of every ray of sunshine", and in another letter she wrote: "let us thank the Almighty for all the good spots we enjoy."

Money was always in short supply as the congregation, and its works, grew, but she did not worry about it, trusting, as she always said, in the "bank of Divine Providence". As she wrote on one occasion, "May all our concerns be in the care of Almighty Providence, and our hearts ever ready to bear the difficulties and disappointments which require our exertions, above all, which call for our entire conformity under what is painful to nature." She was grateful for all the help she received, both from God and from others, and counseled others to vie with each other in proving their gratitude by deeds.

We catch glimpses of Mary's holiness, her spirituality, her faith and trust in God, and her dedication to prayer in the many letters she wrote to her Sisters in the congregation. She constantly encouraged the Sisters to pray for an increase of faith in the Lord she and they loved. She said: "I shall remind you to use the prayer 'O Lord, increase my faith.'"

While she was a woman of prayer herself, and considered it to be "miraculously powerful", she was also a woman of action. The two are constantly mentioned together in her writings. She wrote: "Let us all pray and labor as if all depended on our poor endeavors and, all the while, feel convinced that he alone who is our God and the Anchor of our hope is all sufficient."

Mary was sick for much of her life—inflammation of the spine, which seems to have been badly mismanaged, left her in intense pain. Mary spent twenty-seven years confined to a wheelchair, and in the last years of her life she was entirely confined to her bed, unable even to hold her head up unaided. Yet through all of these sufferings, she never lost her trust in Providence or forgot the importance of laughter and good humor.

After her death in July 1858, a Dominican priest, Father Bartholomew Russell, O.P., an old friend from Cork, described her as a woman to be revered and loved; gifted with high spiritual knowledge and proficiency, "she reminded me of Saint Teresa or Saint Catherine of Siena, with a dash of the Celtic nature."

The gift of Venerable Mary Aikenhead to the Church and to the world is a living gift because it is the gift of the Gospel: the gift of love. It is a free gift, available to those who want to be involved in the great enterprise of loving as Jesus did, of loving as Mary Aikenhead did.

Mary's life teaches us to have faith in God and in ourselves; to dream courageous visions; to reach outward and away from our own preoccupations; to have compassion for human pain and brokenness; to analyze structures that are the cause of poverty; to work with others to solve problems, and to remain resolute in the face of hardship.

The spirit of Mary Aikenhead lives on: it lives on in every health care, pastoral, or educational ministry associated with the Sisters. It lives on in every person who loves and promotes the charism of Mary, and it lives on in every Religious Sister of Charity who has vowed her life to the service of God and to the service of the poor.

Today, the Religious Sisters of Charity are scattered and flourishing across the globe in America, Zambia, Nigeria, Malawi, England, Scotland, and, of course, in its original nursery, Ireland. The Sisters worked for a time in other areas such as Venezuela, Kenya, Ethiopia, and Botswana. The Sisters of Charity of Australia have also flourished spreading Mary's Gospel vision across Australia and beyond.

## Further reading:

Blake, C.F.C., Donal S. *Mary Aikenhead (1787–1858) Servant of the Poor.* Dublin: Caritas, 2001.

Crossan, R.S.C., Rosaleen. *Friend of the Poor, Mary Aikenhead, Woman of Vision, Commitment and Inspiration.* Dublin: Columba Press, 2016. (Quotes from Sister Rosaleen's book have been used here with permission.)

## Further information:

For a history of the cause, see http://rsccaritas.com/who-we-are/history-of-the-cause/.

Literature available from The Mary Aikenhead Heritage Center, Harold's Cross, Dublin 6W; http://www.rscmaheritage.com/ and by email: rsccause @rsccaritas.com. See also: https://www.sistersofcharity.org.au/.

# 8

# The Servant of God
# Sister Alice O'Sullivan

*(1836–1870)*

Consecrated Religious, Missionary, and Martyr, *uti fertur*

*Sister Louise O'Connell, D.C.*

Alice O'Sullivan began her life in Clonmel, Co. Tipperary, in 1836, the second youngest of a family of five children. Her parents were originally from Newry, Co. Down, but had moved to a house in West Gate, Clonmel. Alice's mother died soon after the birth of Francis, the youngest child, leaving the children to be cared for by a nurse, a devoted carer in the family. Alice was educated first at the Presentation Sisters' Convent Schools in Clonmel; later her father sent her to the Dominican Convent in Dun Laoghaire for her further education. It was noted that she showed mature common sense and genuine piety.

When her brother Daniel joined the Vincentian Community, he recommended that Alice should consider joining the Daughters of Charity of Saint Vincent de Paul in Rue du Bac, Paris. Barely nineteen years old, Alice agreed and entered postulancy in Amiens where her vocation was discerned; she entered the Paris Seminary (novitiate) of the congregation on January 31, 1856. This was a step into the unknown, especially because of language and cultural differences. At that time, the seminary had over five hundred Seminary Sisters (novices) coming from many regions. Our Lady had visited the Chapel of the

Motherhouse in 1830 where Saint Catherine Labouré was a Seminary Sister. Our Lady, sitting on a chair in the sanctuary, spoke to Catherine and asked her to promote the Miraculous Medal. The chapel is now called the Chapel of the Miraculous Medal. The formator for the five hundred Seminary Sisters was Sister Azais, who had been serving for twenty years in this role of preparing Sisters for their future apostolates. Sister Azais will be part of Sister Alice's story in China.

Sister Alice, now known in religion as Sister Marie-Louise, was first missioned to Drogheda in her native country in 1857. The Daughters of Charity had arrived there in 1855; this was their first foundation in Ireland. Her apostolate was involvement in an outreach educational program for young workers in factories. It was a night class to encourage literacy, and the venue was an old hayloft.

In 1863, Alice was missioned to China. The first group of Sisters had departed for China in 1848, landing in Macau but moving to Ning-Po. There they gradually opened orphanages for abandoned children, especially for girls and for children challenged by handicapping conditions. Thanks to the support of the Association of the Holy Childhood, these works developed. The impact of the Sisters' presence was so great that requests were made for the presence of the Sisters in Pekin and Tientsin. As a result, two groups of Sisters left the motherhouse in Paris via Marseilles in 1862 and 1863. Alice was among the second group.

Arriving in China, she and some of her companions were assigned to a hospital in Shanghai. The administrators of the hospital were totally unaware of the difficulties involved with Catholic Sisters coming to work in a system that was not Catholic, so at the beginning there were misunderstandings. One of the issues concerned the problem of language—French was spoken and understood by the Sisters. Problems were eventually solved when Sister Alice accompanied the French superior to meetings with the committee. Engaging with the committee with tact and prudence, Alice performed so well that whatever the requests she made were granted. She was humble in response to praise: "Do not be surprised!" she said, "It is Our Lady and my Guardian Angel who have done it all. Before I came out, I confided this affair to them, and it was they who made it a success."

The Sisters of her community often said it was impossible to live with her without loving her. Alice's bright personality and her gift of being able to assist the community at all levels of the apostolates, especially with administrators of the various services offered to the Sisters, made her very popular. But personally, she had great difficulties in trying to accept cultural differences, and she struggled interiorly. In spite of this inner struggle, she continued to give great witness to the charity of Christ with great devotion in her next mission in Pekin.

The Daughters of Charity were engaged with the Association of the Holy Childhood, founded in 1843 in France by the Bishop of Nancy. Its mission was to assist missionaries in China. In Pekin, its activities involved the rescue of abandoned babies and caring for them in an orphanage. Here Alice strove to give a loving service as her inward struggle continued. Eventually, she found strength to write about her difficulties to Father Jean-Baptiste Etienne, Superior General of the Vincentian Fathers in Paris. Father Etienne replied and arranged that she return to Paris, traveling with Sister Azais, her former formator now the superior in charge in China, who was going to Paris for the celebration of Father Etienne's Golden Jubilee. Her companions were shocked to hear that she was leaving them. She prepared to leave Pekin and journey to Tientsin to travel back to Paris by sea. As in Pekin, the Sisters in Tientsin were overwhelmed with work and were delighted to welcome a Sister with knowledge of English and hoped that Alice would change her mind and stay in Tientsin.

In his records, Father David Armand, a Vincentian explorer, describes his visits to the mission in Tientsin during his Second Journey of Exploration. In his diary he notes, "There were ten Sisters in the house in Tientsin, six were French, two Belgian, one English/Irish and one Italian. There were several young Chinese girls, who were postulants for the order." While in Tientsin, Sister Azais wanted to visit the Vincentian Superior, Father Chevrier, and also visit the new Church of Our Lady of Victories. Alice and other Sisters went with her. They visited the church, but Alice remained behind to pray. When she rejoined her companions, they noticed that she had been crying copiously. When they questioned her about her grief, she replied, "If I were to tell you, you would not believe me!" On meeting Sister Azais, she told her she was willing to stay on in China, if it was the will of God. Sister Azais agreed and allowed her to remain in Tientsin, saying, "Goodbye, 'til we meet again." Alice replied, "You will return, and we shall all be gone." In a letter to

Father Etienne, she thanked him for permission to return to France but said, "Today I fully understand why it is more perfect for me to remain till death in this poor country. Please send Sister Azais back to us as soon as possible."

Having made up her mind to remain, Alice set to work with renewed energy. The Sister Servant, Sister Marie-Thérèse Marquet, remarked that the visit to the Church of Our Lady of Victories had given great strength to the community in Tientsin through the presence of Sister Alice. But the storms of unrest were obvious as were the expressions of hatred and scorn for "the devils from the west", as the missionaries were called by xenophobic groups in China. The Sisters were caring for many orphans and disabled children in their "House of Mercy". Its dispensary also cared for numerous patients who were British and American. These patients contributed to the service of the poor by their payments for the medical care they received, so no burden was imposed upon the Chinese. However, storms were brewing among the Chinese fueled by rumors that the Sisters were using the eyes and hearts of Chinese children for medical purposes.

On June 21, 1870, attacks on many Catholic services were gradually fanned into a flame. The French consul, seeing the gathering storm, reported to the Governor that there was a real danger of mob violence. It was too late. The mob suddenly became hostile, and, after an initial confrontation, the consul was brutally attacked and killed; the burning of religious buildings and their occupants began. Given the rumors that had been circulating, the "House of Mercy" was a prime target. The Sisters, aware of this, had been making quiet preparations to meet whatever violence would be afflicted on them. In visits to the Blessed Sacrament, the employees and Sisters had been praying to appease the conflict against the missionaries. Sister Marie-Thérèse Marquet asked everyone to go to the chapel; the children had already been taken to safety, hidden in the crypt; the sacred vessels were also hidden away; all received the Blessed Sacrament.

When the mob arrived at the "House of Mercy", Sister Marquet approached the leader and asked, "What do you want with us? We only do the good we can with the poor and sick." In response, they immediately killed her and, with her, another Sister, Sister Maria Clorinda Andreoni, who was standing nearby. Hearing the commotion, Alice and five others left the chapel to divert attention from the crypt where the children were hidden. Alice was badly scalded with boiling water. As she tried to run back to the chapel, she was killed beside Sister Marquet's body. The mob turned on the rest of the community, and by three o'clock that day, all the Sisters had been brutally murdered and mutilated. As the massacre was going on, a pagan lady saw a brilliant cloud soaring up into Heaven. She ran into the courtyard, telling people they were killing holy people; she too joined the martyrs in their death. These ten Sisters and twenty babies asphyxiated by the mob became the first martyrs of the Holy Childhood Association.

When the news of the massacre reached Shanghai, it caused great distress among the Europeans, quickly becoming an international incident greeted with condemnation. The *North China Daily News* wrote about Sister Alice, noting, "When we recall Sister Louise O'Sullivan, who nursed many of our sick in Shanghai Hospital, our blood boils within us." The writer offered his deepest sympathy and his sincere condolence; "there is one cry of admiration for their heroism", he wrote, "their works of charity and the perfect innocence of their lives. Oh yes, let the Sisters of Charity in China know that at this moment more than one heart deeply sympathizes with them in their afflictions." Father Etienne, the Vincentian Superior General in Paris, was shocked to lose so many of his sons and daughters in one blow. At the motherhouse in Rue du Bac, three hundred Sisters earnestly entreated the favor of being allowed to go and replace their martyred companions.

The Hospital in Tientsin was destroyed, as was the Church of Our Lady of Victories and other religious buildings, but the spirit of the Sisters did not die. Four years later, the Daughters of Charity returned and again began to serve the abandoned and sick children in an orphanage with a dispensary on a very small scale. However, it was not to last: it was destroyed again during the Boxer Rebellion in Tiangin, and later, factories were built on the site of the "House of Mercy".

No memorial, sign, or tombstone marks the site of the martyrdom of the ten Daughters of Charity in 1870. However, people in the area are aware of the historical significance of this place where they live and do business. This interest emerged when the buildings were torn down during a renewal projected for the area, and beneath, the old

Church of God's Mercy was found. In the meantime, the Cause of Beatification for Alice and her martyr companions—her nine Sisters and the two Vincentian priests who served in Tientsin—was introduced and is still under investigation.

## Further reading:

Bishop, George. *Travels in Imperial China. The Exploration and Discoveries of Père David*. London: Cassell Publishers, 1996.

*Pioneer Sisters of Charity of Saint Vincent de Paul in Great Britain and Ireland*. London: privately printed, 1955.

# 9

## The Servant of God
## Father Patrick Ryan

*(1844–1878)*

Priest

*Deacon Gaspar DeGaetano*

The Cause for the Beatification and Canonization of the Servant of God, Father Patrick Ryan, an immigrant from Ireland, was formally opened in the Diocese of Knoxville in June 2016. In the light of the viral pandemic of 2020–2021, it is a cause whose time has come and is being pursued under the new Church category of "offering of life". Father Ryan, pastor of Chattanooga's Saints Peter and Paul's parish from 1872 to 1878, was a shepherd who gave his life in ministering to his flock during the yellow fever epidemic of 1878, dying of the fever himself on September 28 of that year, the day before his thirty-fourth birthday. In the six years he served that parish, he enlarged its little frame church, built a rectory, and zealously tended his flock. He also was responsible for the opening of a school, Notre Dame Academy, under the direction of the Dominican Sisters.

Patrick Ryan was born in 1844 near Nenagh, Co. Tipperary, into a good Christian family. In his childhood, his parents were evicted from their home by a ruthless landlord and forced to emigrate. They settled in New York, where Patrick grew to manhood. In pursuance of his desire to be a priest, he entered Saint Vincent's college, Cape Girardeau, Missouri, in October 1866. Although he was no genius, one of his schoolmates said that he was one of the soundest and most reliable students in the seminary and was noted for his common sense, and he excelled in athletics. He was ordained priest in the summer of 1869 at the Cathedral in Nashville by Bishop Patrick Feehan. The Feehan and Ryan families were close neighbors in Ireland, and this was possibly the reason young Ryan decided to join the Nashville Diocese. Bishop Feehan went on to become the first Archbishop of Chicago. After ordination, Father Ryan was appointed pastor of Clarksville, Tennessee, and its missions, where he served for three years. On July 10, 1872, Bishop Feehan, cognizant of the young priest's prudence and zeal, transferred him to a larger field of labor in the parish of Saints Peter and Paul in Chattanooga. During his first two years at Saints Peter and Paul's, his parish consisted of the city of Chattanooga and most of the southeastern part of the state of Tennessee.

Father Ryan is described as almost impetuous in his efforts to make his parishioners practical as well as professing Catholics. Having recovered somewhat from the ravages of the American civil war, Chattanooga was growing by leaps and bounds. In the decade 1870–1880, the population increased from 6,093 to 12,892. This increase brought challenges for Father Ryan and his parish. For one, the little frame church originally completed in 1847 proved too small for the growing congregation, so he added 30 feet to the building, making it 80 feet long and 20 feet wide. This enlarged church served the parish until the present church, later to become a Minor Basilica, was built under the pastorship of his good friend, Kilkenny born, Father William Walsh. Father Walsh served under Father Ryan for two years following his own ordination in 1874. Father Ryan also procured a church bell that is still in use at the basilica.

The parish, since its beginning, had provided a school for its children under the supervision of the priests. This was a makeshift affair where all grades were taught by one lay man or woman in the basement of the church. Father Ryan was determined to have a first-class school taught by Sisters. He prevailed on the Dominican Sisters of the Saint Cecilia Congregation, established in Nashville sixteen years previously, to send out their first foundation to Chattanooga. On January 6, 1876, four Dominican Sisters arrived and began preparations for the opening of Notre Dame de Lourdes Academy, which has survived as the oldest private school in Chattanooga, a co-educational high school. The Sisters ran two schools, at Father Ryan's request. On their arrival in the parish, he said to them, "In addition to the parochial school, you will find it necessary to carry on a select school, otherwise you will not make support, few as are your needs. My people are numerically small, and also they are poor; the exceptions consist of only two or three families." The parish or free school initially occupied the basement of the church; the Notre Dame de Lourdes Academy was housed in the former rectory, which also served as a home for the Sisters.

The future of the parish seemed exceedingly bright, and Father Ryan was happy. But the school had been in operation for little more than two years when it had to be converted into a hospital and orphanage: yellow fever came to Chattanooga. The city had escaped previous visitations of the plague, so it considered itself protected by its mountains. In offering hospitality to people of neighboring cities, where the fever had broken out, it gave refugees a chance to introduce the scourge within its own limits. People began falling ill on September 18, 1878; within a few days, the fever was declared an epidemic. Four-fifths of the population quickly left the stricken city. Before its deadly work was done, 366 citizens lost their lives to the fever.

Father Ryan was among 1,800 people who remained in the city. An eyewitness described seeing him "going from house to house in the worst-infected section of the city to find what he could do for the sick and needy". On September 26, he contracted the disease himself, yet he continued ministering to his flock. Two days later, the heroic priest died after having received the last sacraments from the hands of his younger brother, Father Michael Ryan. Father Michael, who had just been ordained, had come to Chattanooga a few days previously to spend a short vacation with his brother. The shock of his brother's tragic death so undermined the young priest's health that after a few years' service in Nashville, he retired to St. Louis, where he died shortly afterward.

In accordance with his last request, "Bury me in Chattanooga among my people", Father Ryan's body was buried in the churchyard. For eight years, his grave was a hallowed spot, kept beautiful by the hands of those who revered his memory. When Mount Olivet cemetery, three miles outside the city, was formally opened on November 11, 1886, his remains were carried in solemn procession there. It was a fitting occasion to pay an honorable tribute to a priest who had stuck to his post in the time of trial and offered his life in the cause of charity. On that day, the first Pontifical Requiem Mass ever sung in Chattanooga was celebrated. In his sermon at that Mass, Father William Walsh spoke of the self-sacrifice and generosity of Father Ryan, reading a letter he had received from the priest early in September 1878, in which the latter expressed the wish that he might come to Memphis to help out in the epidemic that was raging there. Father Ryan wrote:

My Dear Father Walsh,

I have written and dispatched to Memphis and cannot hear anything from you. I again try to hear from you, as I know you are still living. Can't I hear from you? Just one line will satisfy. You do not know my anxiety.

I have heard with regret, about the deaths of Fathers Welsh and Meagher. My God! Are we to lose all our priests! I could have been with you about the 15th of last month, but the bishop promising to go to Knoxville, I did not wish to be away. I wished since that I had been to Memphis. Perhaps it's not too late yet. I will go, should the bishop let me. I am going to Nashville this week. I have heard that Fathers Riordan and McNamara are down with the fever; I hope to hear of their recovery.

I have received the circular addressed to the T.A. Societies appealing for aid. Unfortunately, our society could do nothing. I took up a collection for the objects specified in your appeal. The amount is $100, which I am sending you or Father Riordan by express.

I trust in God I shall hear better news from you, and that you are still well. My prayers, if they avail anything, are for your safety. May God, in his great mercy, give you strength and courage to bear up against this terrible calamity.

Will you be kind enough to write or dispatch to me on receipt of this, and believe me to be ever,

Your most faithful friend,

P. RYAN.

P.S.—As I cannot live without ye, I will go and die with ye. P.R.

When the procession left the church, it was more than a mile long. It consisted of more than a hundred carriages, and, as the cortège passed along Market Street, hundreds stopped on the sidewalks to gaze respectfully at the hearse. His remains were interred at the highest spot in the cemetery, on Priests' Mound. In July 2021, the body was exhumed and translated to a new tomb in the Basilica of Saints Peter and Paul. Perhaps no better eulogy of Father Ryan could be written than that which appeared in an editorial in the *Chattanooga Times* on November 12, 1886:

> The reburial of Father Patrick Ryan yesterday roused into vivid realization the terrible scene of September and October 1878, in the retrospective vision of all who were his co-workers in that trying season.
>
> The brave and faithful priest literally laid down his life in the cause of humanity. Only the morning before he was stricken with the deadly pestilence, the writer[1] met him on his rounds of mercy in the worst infected section of the city. Cheerfully but resolutely, he was going from house to house to find what he could do for the sick and needy.
>
> Then the work of the destroyer was upon him, but he looked the one whose spirit had conquered the flesh, like one so absorbed in the dangers of afflictions of his fellow men that he was unconscious of personal suffering, unmindful of personal evil.
>
> We shall never, to the hour we close our eyes for the last time, forget the unselfish and efficient work of Father Ryan and his elder eminent brother, Father John. It was peculiarly meet and very touching the respect shown the dead father's remains yesterday by many of the chief survivors of that terrible fall. This was without regard to religious connections, as it should be. They were on a level then. The yellow scourge was no respecter of persons or creeds.

The Knights of Columbus Council of Chattanooga, in 1915–16, some thirty-seven years after his death, took Father Patrick Ryan for its namesake, in honor of the priest who, by his high ideals, his devotion to duty, his spirit of sacrifice for his congregation and his city, seemed to exemplify the aims and purposes of the new order. The council's name inspired the Knoxville Diocesan Postulator to request that his cause be initiated. The Diocesan Inquiry of the cause of Father Ryan was completed in September 2023 and has now advanced to the Roman Phase.

---

[1] Possibly the Jewish journalist Adolf Ochs, who later owned the *New York Times*.

# 10

# The Servant of God
# Margaret Mary Healy Murphy

## (1833–1907)

### Founder

*Cecilia Gutierrez Venable, Ph.D.*

The gentle bay breeze blew the sea vapors to shore, transporting Mother Margaret back to her childhood home in Ireland. While the parched earth of South Texas little resembled the lush grasses of her youth, the sea air was familiar to her. She lamented to her companion, Sister Alloysius, that if only "she could lie on the seashore and let the waves just touch her ... she would get well"; however, this was not meant to be.[1]

Mother Margaret was born Margaret Mary Healy to Richard Healy and Jane Murphy Healy on May 4, 1833, in Cahersiveen County Kerry, Ireland. Her mother hailed from Carhan, and father from Limerick. Margaret Mary eventually had two brothers and a sister. Her mother died prematurely, and the grieving father felt he had no choice but to allow his boys to travel with his wife's relatives to America. His baby daughter went to live with his sister-in-law, and he and Margaret Mary likely remained in Cahersiveen, where he cared for the sick.

As the Famine ravished the Emerald Isle, Healy reluctantly made the decision to take his daughter to America and rejoin his sons.

[1] Sisters of the Holy Spirit Archives, letter from Gaffney Young to Sister Immaculata Turley (1940). Young was a longtime friend of Mother Margaret.

They reunited with their family in 1845, but the trip took a toll on his health. With some respite, the family eventually moved to New Orleans, but their father became ill and died. The remaining family followed the U.S. army to Matamoros, Mexico, where the troops were stationed in anticipation of trouble from the Mexican government over border issues.

Upon arrival, the Healys and Murphys saw the need for a boarding house and opened the "Healy Hotel". Working in this establishment, Margaret Mary met John Bernard (J.B.) Murphy, an editor and businessman. On her sixteenth birthday, the couple married, and, with the exodus of the army, the family closed the hotel. Margaret Mary, her husband, and aunts moved to Texas.

The family settled in San Patricio, South Texas, where James McGloin and John McMullen brought Irish immigrants to build this town. Margaret Mary developed friendships and stayed close to her family. She worked with the sick, and a friend reported that when a yellow fever epidemic broke out in town, Margaret Mary rode horseback to Corpus Christi, a small city over thirty miles away, to secure medicine for her patients.

One day Margaret Mary encountered a Mexican child who needed help. She brought her home, and after numerous attempts to find her family, the Murphys took her in and cared for her. Margaret Mary also became the guardian for two Irish girls from Roscommon, Ireland, Honora and Mary Gilmore. Honora returned home, and Mary wed Martin Kelly from Galway, Ireland, and they stayed in Texas. While Margaret Mary had no children of her own, she opened her home to others.

The winds of Civil War settled into the area, and Margaret Mary and her family moved to the more populated city of Corpus Christi. J.B. Murphy joined the war, and, although this conflict drenched the South in blood, he and his brother, Patrick, returned unscathed to Corpus Christi.

After the war, yellow fever again scoured the city, leaving over one hundred dead, and Margaret Mary worked with the pastor of St. Patrick Church, Father John Gonnard. He passed away from the disease, but Margaret Mary continued ministering to the sick. One of her patients, Mrs. Delaney, also died and left her orphaned child, Minnie, to Margaret Mary's care. Since the child showed a propensity for learning, the Murphys contacted the Sisters of St. Mary of Namur in New York, where Margaret Mary's cousin and sister (now Sister Angela) operated a school. The Murphys persuaded three bishops to allow the Sisters of St. Mary of Namur to move to Texas, and the Murphys provided a loan for the congregation's expenses. After the Sisters opened their new boarding school in Waco, Texas, the Murphys sent their niece, Elizabeth (Lizzie) Murphy, who was now their ward after her mother died. Both girls, Minnie and Lizzie, entered religious life. Minnie became Sister Bernard with the Incarnate Word and Blessed Sacrament Sisters in Victoria, Texas, and Lizzie became Sister Mary Agnes with the Sisters of the Incarnate Word and Blessed Sacrament in Corpus Christi.

In 1875, J. B. Murphy became a delegate to the Texas State Constitutional Convention in Austin, Texas. In his absence, Margaret Mary bought property and used three buildings for a hospital that people called, "Mrs. Murphy's Hospital for the Poor". One of the houses was for Mexicans, one for Blacks, and one for Whites. Although they were not open for too long, they provided care for hurricane victims and those who were inflicted with other diseases.

When J. B. returned after helping to rewrite the Texas Constitution, he involved himself in local politics and was elected mayor of Corpus Christi in 1880. Just two years into his term, Margaret Mary learned of her brother Thomas' death in a mining accident in New York. A couple of years later, J. B.'s health began to decline, and in 1884, he died.

Still grieving his death and the passing of her aunt, Mary, Margaret Mary opened another hospital for the tuberculosis outbreak exploding in Corpus Christi. She remained active in the church and started a St. Vincent de Paul Society in 1886 to aid the poor in the area. She also bought her niece's ranch before traveling to San Antonio to see friends. While there, she attended Pentecost Mass at St. Mary Church. Father John Maloney, O.M.I., related the message from the Third Plenary Council to the congregation concerning expanding the church to African Americans. After hearing the message, Margaret Mary started building a church with the blessings of the bishop. In 1888, St. Peter Claver opened to Black people in San Antonio. By September of that year, Margaret Mary also had two school buildings that allowed for three classrooms for the city's African American children.

While the school enrollment increased, Margaret Mary was unable to secure more teachers. She consulted the bishop, and he suggested she ask other religious congregations, but they could not accommodate an additional school. She then traveled to see her sister, Sister Angela, and she suggested Margaret Mary start her own order and find women who would support her vision.

Margaret Mary heeded her advice, and, in 1892, Bishop Neraz received a new religious congregation known as the Sisters of the Holy Ghost (now known as the Sisters of the Holy Spirit and Mary Immaculate), and a year later four Sisters pronounced their first vows. Under the guidance of Mother Margaret, this nascent congregation emerged as the first order of Sisters founded in Texas.

Since the school continued to grow, she needed more young women to join her order, so in 1896, she decided to return to her roots, and she traveled to Ireland to entice others to join her mission. Her first trip yielded three women who professed vows in 1899.

By 1901, Bishop Gillow invited the Sisters to operate an orphanage in Oaxaca, Mexico. Mother Margaret allowed five Sisters to manage this new mission, and the Sisters operated this facility until the Mexican Revolution forced them out of the country. In 1903, Mother Margaret was also asked to open a school in Laredo, Texas, for children along the border. She sent three Sisters for this venture, and it, too, proved successful.

In total, Mother Margaret made four trips to Ireland: 1896, 1902, 1906, and 1907. On each trip, she found women to help with her growing congregation. Her extensive travel, however, took a toll on her life, and after her return from Ireland in 1907, her health began to fail. On August 25, 1907, Mother Margaret passed away at her convent, Our Lady of Light in San Antonio. She left behind a congregation of fifteen Sisters, two postulants, and the operation of three missions.

Mother Margaret devoted her whole life to the service of the poor and sick. She ministered to the infirm even though she ran the risk of becoming ill herself. People around her passed away from these various ailments, but she seemed immune to these maladies. As she grew older, she sought to heed the wisdom of the Catholic Church to broaden their scope of teachings to African Americans and other people of color. Mother Margaret trusted in the women of Ireland to help her start a new congregation. Their hard work enticed others to join this order, and it has prospered for over one hundred and thirty years.

In 2023, the Sisters of the Holy Spirit and Mary Immaculate began the process of canonization of Mother Margaret. Her cause has been opened by the Most Reverend Gustavo Garcia-Siller, M.Sp.S., Archbishop of San Antonio. The Sisters have engaged a postulator, Dr. Valentina Culurgioni, for the cause of beatification and canonization of the Servant of God Margaret Mary Healy Murphy.

# The Servant of God
# Father William Doyle

## (1873–1917)

### Priest and Military Chaplain

### Dr. Patrick Kenny

A certain Roman Catholic chaplain ... lies in a soldier's grave in that sinister plain beyond Ypres. He went forward and back over the battlefield with bullets whining about him, seeking out the dying and kneeling in the mud beside them to give them absolution, walking with death with a smile on his face, watched by his men with reverence and a kind of awe until a shell burst near him and he was killed. His familiar figure was seen and welcomed by hundreds of Irishmen who lay in that bloody place. Each time he came back across the field he was begged to remain in comparative safety. Smilingly he shook his head and went again into the storm.... They remember him as a saint—they speak his name with tears.

This *Daily Express* report by the famous war correspondent Sir Percival Phillips records the death of the famous Jesuit military chaplain Father Willie Doyle, who laid down his life for his men at the Battle of Passchendaele in August 1917.

William Joseph Doyle was born on March 3, 1873, in Dalkey, Co. Dublin. He was the youngest of seven children. His father, Hugh, was a clerk of the High Court in Dublin and retired at the age of ninety, following a remarkably long career of seventy-three years. His youngest son seems to have inherited that remarkable work ethic.

Willie was a typical young boy in many respects—he loved sports, in particular swimming and cricket, and was a skilled angler. However, he was not typical when it came to his charity toward others. As a young boy, he regularly helped the servants around the house, sometimes getting up early to light the fire or clean the dishes before they got up. When quite young, he was given his first shilling, but on his way to the local sweet shop, he met a beggar, and, after a severe struggle with himself, he gave the shilling to the poor man, and continued on his way down the road howling with tears, given the effort the sacrifice cost him. He gathered food and money for the local poor and would clean and paint their houses if they were too old to do so themselves. He was even known to shine and clean the coins he gave to the poor, adding a certain dignity to the gift he passed to them.

He entered the Jesuits in 1891. His sixteen years of formation were interspersed with periods spent at home due to ill-health, including a nervous breakdown that he suffered after a fire broke out in his building. It is remarkable to consider how one who suffered so much nervous distress from a fire was subsequently transformed into a rock of courage in the Great War. However, he persevered through his studies and was ordained a priest on July 28, 1907, alongside Blessed John Sullivan, S.J.

His diary entry on the morning of his ordination reveals the character of the man: "My loving Jesus, on this the morning of my ordination to the priesthood, I wish to place in your Sacred Heart, in gratitude for all you have done for me, the resolution from this day forward to go straight for holiness. My earnest wish and firm resolve is to strive with might and main to become a saint." He lived only another ten years; they were nothing more than the living out of this resolution.

Most of his priesthood was spent on the Jesuit mission team, preaching missions and retreats around Ireland. His impact seems to have been electrifying, with many parish priests testifying to the impact of his words, and indeed his mere presence, on their parishes. He sought out those alienated from the Church, visiting them at home or seeking them on their way to work. He seemed to have a special gift for connecting with wounded souls. On one occasion, a gentle word with a prostitute on the street in England ("Don't hurt

Jesus, he loves you") resulted, some years later, in him being asked to assist her in prison prior to her execution for murder.

He undertook a vast range of other apostolic tasks. He was highly sought out as a spiritual director, sometimes receiving several dozen letters per day seeking advice. He was instrumental in founding the Poor Clare convent in Cork; he raised large amounts of money for missions in Africa; helped establish an organization for the spiritual support of priests, and was also on the central council of the Pioneers (a teetotalers' organization). He worked hard to establish a retreat house for working men, but this did not come to fruition until after his death. It was perhaps his work for vocations that had the most lasting impact. He wrote booklets on the topic that sold in the hundreds of thousands, and his work in this area was instrumental in shaping the vocations of countless young people.

It was as a military chaplain in World War I that Father Doyle is best remembered. He served as a chaplain to a variety of different Irish brigades from December 1915 until August 1917. He was present at the Battle of the Somme (for which he was awarded the Military Cross for his bravery), the Battle of Messines Ridge, and the Battle of Passchendaele, in addition to months of stalemate spent in the trenches with his men.

Father Doyle's frequent letters home to his father reveal the sufferings he willingly shared with the soldiers. What shines out from his correspondence is his cheerful acceptance of his tough life:

> I wonder is there a happier man in France than I am? Just now Jesus is giving me great joy in tribulation, though conditions of living are about as uncomfortable as even Saint Teresa could wish—perpetual rain, oceans of mud, damp, cold and a plague of rats.... Sometimes I kneel down with outstretched arms and pray God, if it is a part of his divine plan, to rain down fresh privations and sufferings. But I stopped when the mud wall of my little hut fell in upon me: that was too much of a good joke!

Father Doyle was absolutely loved by the soldiers he served in the war because of his own great love for them, and also because he did not take advantage of the concessions and luxuries that were available to him, preferring to share in all of the privations of the troops. The

famous Jesuit photographer Father Frank Browne served in the war
with Father Doyle. He described him in these terms: "Father Doyle is a
marvel. You may talk of heroes and saints, they are hardly in it!... We
cannot get him away from the line when the men are there.... The
men couldn't stick it half so well if he weren't there ... he wears no tin
hat and he is always so cheery."[1]

He was often to be found in the place of greatest danger—out in
"no man's land" in search of wounded soldiers—precisely because
this was the place of greatest need. It was on one such foray to rescue
some fallen men that he was killed on August 16, 1917, when he was
finally struck by a shell. It is interesting to note that he was attempting
to rescue two wounded Protestant soldiers when he was killed. This
marks him out as an ecumenical martyr of charity, a significant aspect
of his story that has been strangely ignored over the years. All of his
public work, culminating in his cheerful embrace of hardship and
death in order to serve his "poor brave boys" in the trenches, marks
him out as an effective, well-loved, and zealous priest.

But the story does not end there, for there was much more to
Father Willie Doyle than most people suspected. His personal papers
remained in his room back in Dublin with a note asking that they
be destroyed if he died. Thankfully, his superiors did not consent to
this destruction.

Father Doyle's private notes reveal the inner workings of sanctity
in the making. He was not a first-rank theologian or philosopher,
but he was a spiritual tactician of the highest order. He was determined always to go against himself in all things, and his diaries
recount numerous daily successes and failures in this regard. His
spirituality was extremely practical and always focused on the primary duties of one's state in life. As he noted on one occasion: "To
do something great and heroic may never come, but I can make my
life heroic by faithfully and daily putting my best effort into each
duty as it comes round."

While he was always gentle with others, he himself lived a very
austere life, although he had explicit approval from his confessor
and superiors for every aspect of his spiritual life. While he practiced

---

[1] A. O'Rahilly (1939), *Father William Doyle, A Spiritual Study*, 5th ed. (London: Longmans,
Green and Company, 1944), p. 524.

tough personal self-denial (including fasting, all night prayer vigils, and various corporal penances), he always recommended that others focus on doing little things well and fulfilling their daily duties with love. His own penances were unknown to most—he was instead known as a cheerful, practical joker who brought a holy joy and mischief wherever he went.

His love for the priesthood was a significant characteristic of his spiritual life. In fact, he offered many of his sufferings in the war specifically in reparation for the sins of priests. His final entry in his personal diary appeared on the tenth anniversary of his ordination: "I have again offered myself to Jesus as his victim to do with me absolutely as he pleases. I will try to take all that happens, no matter from whom it comes, as sent to me by Jesus, and will bear suffering, heat, cold etc. with joy ... in reparation for the sins of priests. From this day I will bear all little pains in this spirit."

Less than three weeks later he was dead.

It is no exaggeration to say that there was literally a global explosion of devotion to Father Doyle as people got to know of his heroism. His earliest biography went through multiple editions and printings and was translated into all of the major European languages. By the 1930s, the Irish Jesuits had received over 50,000 letters from around the world expressing devotion to Father Doyle, and many thousands of these reported alleged favors through his intercession. Several saints developed a devotion to him, including Saint Teresa of Calcutta and Saint Josemaría Escrivá, the founder of Opus Dei.

There were initial moves to open his cause, but in the 1930s the Irish Jesuits decided to prioritize the cause of John Sullivan, who has since happily been beatified. It was noted that perhaps a later time would come in God's Providence for Father Doyle's cause to be initiated.

That time may be now. Devotion to Father Doyle is growing around the world once again, and the Father Willie Doyle Association was launched in 2022 to spread awareness of his message and to act as petitioner in the cause for his canonization. The initial stages of his cause have begun in the Diocese of Meath.

Father Doyle's example is now more relevant than it was 100 years ago. Saint Paul VI once wrote: "Modern man listens more willingly to witnesses than to teachers, and if he does listen to teachers, it is because they are witnesses." There is no better witness to the Christian call to love all people than the example of one who was willing to die to save your soul or your life, and who did it all in reparation for the sins of priests.

**Further reading:**

Kenny (ed.), Patrick. *To Raise the Fallen: A Selection of the War Letters, Prayers and Spiritual Writings of Father Willie Doyle, S.J.* Dublin: Veritas, 2017.

**Further information:**

The Father Willie Doyle Association (www.williedoyle.org).

# 12

# Blessed Columba Marmion

## *(1858–1923)*

## Abbot

*Father Columba McCann, O.S.B.*

Joseph Marmion was born in 1858, at 57 Queen Street, Dublin. He grew up, the seventh of nine children, in a devoutly religious family and was educated by the Jesuits at Belvedere College, where he ranked among the best pupils. His parents encouraged him from an early age in the direction of the priesthood, and, at the age of seventeen, he began his seminary training at Holy Cross College, Clonliffe. Whatever the intentions of Joseph's parents, God himself had a longer, more adventurous journey lined up for him. Joseph did well in his seminary studies; a lively, popular student, he managed to combine a deep reverence for God with an infectious sense of humor.

In 1897, he was sent by his archbishop to Rome to complete his theological studies, where he again excelled. The attraction of diocesan priesthood gave expression to his desire to bring the Gospel into the lives of others, an instinct that remained with him for his whole life. On the other hand, another deep spiritual desire was awakened within him by God's Providence: on a journey back to Ireland, he stopped at the recently built Benedictine Abbey of Maredsous in Belgium, where the monastic life there struck a deep chord within him. The impression this place made on him never left him, and it was to result in a major change of direction farther down the road.

Joseph was open with his archbishop about the attraction toward monastic life, but the decision was made to continue on the path toward diocesan ministry. He was ordained to the priesthood on June 16, 1881. On his return to Dublin, he was appointed curate in the parish of Dundrum. His ministry here included the spiritual care of those deemed criminally insane in the local mental hospital. He later spoke about the great holiness of many of the people he met there, whatever their perceived mental health or criminal record. A change of appointment in 1882 brought him back to Clonliffe, where he taught philosophy while also serving as chaplain both to the Redemptoristine Sisters in Drumcondra and the women prisoners in Mountjoy prison.

The call to monastic life remained very much alive, and finally, at the age of twenty-eight, he left Dublin and was received as a novice at Maredsous in November 1886. He was given the name Columba, a name that linked him over the centuries to another Irishman who had left his homeland to live the monastic life elsewhere: Saint Columba of Iona. The personal change required to adapt to a very different life and a very different culture made deep, painful demands on the young novice, but he persevered, making solemn profession on February 10, 1891.

From early in his monastic life, Father Columba showed a gift for communication, leading to a life-long ministry of preaching and teaching from within monastic life. There was a growing demand for talks and retreats from this new Irish monk. In 1890, although he was only four years in the monastery, he was appointed prior of a newly founded dependent monastery at Louvain, where he also taught theology and gave spiritual direction. During those years, he gave spiritual talks each week to the monks in his care. The content of these talks was later put together to form three books that were to become spiritual classics for a whole generation: *Christ the Life of the Soul*, *Christ in His Mysteries*, and *Christ the Ideal of the Monk*.

In 1909, the position of abbot of Maredsous became vacant, and the monks of the monastery elected Father Columba to replace him. The outbreak of the First World War led to a major upheaval that called for extraordinary measures on the part of the new abbot. At one stage he left Belgium, disguised as a laborer, in search of a place of refuge for his junior monks, eventually finding a haven for them at Edermine, near Enniscorthy, Co. Wexford. From this time onward, Abbot Columba's health began a slow decline. By January 1923, it had deteriorated to the extent that he received the last sacraments, and on the thirtieth of that month, he breathed his last. Abbot Columba had dreamed of bringing Benedictine life back to Ireland by founding a monastery in his native land. Although he never did this in his lifetime, the Abbey of Maredsous did send a small group of Belgian monks to Ireland four years after his death. They set up their monastery in the recently vacated nineteenth-century castle formerly owned by the Barrington family in Murroe, Co. Limerick. That community remains today as Glenstal Abbey, whose patrons are Saints Joseph and Columba.

The cause for Dom Columba's beatification and canonization was begun in 1955. In the 1990s, after a thorough investigation of medical records and circumstances surrounding an alleged cure, officials in the Vatican concluded that this was indeed a miraculous healing that could be ascribed to the intercession of Dom Columba. Mrs. Patricia Bitzan, of Saint Cloud, Minnesota, had been diagnosed with breast cancer that then spread to her lungs. After a visit to Dom Columba's tomb in 1966, she felt a strong link with him and found a few weeks later that the cancer was beginning to disappear; within a few months it was completely gone. In 1998 Dom Columba was declared Venerable, and on September 3, 2000, he was beatified.

Blessed Columba Marmion's writings were immensely popular. The first edition of *Christ, the Life of the Soul* (1917), comprised of 2,500 copies, was sold out in four weeks; by 1953, 200,000 copies had been sold in French, and 40,000 in Italian; it was translated into nine languages; the first editions of all three books were also published in braille. Blessed Columba clearly had a message for his own time that was joyfully taken up across the globe. It has been remarked that in those days considerable importance was given to the position of law within the Church; it was "flavor of the month" and seemed to provide the answer to almost every question. Blessed Columba was by no means a "loose cannon" regarding law in the Church, but his message and inspiration emphasized other sources, especially the Bible and the liturgy, and people were refreshed by this, because they were being brought to fundamental sources of spiritual nourishment.

He maintained the traditional Benedictine practice of daily *lectio divina*, or Bible meditation. His love for the biblical text was such that he knew the letters of Saint Paul by heart, and his preference was to read the text in its original Greek. His personal notes show how this meditation continually gave rise to new insights and inspirations about the Christian life. The texts of the liturgy also spoke to him and are frequently quoted in his writings. He used the theology of the day, which had a renewed emphasis on the teaching of Saint Thomas Aquinas, to put all of this together in a single synthesis. He rarely got bogged down in details of the spiritual life as regards daily practices; beyond the liturgy itself, he expressed admiration for the Rosary and the Stations of the Cross as very helpful devotions. His primary concern was to give people the bigger picture of the spiritual life, to keep their gaze on the larger story; he wanted them to feel free about their own particular style of spiritual practice. He didn't try to impose any particular approaches as "the only method".

The bigger picture unveiled by Blessed Columba is indeed vast. As the titles of his books suggest, the cornerstone of it all is the person of Jesus Christ himself. In this regard, Blessed Columba is simply re-expressing the advice of Saint Benedict to "prefer nothing whatsoever to Christ." We have heard admonitions to "imitate Christ" or to "do what Jesus would do"; Blessed Columba took it a stage farther: Christ is our model not just in what he does or says, but *in who he is*. Jesus is human-and-divine. His gift to us in Baptism is that we become the same: human beings sharing in his divine nature. All that Christ is, all that he was, all that he ever said, did, or suffered, is now *ours* as a free gift. And all that we do in union with him is his and shares in his redemptive work. We are adopted as sons and daughters, sharing in the *identity* of the Son of God and in his mission. Not just our good deeds, but even our mistakes and weaknesses are his and are part of his work of salvation. Blessed Columba was fond of quoting those words of Jesus, "Without me you can do nothing", and advised those who sought his advice to "lean on Christ." This doctrine was, and remains, a deep source of inner freedom and joy.

When we look at the sources that inspired Blessed Columba, we can see he was ahead of his time, putting into practice something that was later to be proposed by the Second Vatican Council. The Council proposed a renewed veneration for the Scriptures, teaching that they provide us with "food of the soul, the pure and everlasting source of spiritual life". In today's world, where the Church undergoes new pressures and trials, the words of the Council are apt: "The force and power in the word of God is so great that it stands as the support and energy of the Church" (*Dei Verbum* 21). Blessed Columba already knew this from his personal experience. He was already doing what the Council would later exhort: "to learn by frequent reading of the divine Scriptures the 'excellent knowledge of Jesus Christ'" (*Dei Verbum* 25).

The proclamation of the Scriptures finds a uniquely special place in the liturgy, not only in the readings themselves, but also as the inspiration of the prayers, responses, and songs. Blessed Columba saw in the liturgy an extraordinary tapestry woven by the Church in which we contemplate Christ, learn from him, and express our love for him. As a monk with a fluent knowledge of Latin, and as a priest, he had privileged access to the liturgy. In those days, lay people attended the liturgy with devotion and docility to the Holy Spirit, but they tended to do this without much access to the texts and liturgical action itself, often contenting themselves to meditate on aspects of Our Lord's life or pray the Rosary. While these devotions are good, the Second Vatican Council sought to promote for everyone the "close-up" access to the reality of the liturgy that Blessed Columba experienced. Like the writings of Blessed Columba, and even more so, the liturgy puts us into contact with the "big picture" of the whole plan of God revealed in the life, death, and Resurrection of Jesus and our sharing in the Holy Spirit.

Blessed Columba's emphasis on the great plan of God revealed in Jesus brings us back to what is most basic and most wonderful in our faith. He encourages us to refrain from getting wedded too rigidly to this or that "method" of spirituality. His legacy to us is the rediscovery of something that has been there all along: the amazing realization that we are given the gift, not just of imitating Christ, but of sharing in his very identity, so that everything in our life, down to the most mundane, can become an extension of the Incarnation of the Word. Through the Holy Spirit, God becomes incarnate in us as members of the Body of Christ. This is why Blessed Columba is sometimes called the "Doctor of Divine Adoption".

Further information:
A list of publications can be found in the "Columba Marmion" entry of Wikipedia.

The best, up-to-date source is the online page run by the Abbey of Maredsous: http://www.marmion.be/.

# 13

# Venerable Matt Talbot

## *(1856–1925)*

## Layperson

## *Father Brian Lawless*

The drinking had gone on for twelve long years until one Saturday when, for Matt Talbot, the pattern of his life was suddenly, utterly changed. During one week in September 1884, he and his brothers, Phil and Joe, had been out of work and had spent the time drinking; now they were out of money and out of drink. They decided to wait outside O'Meara's pub in the hope that one of their fellow workers would buy them a drink. Matt was always very generous and would often buy a drink for someone if they were short of money. To his dismay, they all passed by with hardly as much as a good day.

Matt was cut to the heart. He left his brothers and began walking home toward Newcomen Bridge. There, on the bridge, something extraordinary happened. For the first time in his life, he realized what a fool he had been: a man of twenty-eight years of age with nothing to show for his life but the pain and suffering of addiction. What a waste of a life. Matt was determined to change. He returned home to be greeted by his mother, who expressed her surprise at seeing him home so early and sober. She was still more surprised when he announced that he was going to Holy Cross College, Clonliffe, to take the pledge. Could Elizabeth dare to hope that this was the conversion for which she had prayed and longed for so many years? She told him not to take the pledge unless he meant to keep it, and with tears welling up as he left the house, she softly said, "God give you the strength to keep the pledge." He did.

Born in Dublin on May 2, 1856, Matt Talbot was the second eldest of twelve children. His twin brothers Charles and Edward died in infancy, leaving ten children, eight boys and two girls. The family should have been relatively well off, but because his father, Charlie, drank very heavily, they were always poor, moving from one tenement to another. Life was very difficult for the Talbots, living in cramped and squalid conditions with no proper sanitation or running water.

Matt did not begin school until he was eleven, and like many children of the time, the main reason why he went to school at all was so that he could be prepared for the sacraments of First Communion and Confirmation. He went to O'Connell's Primary School, opened by and named after Daniel O'Connell. He rarely attended school; as the family was poor because of his father's drinking, Matt's mother had to work as a cleaner to earn extra money while Matt stayed at home to look after his younger siblings. His teacher, Brother Ryan, sums up his time in O'Connell's by noting in the remarks column of the class roll book that Matt was "a mitcher", or truant. When he left school at the age of twelve, he could hardly read or write.

He found a job working for E&J Burke, a bottling company for Guinness; it was here that he got his first taste for alcohol. By the age of sixteen, Matt was a confirmed alcoholic, and all his money went to buy drink. A niece recalled hearing her grandmother relate how he would come home on Saturdays, hand his mother a shilling, all that remained of his week's wages, and say, "Here, Mother. Is that any good to you?" Elizabeth, a very patient woman, would reply, "God forgive you, Matt! Is that the way to treat your mother?" Matt himself recalls how his addiction to alcohol reached its lowest point when he and his brothers stole a fiddle from a blind street player and sold it for the price of a drink.

By 1882, Matt had reached the darkest period of his life. He had ceased going to the sacraments, though he continued to attend Mass on Sundays. On the few occasions in later life when he referred to his youth, he admitted that from his early teens until his late twenties his only aim in life was heavy drinking. That September afternoon outside O'Meara's pub was the end of his old life and the beginning of a new one; when he returned from Clonliffe having taken the pledge, he realized his whole life would have to change if he was to keep it.

In the years after his conversion, the portrait of Matt Talbot that emerges is one of a man intent on humbling and hiding himself, a man mindful of his soul and its progress, a working man diligent and faithful. His spiritual life deepened. Guided by his spiritual directors, Father James Walsh and later Monsignor Michael Hickey, he began to study early Irish monasticism and was profoundly influenced by the Celtic spirituality of the Irish monks, rising at 2 A.M. to pray, attending Mass at 5 A.M., returning home for a small breakfast of dry bread and a mixture of tea and cocoa.

Matt now gave most of his wages to his mother and, with the enthusiasm of the newly converted, tried to reform his hard-drinking brothers. He failed in this regard and decided to leave home to live in a rented flat a few streets away. It was at this time that he became one of the first members of the Pioneer Total Abstinence Association of the Sacred Heart on May 4, 1890. Matt understood the human condition with all its weakness and frailties. He once said to his sister Susan, "never think harshly of a person because of the drink; it's easier to get out of hell than to give up the drink; for me it was only possible with the help of God and Our Blessed Mother." Eventually he moved back to live with his parents. After his father died, Matt and his mother moved to 18 Upper Rutland Street, where Elizabeth spent the last twelve years of her life looked after by Matt, who more than made it up to her for the thoughtlessness of his youth.

The 1880s saw great victories over old temptations and habits, the conquest of discouragement, and the laboriously acquired ability to read. His delight was to spell through a text of Scripture or to pour over a paragraph of that great convert, Saint Augustine: as often happens with friendship, the friends of Jesus became Matt's friends. He loved to read the lives of the saints and called Saint Thérèse of Lisieux, Saint Catherine of Siena, and Saint Teresa of Ávila, "grand girls". Prayer and spiritual reading had taken the place of his former drinking companions.

His life had become one of prayer, penance, fasting, and daily acts of charity. He had a thing about honesty. For years after 1884, he went back to pubs where he used to drink, paying back arrears he owed for

drink. He would go in, hand over the amount he owed in an enve-
lope, and hurry away. He did this until he had repaid every last penny.
A seven-year search for the fiddler whose fiddle the Talbot boys had
stolen proved fruitless. Matt was very upset by this and tramped the city
enquiring after the man's whereabouts but to no avail.

At this time Matt read a book entitled *True Devotion to the Blessed
Virgin* by Saint Louis-Marie de Montfort, a spiritual work that would
have a profound influence on him. In this book, Saint Louis' aim is
to lead us to a closer union with Christ through a more faithful obser-
vance of our baptismal promises. Saint Louis teaches that, "we come
to Jesus through the hands of Mary." The more one is consecrated to
Mary, the more one is consecrated to Jesus. One of the practices
described by Saint Louis is the wearing of a little chain as a symbol of
consecration. While not essential, this is to remind those who wear it
that they have shaken off the chains of sin and have put on the chains
of Jesus Christ. Although his words were clear enough, Matt, in his
usual zealous manner, chose to understand this as a call not only for
a chain that would be a sign of his bondage to Christ, but a chain
uncomfortable enough to remind him of Christ's suffering.

Matt had no concern for worldly possessions, whatever remained
of his wages after paying his rent and buying the little food he
allowed himself, went to the foreign missions and other charities;
he also saw when neighbors were in need, and he came to their aid.
Of all the charities he supported, the one that inspired him most,
and to which he gave the greatest amount out of the little he had,
was the Maynooth Mission to China, later known as the Columban
Fathers. The only known letter Matt ever wrote was to them. He
was very ill at the time, in December 1924, and in a very poignant
letter he writes:

> Matt Talbot have done no work for past 18 months. I have been sick
> and given over by Priest and Doctor. I don't think I will work any
> more. There one pound from me and ten Shillings from my sister.

On Trinity Sunday, June 7, 1925, as Matt was on his way to Mass,
turning into Granby Lane, a shortcut to the church, he stumbled
and collapsed. Passersby came to his aid, people coming from an earlier Mass in Dominick Street Church, and called for help. There

he passed away. The last sound he heard was the church bell calling the faithful to Mass, and Matt to the Eternal Banquet. If he had known that morning what was going to happen, he would not have worn the chains. He had, and through them God would reveal to the world the hidden aspects of his life of holiness.

The story of Matt Talbot, a poor worker who was born in a Dublin tenement, inspired the hearts of the nation and eventually the world. Such was the demand from the faithful that in 1931, Archbishop Edward J. Byrne of Dublin opened the process for his beatification. He was declared Venerable in 1975; a miracle is now being sought so he may be declared Blessed.

We live in an age of addictions more sophisticated, perhaps, than those of Matt's day; addictions to substances such as alcohol and other drugs, soft or hard, prescription or illegal; addictions to gambling, pornography, and the internet; addictions to work, professional advancement, sex, money, and power. Matt sets before us a radical example that demonstrates that ordinary people can do extraordinary things. He gradually came to this awareness, and from the time of his conversion, from alcoholism to sobriety, as a young man of twenty-eight, he spent the rest of his life living, to a heroic extent, the Christian virtues through prayer, spiritual reading, work, and caring for others. His life is a witness to the fact that people can by God's grace and their own self-acceptance say no to that which leads to addiction or addictive behaviors.

Matt's example has inspired many institutions, movements, and individuals around the world, giving hope of recovery to those who are willing to accept their weakness and need. Such people stand as beacons in our world to the truth that we can overcome addiction, rise above our weakness, and achieve great things—even sainthood. At this time when so many of our communities are affected by the scourge of alcohol and substance misuse, God has chosen Matt to be a model of temperance and a source of strength and support to all who suffer from addiction or compulsive behaviors.

Christ told his followers, "You therefore must be perfect as your heavenly Father is perfect" (Mt 5:48). When Matt Talbot found sobriety through prayer, his desire for alcohol was replaced by a desire for Christian perfection.

# 14

# Blessed John Sullivan

## *(1861–1933)*

### Priest

## *Father Conor Harper, S.J.*


Father John Sullivan, S.J., was declared Blessed on Saturday, May 11, 2017, by Angelo Cardinal Amato, representing Pope Francis, in the Church of Saint Francis Xavier, Gardiner Street, Dublin. The two Solemn Petitioners at the ceremony were Archbishop Diarmuid Martin, Roman Catholic Archbishop of Dublin, and Archbishop Michael Jackson, Church of Ireland (Anglican) Archbishop of Dublin, made in the name of the two traditions shared by John Sullivan.

John was born on May 8, 1861, at 41 Eccles Street in the heart of old Georgian Dublin. The house is situated opposite the hall-door of the old Mater Nursing Home. The street sweeps down with a wonderful vista toward Saint George's Church, where John was baptized on July 15, 1861. His father, Sir Edward Sullivan, was a member of the Church of Ireland; his mother, Bessie Josephine, was Roman Catholic. John and his three brothers were raised in the Protestant tradition of their father, and his only sister, Annie, as a Catholic, like her mother.

John's father was a barrister and had an illustrious legal career that was to be crowned with success in 1865 when he was first appointed Solicitor-General, then Master of the Rolls, and, finally, in 1883 he became Lord Chancellor of Ireland. In 1881, he was created a baronet, becoming Sir Edward Sullivan. He was known to be a firm judge, and he delivered many notable judgments at a time of great political upheaval in Ireland, while also playing a leading role in the Disestablishment of the Church of Ireland in 1869–1871. He once entertained the British Prime Minister, W. E. Gladstone, at his residence, 32 Fitzwilliam Place, where the eight-year-old John may well have heard conversation between his father and the Grand Old Man of the Liberal Party.

In 1873, John and his brother William were sent to Portora Royal School, Enniskillen, following in the footsteps of the older brothers, Edward and Robert. John's years in Portora were happy. In later years, John admitted that he went to Portora for the first time "bathed in tears", but when the time came to leave, he wept "more plentiful tears"! Contemporaries of the young John Sullivan recall him as a popular boy who was always gentle and kind to the new boys who found the new life in a boarding school to be difficult.

After Portora, John went to Trinity. Unlike his father and brothers, he does not seem to have been an active member of the many societies that flourished in Trinity at the time. He did distinguish himself in his studies, and in 1883 he was awarded the Gold Medal in Classics. After achieving a Senior Moderatorship in Classics, the promising young scholar left Trinity to study law at Lincoln's Inn, London. It was at this time that his father died suddenly on April 13, 1885. The shock had a devastating effect on John. Completing his training, he was called to the Bar in 1888.

Financially, he was left very comfortable, and he was noted for his fashionable dress and handsome good looks. He traveled a great deal and was a keen cycling enthusiast. Little is known of his inner feelings at this period of his life. Like many young adults, he probably set out on the marvelous adventure of life, not very sure of where life would lead him. There must have been some times of uncertainty—but he continued to search. During this period, he went on continental trips across Europe and on walking trips in Greece and Asia Minor. It was while he was in Greece that he visited the Greek Orthodox monastery at Mount Athos. He spent three months there and considered joining the monastery as a monk, a very rare insight into his spiritual thinking at this time.

At the end of 1896, at the age of thirty-five, he made a momentous decision to become a Catholic and was received into the Catholic

Church in the Jesuit Church, Farm Street, London. To say that the family was "shell-shocked" was an understatement. Not that the family members were in any way hostile to John's decision; after all, John's mother, whom they all loved, was a devout Catholic. It was simply that John had never expressed any great interest in theological matters and seemed to be a good "typical Protestant". We can only imagine the reaction of Lady Sullivan on receiving the news. It was probably an answer to her prayers.

On his return to Dublin, John's life changed dramatically. From the young man who had been referred to as "the best-dressed man" in Dublin, his new style was of the simplest. He stripped his room of anything that reflected luxury or ostentation. He was immediately drawn toward the poor and the needy. He visited the schools and the Night Refuges of the homeless. He was always a welcome visitor to Our Lady's Hospice for the Dying. His good works brought him into contact with some of the convents and religious houses in Dublin, where he made some lasting friendships.

Then in 1900, the family was given another profound surprise when John decided to become a priest and to enter the Society of Jesus. His training as a Jesuit followed the usual pattern. The program of formation began with a two-year novitiate at Tullabeg, Co. Offaly. This was followed by studies in philosophy at Stonyhurst (Lancashire) and then theology in Milltown Park, Dublin. From the beginning, it was noticed that he was different. He gave himself completely to his new way of life. All who lived with him could not fail to notice his holiness and devotion to deep prayer. Throughout the years of formation, he never paraded his superior intellectual gifts; he was always available to help in any way possible, especially in the most menial of tasks.

He was ordained a priest at Milltown Park on Sunday, July 28, 1907, and was then sent to join the community at Clongowes Wood College, Co. Kildare, to begin a life of priestly, pastoral service. Apart from the period 1919–1924, when he was appointed Rector of Rathfarnham Castle, the rest of his Jesuit life was spent in Clongowes.

Many of the boys who were in his care remembered him as someone who was "different" and "special". He was a good counselor—but not a good teacher. The boys often considered that they passed their exams more through the power of his prayers than the quality of his teaching, despite his brilliant mind and intellectual achievement. The brilliant scholar is not always the best teacher, but a holy man is always a holy man, and the power and influence of that holiness were acknowledged and recognized. For many of his former pupils, it was only in later years that they realized how extraordinary it was to be "taught by a saint".

Father John was known far beyond the confines of Clongowes. He was a constant friend to the sick, the poor, and to anyone who was in distress or need. He had the reputation for the strange gift of healing of the body and the spirit. The accounts of his reputed cures are legion, although he would have been appalled at any effort to imply that he had cured anybody. He always insisted that it was not his achievement or influence, but his many friends recognized the power of God working in him. There are many families who treasure the records of the past, records of how Father John brought healing and peace to many troubled lives.

The years in Clongowes are a spiritual testimony to John Sullivan. He lived a very rugged and ascetical life. His meals were of the simplest; he lived mainly on a diet of dry bread, porridge, rice, and cold tea. He slept little, spending most of the night in prayer. His room lacked even the ordinary comforts of life. The fire was lit only in winter when he was expecting a visitor. The stylish dress of his earlier years was gone forever; he now wore the patched garments of the poor. His life-style reflected the simplicity and hardship of the Desert Fathers—it was a life of austerity and prayer.

One interest that he maintained from the past was his interest in cycling. His old-fashioned bicycle was a familiar sight around the roads of Kildare. He was known to have cycled to Dublin, on more than one occasion, to visit the sick. Having prayed with the sick person, he would then set out immediately on the return journey. His passion, for what in his younger days was a newfangled invention, stood him in good stead in later years. When not traveling by bicycle, he usually walked. His stooped, shuffling figure was well known, and it was always presumed, when he was seen along the roads, that he was on his way to attend someone who needed his presence and prayers.

Father John's reputation as a saint grew rapidly during his time in Clongowes. Very few knew of his illustrious family history or of his previous life as a fashionable well-dressed young man, so much in contrast with the humble poor man who was their priest and friend. He died at Saint Vincent's Nursing Home on Leeson Street in Dublin on February 19, 1933. Great crowds gathered in Clongowes for his funeral Mass presided over by the Bishop of Kildare and Leighlin, Matthew Cullen.

During his lifetime, and even more so after his death, there was a deep conviction about the genuine holiness of this good priest. His grave became a place of pilgrimage, and there was a constant demand for keepsakes and pieces of his clothing, which were treasured as relics. In 1947, it was decided to propose Father John as a candidate for beatification. As a result of this initial inquiry, the first stage in the process was completed, and he was declared Servant of God in September 1960. His mortal remains were removed from Clongowes and brought to a special tomb in the Jesuit Church, Gardiner Street, Dublin.

A remarkable feature of the beatification cause has been the most welcome support and encouragement from the Church of Ireland in ceremonies to honor this extraordinary Jesuit. It is not forgotten that Father John was a member of the Church of Ireland into his mid-thirties. One of his great admirers was the late Archbishop of Dublin, George Otto Simms.

The life of Blessed John Sullivan, S.J., sets an example to all who seek God. It is the story of a most extraordinary pilgrimage. The path traveled often reveals a ruggedness that matures the soul's search for God. It is a life that radiates authenticity. This holy man made a profound effect on those he met. His secret? One elderly woman whom he had helped perhaps provides the key: "Father Sullivan is very hard on himself, but not on others."

# 15

# The Servant of God
# Bishop Joseph Shanahan

## (1871–1943)

## Bishop, Founder, and Vicar Apostolic of Southern Nigeria

### Sister Angela Ruddy, M.S.H.R.

On Christmas morning 1943, Bishop Joseph Shanahan died in the Maia Carberry hospital in Nairobi, Kenya. The matron came on duty shortly after he had received Holy Communion and went to check on him. She thought he was sleeping but noticed that the light was shining over his bed and thought it might disturb him. She went to turn it off. She found that he was not sleeping but dead—and there was no light turned on.

Joseph Shanahan was born in Glankeen, Borrisoleigh, Co. Tipperary, on June 4, 1871. He was the fourth of eleven children, his parents being Daniel Shanahan and Margaret Walsh. Joseph had four sisters and six brothers. Young Joseph had a very happy home environment. John Jordan, C.S.Sp., remarked "that he had a deep supernatural home life where faith was the very air one breathed".[1] Joseph had an easy, natural, open affectionate relationship with his family. One can presuppose that those warm and affectionate familial relationships influenced his relationships both with God and with others and were to have far-reaching effects in his later life as an evangelizer. Joseph

---

[1] P. J. Jordan, *Bishop Shanahan of Southern Nigeria* (Dublin: Elo Press, 1971), p. 2.

attended the nearby Clohinch Primary School, where the Catholic ethos was a continuation of the ethos of his home.

At the age of fifteen, Joseph had a great desire to become a priest and a missionary. This would mean attending a secondary school, but his parents were poor. Joseph's maternal uncle, Patrick Walsh (Brother Adelm, C.S.Sp.), was working in a Spiritan Missionary school in Beauvais, France. He approached Father Limbour, C.S.Sp., the priest in charge, and asked him to take Joseph into the school. He agreed, and Joseph's parents gave their consent. On August 16, 1886, Joseph left his home in Ireland and set out on the long road that led to Beauvais and priesthood.

In those years of his secondary education, his willingness to acculturate, to gain proficiency in a new language, to overcome loneliness and isolation, to socialize in a multicultural situation, as well as his pioneering spirit, were very evident. There he learned to respect other cultures and values, to form relationships with people of different backgrounds and to respect their values. All of this stood him in good stead and were to have far-reaching effects later in life when he took over as Prefect Apostolic of the Spiritan mission in Southern Nigeria. His spiritual diary indicates that all of this was not accomplished without a struggle. At the close of his secondary studies, he took his baccalaureate with distinction.

By August 1896, Joseph had completed his philosophy and part of his theology courses but had to interrupt his studies to begin his novitiate year. His novitiate was an extraordinary year of grace for him as the lofty ideal of being a compassionate missionary and the desire for holiness of life were engraved on his heart. He wrote in his spiritual notebook: "I must be a saint ... but above all because of the priesthood ... because of my vocation, work to become a saint. Do it perseveringly, seriously, but with trust and without anxiety." He came to the end of his novitiate with an intense desire to become a saint and with a resolution for the future, "Love will be the one driving force of my life ... and I also wish to become a good and valiant missionary."[2]

Straight from his novitiate in Chevilly, after eleven years in France, he found himself as Prefect at Rockwell College near his family home

[2] Missionary Sisters of the Holy Rosary Archive, Dublin, MSHR/3/3/1, 1897.

in Tipperary. He combined the duties of prefect and teacher with those of a theology student. His first profession took place on April 10, 1898, in Rockwell College chapel. He was ordained a priest on April 22, 1900, in Blackrock College, Dublin, and made his perpetual vows the following year. He was assigned to the Spiritan mission of Southern Nigeria in 1902.

Arriving on the banks of the Niger at Onitsha on November 13, 1902, the thirty-one-year-old stepped into a dynamic mission of faith-filled and heroic missionaries, mainly French Spiritans. Up to 1902, the missionaries had set up orphanages for slaves and outcasts, built and staffed primary schools, and bought slaves in order to restore to them their dignity. Father Shanahan inherited this particular approach to evangelization.

Just three years later, on September 28, 1905, at thirty-four years old, he was appointed Prefect Apostolic of Southern Nigeria. His initial missionary strategy was evangelization through schools. He took seriously the insights of Venerable Francis Libermann, co-founder of the Spiritans, regarding the idea of teacher-catechists and set out to actualize this idea on a grand scale. Those teacher-catechists would become his colleagues in his missionary work: he understood the apostolate of the laity long before Vatican II. His Catholic schools would not only spread the Gospel message but would attack slavery at its roots. Open to all, rich, poor, slave, and free, they would in time transform the interior of that unexplored country. In 1913, when Propaganda Fide in Rome raised some question about Father Shanahan's diverting the anti-slavery subsidy to the schools, he wrote to the Cardinal Prefect, "I have regarded the work of the mission as one great struggle against slavery. The Africa of today is not the Africa of twenty years ago. Those who hold the school hold the country, hold its religion, and hold its future."[3] For Shanahan, education was the one permanent bulwark against slavery. Rome did not withdraw the subsidy.

Not all the French Spiritan priests approved of his schools' strategy, and he suffered greatly from opposition. Their main objection had to do with the government grants-in-aid and the right of inspection that he had accepted. Against all opposition and nourished by

[3] Jordan, *Bishop Shanahan*, p. 86.

hours praying before the Blessed Sacrament, he held on to his vision and pushed ahead. When he had first arrived in Nigeria, there were thirteen schools with an enrollment of 800; when he retired from the Vicariate in 1932, there were 1,386 schools with an enrollment of 30,390.

In April 1916, he went for three weeks to Cameroon to visit the mission stations and assess a developing situation. Nigeria's neighboring country, Cameroon was at that time under German administration, and during World War I, German missionaries were being forcibly evacuated. Father Shanahan saw this situation as an ecclesiastical one and acted immediately. He sent a report to the Prefect of the Sacred Congregation of Propaganda Fide in Rome outlining what was happening; in response, the congregation appointed him "*ad interim*" to the administration of the Adamaua Prefecture in Cameroon for the duration of the war.

In the first week of December 1918, he visited the mission stations in Adamaua, administering the sacraments, speaking to the chiefs of the area, and meeting representatives of the British government. He trekked 1,200 kilometers (746 miles) on foot over six months. He wrote, "The Christians are few in number, scattered, without any pastors or any help, without sacraments.... The sacred fire of faith, of hope, of charity, has never gone out of their souls.... In the Catacombs people did not pray with a more sincere devotion.... I would do them again, these 1,000 kilometers (621 miles), a thousand times if it was necessary, to visit even one Christian ... or rather, divine soul among thousands, [a] soul loved by God and destined to Heaven."[4] At the end of the trek, he became seriously ill and was hospitalized. In 1919, he returned to Nigeria.

Returning to Ireland the following year, he was appointed Vicar Apostolic of Southern Nigeria, and on June 6, 1920, he was ordained bishop in the chapel of Maynooth College. Back in Africa, he devised a second missionary strategy: to establish Christian families in his vast missionary territory. Boys were being educated but not girls; both were needed to form the Christian family. He put great emphasis on the need to present an image of true Christian womanhood in Africa. To accomplish this, he founded the Missionary Sisters of Our Lady of

[4] Spiritan (C.S.Sp.) Archive, Chevilly, France, 2 J.1.1. a4, March 1919.

the Holy Rosary at Killeshandra, Co. Cavan, in 1924 with the blessing of Pope Pius XI. He firmly laid the foundation for the status of
the Sisters as missionaries; they needed "careful preparation and training for their special work of evangelization, just as the priest does."[5]
To the Sisters he imparted the flame of his own apostolic spirit.

His innovative proposal to enlist Irish diocesan volunteer priests
was his third missionary strategy. Due to the rapid expansion of the
mission in Nigeria, he realized the need for more priests. He was
given an opportunity to appeal to seminarians in Maynooth College
in 1920, and a number of them volunteered for Nigeria. In the mid-
1920s, in discussion with the volunteer priests, he realized the need for
a society of secular missionary priests. He got full approval from the
pope to establish such a society, but, due to opposition and misunderstandings from fellow missionaries and others, he could not carry out
this undertaking. This caused him great suffering and mental anguish,
but he was sustained by hours of Adoration, sometimes throughout
the night. In time his idea came to fruition when Saint Patrick's Missionary Society was established in 1932 at Kiltegan, Co. Wicklow,
along the lines he had envisaged.

Beset by health problems, Bishop Shanahan decided to submit
his resignation to the pope, who refused to accept it and asked him
to select a coadjutor. Charles Heerey, C.S.Sp., who had worked
with him in Nigeria, was chosen and ordained bishop in 1927. In
1932, the pope finally accepted Bishop Shanahan's resignation, and
he returned to Ireland. He deeply longed to retire in Nigeria, but
this was not made possible for him; he always felt himself to be an
exile in Ireland. In 1938, the Vicar Apostolic of Zanzibar, Bishop J.
Heffernan, C.S.Sp., invited him to Kenya. With great joy he set off
on November 24, 1938, where, in Nairobi, he became chaplain to
Carmelite Sisters.

While in Kenya, he suffered from ill health and many misunderstandings. Because of the intensity of his prayer life and deep faith, he
never harbored bitterness, "Always forgive", he said. He saw God's
hand in all and accepted all. The Carmelite Sisters said that sometimes
the bishop looked as if his skin were parchment and as if a lamp were
burning within and shining out through his face. They said that he

---

[5] Missionary Sisters of the Holy Rosary Archive, Dublin, MSHR/1/1/1, November 1923.

was a saint. Dr. J.R. Gregory, who attended him shortly before his death, wrote, "I was called to the presbytery, and there I met the most holy man I have ever seen in my life. He had such a beautiful face and charming expression ... he was in great pain.... I am sure that Heaven is enriched by his presence there, and I can never hope to meet his like."[6]

Bishop Shanahan died on Christmas morning 1943 and was buried in Nairobi, but the Igbo people of Nigeria sought his interment among them. The exhumation took place on December 20, 1955, and the remains were flown back to Nigeria; the casket returned to a tumultuous welcome and a tour of all the missions where night vigils were held. Thousands of people lined the roads to welcome back "Our Saint Patrick". After an open air Mass in Onitsha, the casket was brought into the cathedral and interred beneath the floor of the east transept, in front of the altar of the Blessed Virgin.

On November 15, 1997, Bishop Shanahan's cause for canonization was opened in the Archdiocese of Onitsha. The diocesan inquiry into his life and heroic virtue is completed, but the inquiry in the Archdiocese of Dublin is still ongoing. Bishop Joseph Shanahan, C.S.Sp., was one of the greatest missionaries of the twentieth century. His vision for the evangelization of Nigeria was matched only by his passionate apostolic spirit. He is worthy to be counted among the saints of the Church.

## Further reading:

Dynan, E. *A Man for Everybody: The Story of Bishop Joseph Shanahan*. Dublin: Veritas, 2001.

Forristal, D. *The Second Burial of Bishop Shanahan*. Dublin: Veritas, 1990.

Jordan, J.P. *Bishop Shanahan of Southern Nigeria*. Dublin: Elo Press, 1971.

Kiggins, T. *Maynooth Mission to Africa: The Story of Saint Patrick's, Kiltegan*. Dublin: Gill and MacMillan, 2001.

---

[6] Ibid., MSHR/3/6/2/1/(i), February 1969.

# 16

# Venerable Edel Quinn

## *(1907–1944)*

## Layperson, Legion of Mary Envoy, and Missionary

### *Father John S. Hogan*

The vast expanse of Africa did not intimidate Edel Quinn; it invigo-rated her. As soon as she caught sight of it for the first time, she was eager to begin her work. The boat carrying her from Dublin docked for a brief respite at Port Sudan, and she was off it, setting foot on the land that would be her last home. For eight years, possessed with a singular zeal, she covered huge distances in East Africa, establishing the Legion of Mary and serving the Church as a missionary to grow-ing Christian communities. Her lungs racked with the illness that would eventually claim her, she drove herself on to the astonishment of those she had left behind in Ireland. To many of them, Edel was an enigma, even to members of her family. Quiet and amiable, strong-willed, and passionate, what emerged in the woman tracking across Africa surprised, even shocked those who thought they knew her. By the time of her death, Edel had left an extraordinary legacy that dumbfounded many but also opened their eyes to something they had not realized about her: this was a woman through whom God did the most tremendous things.

Edel was born in Kanturk, Cork, on September 14, 1907, the feast of the Exaltation of the Holy Cross. Her father, Charles, was a bank official, which meant the family had to move regularly from place to place as he filled various positions. She was educated by the Loreto

Sisters and Presentation Sisters and later sent to a boarding school in Liverpool. Bright and vivacious, she was possessed of great charm, intelligence, and elegance. Deeply religious from a young age, she also harbored a desire to enter religious life.

In 1924, her father's dire financial situation was exposed. He was a compulsive gambler, and his debts had become unmanageable; the family was in dire straits. To make things worse, he had been embezzling money from the bank to keep his creditors at bay. As the Quinns expected the worst, the bank chose a merciful solution; instead of pressing charges and bringing disgrace on an innocent family, driving them into poverty, Charles was transferred to a Dublin branch to work in the lowly position of a ledger clerk on a much-reduced salary. Living in cramped conditions in Monkstown, facing mounting bills and surviving on a meager income, Edel took charge and sought employment. She trained as a secretary and applied for the civil service. She failed to get a position because her Irish was quite poor; however, she secured a secretarial position in a small Dublin business.

These years were difficult for Edel. She impressed her employer and all who knew her. Though still only eighteen, inwardly she had to abandon whatever hopes she had for her life for the sake of her family. However, she trusted in God to bring them to fruition, if it was his will. In the meantime, she caught the attention of a young Frenchman, Pierre Landrin, her employer. She had had an impact on his life—her faith had rekindled his and brought him back to the Church, but he had also fallen in love with her. In September 1927, he revealed his feelings to her. Edel had to let him down gently; her family situation was bad, but her heart belonged to God and when circumstances improved, she would enter a convent. Though devastated, Pierre accepted her decision; he would later marry and have children. However, though she had not let herself reveal it, she too had feelings for him, and her decision was a difficult one; remaining true to her vocation had been a sacrifice.

By 1928, Edel was running the company, revealing extraordinary administrative and diplomatic skills. She had to deal with a workers' strike and did so with competence and firmness. In 1929, she joined the Legion of Mary and took to it immediately. By now she was immersed in a life of deep prayer and reading about the Faith; practical works of charity emerged naturally from her interior life. As the legionaries became more familiar with her, they were impressed with her ability and holiness of life; they spoke to Frank Duff, the founder of the Legion, about her. In conversations with her, Frank realized that they had a singular legionary in Edel, and he soon asked her to take charge of difficult situations, which she did with great competence. In the meantime, as family circumstances improved, she began making preparations to enter religious life; she planned to enter the Poor Clares in Belfast on March 25, 1932.

Quite suddenly Edel's plans came crashing down; not long before she was due to leave, she had a hemorrhage that turned out to be a symptom of TB. Following a medical examination, it was discovered that she was in an advanced stage of the disease. As always, she embraced this development with generosity and left it all in the hands of God; he knew the plan he had for her life, and this would not confound it. On February 5, 1932, she was admitted to a sanatorium in Wicklow; there she endured the treatment that doctors hoped would ease the progress of the disease if not cure it. Though she suffered a great deal, she was still vivacious and charming. Her spiritual life deepened even further, and before long her desire for apostolic work found expression in helping around the sanatorium. After eighteen months, her health a little improved, she decided she might as well leave and get back to her work.

Life resumed as per normal for Edel in the years following her discharge. Religious life was no longer a possibility, but her work for the Legion increased—she realized that this was where God wanted her. In 1934, she took part in a project in England and Wales and returned healthier than when she left, which was noted by her fellow legionaries. She asked to be sent back to Wales to work full time for the Legion there. At that time, Concilium, the Legion's head council, was considering a request to send an envoy to Africa; Frank Duff thought of Edel and speaking with her asked if she might consider it. She agreed immediately—the climate might even benefit her health. Concilium would have to be convinced. The meeting that followed was stormy. For many in the Legion, Edel was the last person who should be sent—no one doubted her ability or zeal; it was her precarious health that was the issue. She had spent eighteen months in a sanatorium suffering from TB; she was frail; to send her to Africa would be to condemn her to death, as one legionary said to Frank. Yet, he knew that this was a woman not marked with death, but with life and a mission—there was a surprising providence at work in this woman's life. Edel spoke up for herself, and this seemed to ease tensions. When the matter came to a vote, the decision was unanimous; she was appointed. East Africa, 750,000 square miles of the continent, was entrusted to her to further the Legion and its mission.

Edel left Ireland on October 4, 1936; she knew she would never return. She arrived at Mombasa on November 23, the feast of the great Irish missionary Saint Columbanus. She made her way to Nairobi in Kenya. Hungry to get going, she immediately began to speak to priests and laity, gathered groups, founded praesidia, and urged them out into the mission of the Church in Africa. This was to be the pattern of her life, and there was little doubt that she was being led by the Spirit. There seemed to be no planned organization to her itinerary: she dashed all over Kenya, Uganda, Tanzania, Malawi, and Mauritius with abandon as opportunities arose, as if she were being spirited by a supernatural force. As her letters and reports arrived at Concilium, they were read with astonishment. There were no surprises for Frank; he was overjoyed at her successes, but he had discerned the hand of God; others reassessed their view. She was traversing Africa, deserts and wilderness, first with the help of other missionaries and then with her own car. Praesidia and higher councils were being founded, and African lay Catholics were taking their place in the life and mission of the Church.

She faced many challenges and disappointments, but overall, there was a great fruitfulness to her mission. Mysteriously, her health was stable enough, though she was grounded at times with fever, malaria, or the effects of the TB. What her body seemed unable to do, her spirit supplied. Indifference and opposition from priests were a constant barrier, but she endured it with charity, gentleness, and creativity. She was, of course, being watched, most attentively. Fellow missionaries took note of what she did and said and came to their own conclusions. All of them agreed: not only was this young woman extraordinary, she was a saint.

In 1941, Edel's health collapsed, and she was admitted to a sanatorium in South Africa. For six months she endured, not only the ravages of her disease, but an intense loneliness—it was a dark night. As she always did, she embraced it with generosity; in those months, it was the Eucharist that sustained her. As her condition gradually improved, she was eager to get back to the mission. She discharged herself in October 1942, she was not better—she never would be—but she had to continue her work. Offered a place in Zululand, she declined and made for Nairobi. Living in a small room in Saint Teresa's Convent, she resumed her work, visiting praesidia, dealing with correspondence, and setting off on journeys to inspect and support praesidia and councils and to lay the foundation for more. Her hectic life continued to be sustained by daily Mass and personal prayer; she spent long hours in the chapel.

Christmas 1943 saw a turn for the worse in Edel's health. Staying with Carmelite nuns for the season, she suffered a heart attack, but somehow she recovered and got back to her work after a brief respite. The new year saw her slow down as the TB began to claim her strength more and more. In March 1944, she left on a mission to Kisumu to help revitalize praesidia she had founded, but her health collapsed again. She was unable to finish the mission and returned to Nairobi exhausted. Now she understood that the work was done. In her little room in Saint Teresa's convent, she spent her mornings in bed and afternoons resting in the garden dealing with correspondence, all the time immersed in prayer; she was waiting.

On May 12, Edel suffered another heart attack as she was resting in the garden. Carried back to her room, a priest was called, and she was given the Last Rites as she drifted in and out of consciousness. At one point she opened her eyes to see the priest holding up her statue of Our Lady. Gazing at it she said "Jesus, Jesus", and as the priest continued the prayers for the dying, she died. Two days later, she was buried in the missionaries' cemetery in Nairobi followed by a Requiem Mass. Not long after, reports of favors were being received, and Concilium realized that it was time for the Legion to begin, for the first time, a process of beatification for one of its members. It was no surprise to Frank Duff that it was Edel. Edel was declared Venerable on December 15, 1994, and a miracle to see her beatified is being sought.

**Further reading:**
Suenens, Leon-Joseph. *Edel Quinn, Envoy of the Legion of Mary to Africa.* Dublin: C.J. Fallon, 1953.

**Further information:**
See www.legionofmary.ie.

# 17

# The Servant of God
# Father Edward J. Flanagan

## *(1886–1948)*

### Priest

*Steven R. Wolf*

Edward J. Flanagan was born in a thatched cottage at Leabeg, Co. Roscommon, on July 13, 1886. It is believed that he was born prematurely, leading to respiratory problems that he struggled with for the remainder of his life. Young Edward attended Drimatemple National School just across the field from his home in County Roscommon and completed secondary school with honors at Summerhill College, Sligo. The Flanagans were sheep farmers, and Edward often minded the sheep in the fields. They were a devout Catholic family, and Father Flanagan felt the first stirrings of his vocation to the priesthood from a very early age.

He emigrated to the United States in 1904 and permanently located in Omaha, Nebraska, in 1906. He was ordained to the priesthood in 1912 at the Royal Imperial Leopold Francis University, Innsbruck, Austria. He returned to Nebraska, where his first parish assignment was at Saint Patrick's Church in O'Neill, Nebraska. Around this time, he began mission work with homeless men. Through hearing of their backgrounds and experiences, he came to understand the importance of a healthy childhood, and he saw that pastoral work with needy young people was the best possible way to prevent them from ultimately becoming another generation of broken men and criminals.

In 1917, he founded what has become a world-famous youth-care institution and village on the outskirts of Omaha, called Boys Town. He was a revolutionary in his time, bringing together youth of all races, creeds, and color under one roof without any segregation. This was unheard of in the United States and decades ahead of the civil rights movement of the 1960s. He faced open and harsh criticism for his methods, which included allowing orphaned and troubled children from all races to live openly together as equals and independently govern themselves at Boys Town without fences, barred windows, or locked doors. When the number of children he was caring for outgrew the second facility they occupied, no one would sell or lease him a property within the city of Omaha. Not one to be deterred, he ended up purchasing Overlook Farm, which was several miles beyond the outskirts of Omaha in 1921. This farm became what it remains today—an incorporated village in the State of Nebraska, named Boys Town. To this day it is still a sanctuary for children in need and a beacon of the best possible youth care practices for the whole world.

Bigotry followed Father Flanagan even to Overlook Farm. The local Ku Klux Klan threatened to kill him and burn Boys Town to the ground if he did not send away the Black children under his care. When threats were of no avail, financial bribes were offered. A man offered him $1 million, but only if Father Flanagan removed all the Black and Jewish children from Boys Town. Father Flanagan had significant debts; he always struggled financially to keep food on the table and clothes on the backs of the children; this money would have wiped all of his financial concerns away, but he remained unmoved in the face of this prejudice. His response to the bigotry he was faced with was to ask, "What color is a man's soul?"

After the attack by the Japanese on the American military bases in Hawaii on December 7, 1942, the United States entered into World War II. One of the ugliest turn of events domestically was the rounding up of American citizens of Japanese descent and their forced placement in internment camps. These mostly second-generation ethnic Japanese, known as the Nisei, were stripped of their private property and treated as less than second-class citizens. In the midst of war, fear, and unfounded bigotry, Father Flanagan entered into this fray, liberating approximately 200 American Nisei from these camps by personally sponsoring each one and bringing them to the freedom and dignity found at Boys Town.

Father Flanagan became recognized as a world-renowned expert in advanced youth-care methods for disadvantaged and neglected children and an advisor to presidents and other world leaders on the best practice in child care. His mission brought him back home to Ireland in 1946, where he admonished the treatment of children at industrial schools operated by the government and religious orders. When he returned to the United States, he had the audacity to call out the religious and governmental leaders at the head of these abuses. Father Flanagan said, "What you need over there is to have someone shake you loose from your smugness and satisfactions and set an example by punishing those who are guilty of cruelty, ignorance, and neglect of their duties in high places. I wonder what God's judgment will be with reference to those who hold the deposit of faith and fail in their God-given stewardship of little children." Father Flanagan was practically the only voice criticizing the bad practices of that time in Ireland. He loved the land in which he was born and reared and wanted to help solve the child-care problems he saw in Ireland. He was not a mere critic, but an Irishman with a proven solution that could have been applied in Ireland. His condemnations were not merely ignored or dismissed; instead, the Irish establishment set upon him and sought to shred his integrity and reputation in a public fashion. Father Flanagan vowed that he would return home to Ireland and close down every last institution in Ireland in which he saw children being mistreated. "I do not believe that a child can be reformed by lock and key and bars, or that fear can ever develop a child's character", he said. He gave notice that he would take leave of his work at Boys Town to return home to Ireland, but another urgent call came in to help youth in critical need, and he never got the chance.

Following the end of World War II, he was asked to help with the orphan crisis in the Philippines, Korea, and Japan by General Douglas MacArthur. After successful work there, President Harry Truman then asked him to provide the same assistance for war orphans in Austria and Germany. In the course of this mission, he died of a massive heart attack in Berlin, Germany, on May 15, 1948, literally giving his last breath in the service to children in need.

Father Flanagan left behind an enormous legacy. Even during his lifetime, his example and methods inspired eighty youth-care programs modeled on his philosophies and the operations of Boys Town across the globe. He transformed the juvenile justice system across the United States and changed the way America takes care of its most vulnerable and abused children. He spoke truth to power in Ireland, and had he not been rebuked by the Irish establishment at the time, he could have prevented decades of additional suffering for children, a legacy that is still tearing at the fabric of Irish culture and its people's relationship with the Catholic Church.

A world leader for youth care, and a civil-rights champion clearly decades ahead of his time, his legacy sprang from his deep life of faith and prayer. He trusted completely that Christ and the Gospel are the way, the truth, and the life. It is legitimate to recognize him as among the greatest humanitarians of the twentieth century and among the greatest sons of Ireland. He is an icon for the Catholic virtue of Ireland and the antidote for the poison of the clergy abuse of youth scandals rocking the universal Church.

Father Flanagan has the twin distinction of appearing on a U.S. postage stamp and being the only Catholic priest ever to appear on a U.S. Mint coin, a gold coin no less, minted in 2017. But, more importantly, his mission work continues today; Boys Town recently celebrated the 100th anniversary of its founding. This program has grown to other locations across the United States and provides direct aid to more than one million children and families each year. Boys Town took in its first native Irish youth in the early 2000s, a teenager who happened to be from County Roscommon, the county of Father Flanagan's birth. Several other troubled Irish boys and girls have taken residence at Boys Town for assistance and returned to Ireland to lead productive lives. Ireland's Western Health Board staff have collaborated with Boys Town officials for program development and staff training, all important steps in fulfilling Father Flanagan's desire to bring his mission work home to his people.

Father Edward Flanagan's cause was initiated thanks to a groundswell of devotion spread by former youth of Boys Town in 1999 in cooperation with the Holy Spirit. The official opening of the cause was March 17, 2012, the feast day of Ireland's patron, Saint Patrick. The diocesan investigation was sent to the Vatican in September of

2015. The Dicastery for the Causes of Saints issued a decree of Judicial Validity for the cause in 2017. The *Positio*, which makes the closing argument and offers proof of his heroic virtue, was officially submitted to the congregation, and the historical commission completed its review in December 2019. At the time of writing, there have been twenty-three alleged miracles attributed to his intercession. Two tribunals have been held so far, but the investigations allowed that some small margin of human intervention may have been involved in these individual healings. The Servant of God Father Flanagan himself encouraged "Pray, for prayers work miracles." The Father Flanagan League Society of Devotion asks that you join them in beseeching the intercession of Servant of God Edward J. Flanagan with your prayers. May you have your intention met, and the recognition that Father Flanagan, a son of Ballymoe, Ireland, is among the Communion of Saints for the greater glory of Christ Our Lord.

### Further reading:
Stevens, Father Clifford J. *Legacy of Devotion, Father Edward J. Flanagan of Boys Town*. Boys Town: Boys Town Press, 2019.

### Further information:
See www.fatherflanagan.org and https://www.facebook.com/Flanagan League/.

# 18

# The Columban Martyrs of Korea

The Servants of God
Father Anthony Collier, Monsignor Patrick Brennan,
Father James Maginn, Father Patrick Reilly,
Father Thomas Cusack, Father John O'Brien,
and Father Francis Canavan

*(Died 1950)*

Priests and Missionaries

*Father Seán Coyle, S.S.C.*

Columban Father Ray Collier recalls that in October 1950, when he was eight or nine, the parish priest of Clogherhead, Co. Louth, came to his school and announced to the assembled pupils and teachers that Father Anthony Collier (Ray's uncle) had died in Korea. Earlier that year, the young Ray had been serving his uncle's Mass daily. Father Anthony was a Columban priest who went to Korea in 1939. He had just completed language studies and begun missionary work when he and other Columbans were placed under house arrest by the Japanese, who had occupied Korea since 1910 and entered World War II in December 1941. Father Ray remembered his uncle as easygoing and delighting in making films of his family, unknown to them, with his cinecamera; something rare at the time. He recalled, too, that before he returned to Korea in the early summer of 1950, Father Anthony told the family that North Korea would probably invade the South.

This they did on the morning of Sunday, June 25, beginning a war that ended on July 27, 1953, with the signing of the Korean Armistice Agreement.

After Sunday Mass on the morning of the invasion, Father Anthony, who was parish priest of Suyangno, Chunchon city, met with Monsignor Thomas Quinlan, the Prelate of the Prefecture Apostolic of Chunchon and Father Francis Canavan. Father Anthony turned down the offer of an American officer to take the priests to safety, saying, "I want to be with my parishioners." Two days later, North Korean soldiers arrested him and Gabriel Kim, a parish catechist. They tied them together, shot them, and left, thinking both were dead. But Gabriel survived and reported Father Anthony's death to the Columbans. The Clogherhead priest was the first foreigner to die in the Korean War.

Six other Columbans were to die within months as a result of the Korean War. They were Monsignor Patrick Brennan, Fathers James Maginn, Patrick Reilly, Thomas Cusack, John O'Brien, and Francis Canavan. All seven are included in a list of eighty-one martyrs of the twentieth century, fifty-eight Korean and twenty-three foreign, proposed for beatification in a list finalized by the bishops of Korea in 2012, now under the title "Bishop Francis Borgia Hong Yong-ho and Companions".

Father James Maginn was based in Samcheok city on the east coast of South Korea. Born in Butte, Montana, in 1911, he grew up in Newcastle, Co. Down, after his family moved back there when he was nine or ten. He studied in Saint Malachy's College, Belfast, before entering the Columbans in 1929 and was ordained in December 1935. He went to Korea in 1936, three years after the Columbans had opened their first mission there. He, too, was under house arrest during World War II. After the invasion from the north, Father James' parishioners pleaded with him to flee, but, as many of them testified later, he said, "As pastor I am staying here in the church." The North Koreans arrested him and shot him on July 4, 1950.

Teresa Maginn Dunne, a first cousin of Father James, speaks of "such a sense of loss and grieving" when the family learned of his death in 1952. His body had been located by Father Brian Geraghty, the Columban superior in Korea and one of a pioneering group of Columbans that went there in 1933. Some years later, Teresa trained as a nurse in the Mater Hospital, Belfast. She asked a priest from Saint Malachy's College, where her cousin had done his secondary studies, to offer Mass for her. He told her to pray through the intercession of Father James. She did so, asking that God would guide her to meet the person he had selected to be her spouse. When Teresa eventually met Jack, she showed him a photo of Father James' grave in Chunchon. Jack, who had served in the U.S. Army in Korea during the war, told her that he had visited the grave and that he had also given money to rebuild the church there. In 2003, she and Jack visited Chunchon, and Teresa was very much aware that she was, at that time, the only blood relative to visit Father James' grave.

Father Patrick Reilly was a parish priest in Mukho, north of Samcheok. From Drumraney, Co. Westmeath, he did his secondary studies in Saint Finian's, Mullingar. He was ordained in December 1940. Because of World War II, he was unable to go to Korea until 1947; he spent the intervening years in the Diocese of Clifton, England. On the day of the invasion, he too said to parishioners who advised him to leave, "A pastor cannot desert the flock." He stayed in the house of a catechist but was arrested on August 29. His body was found on a mountain path where he had been shot.

When the Korean War began, Monsignor Patrick Brennan was Prefect Apostolic of Kwangju in the southwest of South Korea. Of Irish ancestry, he was born in Chicago in 1901 and ordained a priest for the Archdiocese of Chicago in 1928. He became a Columban in 1936 and was sent to Korea in 1937. He was known for his warm, generous-hearted nature. He, with two other priests, Father Thomas Cusack, parish priest of Mokpo, and his assistant, Father John O'Brien, were taken by the North Korean army and died in a massacre of prisoners in Taejon on the night of September 24.

Father Thomas Cusack was born in Liscannor, Co. Clare, in 1910. He studied at Saint Mary's College, Galway, before entering Saint Columban's in Shrule, on the Galway-Mayo border, in 1928. He was ordained in 1934, when he went to Korea, remaining there without a break until 1947. After a holiday at home, he returned to Korea in 1949, where he was assigned to Kwangju. He wrote home after the Korean War broke out, "Mother, if I were to leave my people, I would never have a sound night's sleep again." When she read this, she said, "Had I been there with him, I would have told him the same thing."

Father Thomas' cousin, Columban priest, Father Tom Cusack, speaks of the physical strength of his older cousin, who survived peritonitis when a student, his life being saved by a surgeon from Galway. He was known to his parishioners in Korea as "The Iron Man". When Father Thomas came home in 1947, he spent a month with the family of young Tom, who was then fourteen. Tom was acquainted with many priests, but this was his first time to come to know one. He described Father Thomas as "a joy ... totally human, great fun, even to relate to us children very, very beautifully".

Father John O'Brien was born in Donamon, Co. Roscommon, in 1918. After five years in Saint Nathy's, Ballaghaderreen, he entered the Columbans in 1936 and was ordained in 1942. He was a chaplain in the British Army until 1948, when he finally got to Korea. His younger brother Vincent also became a Columban priest and served in the Philippines for many years.

During the priests' imprisonment prior to martyrdom, Lieutenant Alexander Makarounis, an American soldier who shared a prison cell with them, wrote in *The Far East*, the Columban magazine, in May 1951: "Father O'Brien had a good voice, and the way he sang *Far Away Places* sort of made you forget that you were cooped up in a prison cell and sent your thoughts flying back home." Lt. Makarounis said of the three Columbans, "I shall always remember them for the comfort, cheerfulness, kindness, and courage they somehow communicated to us when they were no better off themselves."

In July 1950, three other Columbans were taken prisoner in Chunchon: Monsignor Thomas Quinlan, Father Phil Crosbie, and Father Francis Canavan. Monsignor Quinlan, from Borrisoleigh, Co. Tipperary, was Prefect Apostolic of Chunchon and later bishop of the Diocese of Chunchon. Father Phil Crosbie was from Victoria, Australia, while Father Francis Canavan was from near Headford, Co. Galway. After his secondary studies in Saint Mary's, Galway, Father Francis joined the Columbans and was ordained in December 1940. He worked in the Diocese of Galway until 1949, when he went to Korea.

The three were interned in a school outside Pyongyang and later forced to take part in a notorious "death march" that ended on November 8 in Linjiang. Ninety-six prisoners, many of them missionaries, Catholic and Protestant, some American soldiers, died along the way. Father Canavan died in a prison camp on December 6, 1950. Monsignor Quinlan, Father Crosbie, and the other prisoners were released in 1953. Father Crosbie wrote about the experience in his book *Three Winters Cold*, published in Ireland in 1955 by Browne and Nolan and in some countries with the title *Pencilling Prisoner*.

The remains of Fathers Anthony Collier, James Maginn, and Patrick Reilly were recovered and eventually buried in the grounds of Chunchon Cathedral. The bodies of Monsignor Patrick Brennan, Fathers John O'Brien, and Thomas Cusack were buried with others killed in the massacre in a mass grave. Exhumed in 1952, all the bodies were cremated together and reburied. These ashes were later laid to rest in a memorial in Daejeon. The body of Francis Canavan was buried where he died on the death march; a memorial to him stands over an empty grave at Chunchon Cathedral.

These seven Columban priests were products of a time when the Church in the Western world was very outward looking. The first half of the twentieth century saw an extraordinary growth in the missionary dimension of the Irish Church, including the Legion of Mary, a lay movement. There was an idealism that also led to the independence of most of Ireland and a willingness to sacrifice. That era is often depicted in very negative, dark terms. Awful poverty, high emigration, unemployment, and poor housing were realities, but successive governments tried to deal with these issues. The young men and women who became missionaries were well aware of the dangers that might await them.

Those who joined the Columbans in the 1950s and 1960s were familiar with the stories of the Korean martyrs and with those of Columbans who had been imprisoned in and expelled from China during the same years, and with those who died during the Battle of Manila in February 1945. The decisions that the seven Columbans in Korea made to stay with their people is something that touches the hearts of those today who are trying to follow Jesus Christ faithfully. The contemporary Western world does not encourage long-term commitments of any kind, never mind laying down one's life for others. And yet when such happens, people are truly inspired. And this century has produced many martyrs.

The Church in Korea sees these priests as martyrs because, though each had a chance to escape, each chose to stay with his parishioners.

The cause for their beatification, among the eighty-one, has been opened and is advancing in Korea. Two dossiers of a proposed five of documentation on the group to be presented to Rome had been completed by the summer of 2019; the second dossier includes the documentation on the Columbans. In June of 2022, the Diocesan Inquiry into the cause was concluded and the Acts sent to the Dicastery for the Causes of Saints. The process now moves to the Roman Phase, where the *Positio* will be written and submitted to the various consultors for examination.

Further information:

More information about the seven Columban martyrs of Korea can be found on the website of the Columban Missionaries: https://columbans.ie/about-us/columban-martyrs/.

# 19

# The Servant of God
# Mother Mary Kevin Kearney

## *(1875–1957)*

## Missionary and Founder

### *Sister Cecilia Sweeney, F.M.S.A.*

I remember being almost crazy and desperate because of my temptations. I came to Mother in floods of tears to tell her of my despair. After talking kindly to me for a few minutes, she picked up a basket with four little kittens in it. Mother lifted each little kitten and tried to put it down on the floor, but each one clung to her hands, digging tiny claws into her sleeves. Then she smiled at me and said: "Be like the little kittens. Cling on! God is your heavenly Father. If you cling to Him, nothing evil can happen to you. Fear nothing child! Trust in God."

This was the testimony of a young Sister, speaking of her Founder, Mother Mary Kevin Kearney. Mother Kevin left her mark on those she met and the Sisters she formed, though, in humility, she saw herself merely as a poor servant. She once said, "I have done so little for God in my life, and he has given me so much grace; but he knows that I tried to love him, poor and weak as I am. In time and eternity he will deal with us in mercy. He knows our weakness and loves us just the same." But to many in Africa she was known as "Mama Kevina", and she found joy in using her talents to help others.

The future Mother Kevin was born Teresa Kearney at Knockenrahen, Arklow, Co. Wicklow, on April 28, 1875. Her parents, Michael

Kearney and Teresa Grennell, had happily been blessed by the birth of two daughters, Elizabeth and Ann. But in January 1875, tragedy entered their lives when Michael, returning from a sheep sale in a neighboring town, met with a fatal accident and died before the birth of their third daughter. Teresa's birth was therefore an event marked by joy and sorrow. She was to encounter more sorrow when she was only ten years old and her mother died, and she experienced the trauma of separation as family members were scattered. The final blow for her was the death of her beloved grandmother ten years after her mother. With an early life that was so traumatized, we might expect a needy, disturbed character to develop—a fit subject for a psychiatrist's couch! Far from it. Teresa Kearney was a lively, warm-hearted young girl who loved nature and never settled for half-measures. Her early encounter with family tragedy, as well as the struggle of growing up in rural Ireland in the wake of the Great Famine, may have begun to prepare her for her great mission of bringing love and solace to sick and suffering people. She drew strength from reflecting on the Passion of Christ and made it her special dedication at her Profession.

From early in her life, Teresa seems to have had the heart of a missionary disciple; thus, she took "de Paul" as her Confirmation name. Her vocation came from a strong sense of conviction, a belief in the Spirit at work and a strong commitment to live according to God's plan as it unfolded in her life. Moving to England, she entered the Franciscan Missionary Sisters of the Five Wounds at Saint Mary's Abbey, Mill Hill, London. This was the Victorian era, the suffragette movement had not even begun; it was a generally rigid but safe and predictable time. No scandal rocked the Church, and the missionary vocation was tremendously esteemed, particularly the vocation to the "foreign mission", and in choosing to go to the Abbey, Teresa Kearney knew that she was going to a center of missionary zeal. She connected with this spirit. Making profession in the congregation, she was now known as Sister Mary Kevin of the Sacred Passion.

In December 1902, Sister Kevin and five companions were sent from their convent in Mill Hill, London, bound for Uganda. Archbishop Henry Hanlon, M.H.M., in Kampala, had requested Sisters to come to Uganda to promote, in particular, the human and spiritual development of women and girls. The six companions arrived on January 15, 1903. The interior of Uganda was almost uncharted territory, and the task ahead of them was onerous, but the Sisters responded to the task, and the epic journey involved, with eagerness and zeal. A look at what they packed shows the total contrast with modern missionary travel and modern Africa. They had a stove, a coffee-grinder, a washtub, and sun helmets.

The Uganda they finally reached was both a natural paradise and a place of fear, sickness, and hardship. The people had come through the Arab slave trade and were exhausted from wars and oppression and confused by the sectarian strife and mistrust between religious bodies. Uganda had become a British Protectorate, but medical service was in its infancy and the people were plagued by many illnesses: malaria, virulent fever, leprosy, sleeping sickness, and a terrible incidence of child mortality and maternal death. The Sisters were few in number, just as today, but they were not deterred, and their response to the medical needs began with the setting up of a dispensary under a mango tree in Nsambya, Kampala. Sister Kevin and her companions dispensed what remedies they could to those who came seeking help. With the lack of adequate staff, they also battled with superstition, lack of medicine, equipment, and transport. She also visited people in their homes bringing medicine and comfort. Her greatness of heart and mind endeared her to many, but she also challenged injustice and exploitation wherever she found it. So much was she associated with healing and providing that the Bagandan soldiers in Burma in the war years called the plane that brought their provisions "The Mama Kevina".

From the start, Mother Kevin responded to Africa and its people with the very qualities and values that we ourselves aspire to today. She showed vision and courage in entering the unexplored world of the African interior and approached her work in a spirit of contemplation, welcoming the wonderful diversity she found. She was remarkably inclusive, loved people, and celebrated life with them. Mother Kevin showed herself to be prophetic and forward thinking—in many ways a woman ahead of her time. Her advanced thinking was evident on the issue of midwifery. Her concern for what mothers endured in preparing for and giving birth, and the rate of maternal death, drove her to help procure more liberal legislation from Rome in 1936, allowing Sisters to engage in midwifery, which had been previously forbidden.

Her missionary initiatives encompassed both educational and medical programs. She fought for the right of education for African women and for African girls to join the Sisterhood, meeting all opposition by saying: "We are pledged to do everything possible for the welfare of women in this country." She wanted a better world and a better life for them. Keenly aware of the importance of the involvement of the laity, she made radical calls on people in "home" territories to be part of the missionary work. The Director of Education in Uganda described her work as: "Potentially the most productive that I ever knew; a real source of inspiration for anyone who believed in the spiritual values in education".

In the treatment of leprosy, she understood the fear that the disease inspired and saw it as a grave social problem as well as a medical one. In 1932, she set up the first leprosarium at Nyenga, five miles from the source of the Nile, and later at Buluba, which is situated on the great Lake Victoria/Nyanza. Here the lives of sufferers were transformed thanks to treatment and rehabilitation; and attitudes began to change from dread to the acceptance of leprosy as another illness, one that was treatable when attended to in good time.

Mother Kevin also helped people become pioneers in their own right in many fields. In 1923, when a group of Ugandan girls came to her and asked to be Sisters, she realized that it was an audacious proposal, but with a profound act of faith in the Providence of God, she started plans for a local congregation that would grow and develop close to its roots. "Her crowning glory and the achievement which made Mother most happy", notes Eleanor A. Kearney in her *History of the Kearney Family*, "is the large congregation of African Sisters, the Little Sisters of Saint Francis, founded by her in 1923."

While Mother Kevin received recognition and many tributes for her great zeal and her respectful approach to people, she remained kind, humble, and practical. When she received the MBE [Most Excellent Order of the British Empire] from King George V in 1918, she held a children's party to celebrate the event. W. A. Sheridan, D.C.L., said of her that her boundless charity for her neighbor, manifested by great sacrifice and great zeal, proved the intensity of her love for God. Sheridan notes that it is never easy to assess or evaluate the stature of contemporaries, but there was no doubt that Mother Kevin was one of the great missionary figures of her age. One of her most important achievements, perhaps, was the fact that she succeeded in having women admitted to many spheres of missionary activity that had been forbidden to them before. Demonstrating the heights to which Christianity had elevated women, he continued, she

established not only the usefulness, but also the absolute indispens-
ability of Sisters in missionary apostolate.

Mother Kevin's initiative and spirit formed the missionary group
from Mill Hill Abbey into the nucleus of a new missionary congregation, the second she would found. In 1952, the African Province
of the Mill Hill Sisters became the Franciscan Missionary Sisters for
Africa, and Mother Kevin was appointed its first Superior General.
This was the culmination of many years of journeying in faith, hope,
and love. In Mother's Kevin's later years, when the leadership passed
out of her hands, she easily stepped aside. Freedom within allowed
her to be led by God through the voices of her superiors. For this to
happen in anyone's life is challenging. For Mother Kevin, it was done
with considerable ease and joy.

On October 16, 1957, Mother Kevin died peacefully in her sleep
after a period of work in Boston, U.S., where she was promoting, as
always, an awareness of the missionary role of the Church. She was
buried in the cemetery in Mount Oliver near Dundalk, the motherhouse of the Franciscan Missionary Sisters. However, the people of
Uganda insisted that she be brought back and buried among them,
saying: "She must come home." This was done, and on December 3,
1957, fifty years since she had first sailed to Africa, Mother Kevin was
finally laid to rest in Nkokonjeru, among the people she had loved
and served.

On November 6, 2016, Mother Mary Kevin Kearney was declared
Servant of God at a ceremony in Rubaga Cathedral, Kampala,
Uganda. Aware of her compassion, her love for the poor, zeal, and
reputation for holiness, Bishop Christopher Kakoza, Bishop of Lugazi
Diocese, had asked and obtained from the Dicastery for the Causes of
Saints the rescripts of *Competentia fori* on May 6, 2016, and the *Nihil
Obstat* on July 8, 2016. On October 20, 2016, on the direction of the
Postulator, Dr. Waldery Hilgeman, the Diocesan Inquiry was begun.

**Further reading:**

O'Hara, Sister Louis. *Love Is the Answer.* Dublin: Fallon Educational Supply
  Co., 1964.
————. *The Unfinished Canticle: The Mother Kevin Story.* Serialized in *The
  Curate's Diary*, 2016–2018.

# 20

# The Servant of God
# Alfie Lambe

## *(1932–1959)*

## Layperson and Legion of Mary Envoy

### *Father Oliver Skelly*

Alphonsus Lambe was born in Tullamore, Co. Offaly, on the feast of the Nativity of Saint John the Baptist, June 24, 1932; the year that Ireland first hosted the International Eucharistic Congress. The house in which he was born no longer exists, but the house on the Arden Road where he grew up with his seven brothers and sisters has become a shrine to his memory and is diligently maintained by the Tullamore Curia of the Legion of Mary.

Alfie, as he was known, was educated by the Sisters of Mercy at Saint Joseph's (now Saint Philomena's) Primary School and by the Christian Brothers, first at Saint Brigid's Primary School, Harbour Place, and later at the secondary school on High Street. Prayer was central to his family life: morning and night prayers, daily family recitation of the Rosary, assistance at the Holy Sacrifice of the Mass, and regular confession meant that prayer was as natural to him as the oxygen he breathed. The inspiration he received from the Christian Brothers encouraged Alfie to try his hand at teaching once he left school. At sixteen years of age, he was received into the novitiate, where he chose his religious name, Ignatius, inspired as he was by Saint Ignatius of Loyola, whose motto, "To give and not to count the cost; to fight and not to heed the wounds; to toil, and not to seek for rest; to labor, and not to ask for reward except to know that I am doing your will", struck a chord with him. The following year he began his teacher training at Saint Mary's Teacher Training College in Marino, Dublin, and it was here that he became involved with the Legion of Mary, which had been founded in 1921, the same year as the Irish Free State.

Alfie suffered from indifferent health, and, on medical advice, he reluctantly admitted that God was not calling him to be a Christian Brother. He returned home to work in Salts' textile factory in Tullamore. During his novitiate years, his fellow students had remarked on his devotion to the Mother of God. Now he was in a position to follow that devotion—spiritually by praying the Rosary and practically by immersing himself in the work of the local Curia of the Legion of Mary. Among the acts of charity he engaged in was to work with groups of Travelling People who struggled financially during hard economic times following the Emergency, as World War II was known in Ireland.

Since 1921, the Legion of Mary had been based in Dublin, assisting the materially poor whom the Irish Free State had no money to support. In 1933, the movement spread to the United States of America. Séamus Grace, a Concilium officer in Dublin, wished to extend the movement outside the capital and the main cities and towns to rural areas around Ireland and needed assistance. Back in Tullamore, Alfie's mentor in the Curia was another Dubliner, Tom Cowley, who recognized his potential and introduced the teenager to Grace. Very shortly, Alfie was working full time for the Legion at Concilium, where he was given the task of founding new branches and guiding praesidia. Alfie was acutely aware of his unworthiness to be a member of the Legion of Mary: "I am really very weak," he wrote, "but I know that Our Lady uses the weak to show her power. For some time past I have made it a practice of reciting the Legion Prayer daily toward the end of Mass. Every line of it is full of consolation for weak people."

In 1953, Séamus Grace offered himself to Frank Duff, the founder of the Legion, for service as a Legion envoy. Frank accepted the offer and appointed him envoy to South America; he also suggested that Grace might take the enthusiastic Alfie with him. Thus it was that on the feast of Our Lady of Mount Carmel, July 16, 1953, the two men left Shannon Airport for New York and on to Bogotá, Colombia. There Alfie immediately threw himself into Legion work, helping to found praesidia and engaging in pastoral work, including winning back lapsed Catholics, encouraging couples to regularize their unions, and persuading parents to have their children baptized. He had trouble learning Spanish, but he made every effort to communicate, smiling, gesticulating, and endearing himself to people.

From Colombia, Alfie went on to Ecuador in 1954. As he was about to board the plane, he said farewell to Séamus Grace; the two would never meet again. Arriving in Quito, a whole host of unique challenges awaited him, but he was undeterred and entrusted the work to Our Lady; he was as successful here as in his other assignments. He rallied new legionaries to his cause, reached out to the indigenous peoples, and even founded praesidia in a leprosarium. Though his health was still frail, and he was often ill, he continued to work. However, when he contracted dysentery, his health was impaired even further, and this condition would lead to gradual deterioration in his physical well-being.

Recovering from this bout of dysentery, he was asked to come to Bolivia; he agreed and decided to stop off in Peru on the way. This was to be a holiday, but for Alfie it was a busman's holiday, and he got to work to establish the Legion in Lima and beyond. He then went to Bolivia to do the same there. Following this, Alfie moved to Brazil, learning Portuguese to facilitate his work, and he remained there working with another Irish legionary, Mary Clerkin, until he was called to Argentina in 1955.

When Alfie arrived in Argentina, he found himself in a country in the throes of revolution. Great caution, prudence, and patience would be necessary if he was to make any headway in the country. He was fortunate to have the papal nuncio on his side, and it was the nuncio who persuaded the Argentinian bishops to facilitate Alfie in his work. Not all of the bishops were inclined to help him: initially the Archbishop of Buenos Aires said no; Alfie turned to other dioceses to begin his mission, and he had a great deal of success.

From Argentina, he set out on missions to Bolivia and Paraguay and then back to Ecuador to see how the seeds he had planted were growing. In each country, he was zealous in his efforts, and the numerous branches of the Legion of Mary that he founded flourish to this day. He then returned to Argentina in response to an urgent request by bishops to continue his work there. It was then that he began to express the hope of bringing the Legion of Mary to the Soviet Union; he began to learn Russian and translated the *Legion Handbook* into that language. He also nurtured an ecumenical development: contacting an Orthodox bishop, engaging with him to see if the Legion could be established among the Orthodox. He was successful in this, and on December 12, 1957, the feast of Our Lady of Guadalupe, the first meeting of an Orthodox praesidium took place. It was a praesidium of men, and its members all hailed from Syria.

Buenos Aires was in a bad state. He discovered that 70 percent of Catholics did not practice their faith and that those who did often preferred to attend Orthodox liturgies and receive Holy Communion there rather than attend Mass. He also learned that the local university was a hotbed of Marxism, and this was proving to be a threat to Christianity in the city. This enlivened him; he knew he had to found and direct praesidia in the city to meet these problems head on and draw Catholics back to the understanding and practice of their faith, but the archbishop still refused permission. However, the establishment of four new dioceses in the outskirts of Buenos Aires would change everything. As the new bishops invited Alfie into their dioceses to establish the Legion, the archbishop saw at firsthand the extraordinary work this young man was doing. On December 9, 1957, the Archbishop of Buenos Aires invited Alfie to bring the Legion to his city.

The South Americans took Alfie to their hearts and, in a fond play on his surname, nicknamed him "*el corderito*": "the little lamb" or "lambkin". His letters home to his mother in Tullamore and his reports to Concilium in Dublin are full of details of new praesidia that began to spring up all over Buenos Aires and Argentina, including at the Communist university where he was gradually undermining Marxism, so much so that demands for his deportation were being made. In January 1958, he was called to Uruguay, where the Legion was introduced in the Archdiocese of Montevideo. While there, he suffered stomach pains, a result of the dysentery he had contracted in Ecuador.

Alfie returned to Buenos Aires in February 1958, but his health was in a bad state. He continued to travel and work. Despite the challenges, Alfie's zeal urged him on through the year. Concerned about his workload, Concilium made the decision to send a young legionary, Noel Lynch, to assist him. When he was in Cordoba that December, he fell seriously ill. He spent Christmas in the hospital but continued to write letters and reports from his bed. He was planning to return to Uruguay, but it was obvious he was too ill. Suspecting an ulcer, an operation was scheduled for January 9, 1959, but when they opened him up, they discovered cancer; there were malignant tumors everywhere, and there was nothing that could be done. Whatever time Alfie may have had to live, the operation accelerated his decline, and, in the days following, he endured a terrible agony as death approached. He bore the agony of his last days with serenity and was overjoyed to hear that Noel Lynch was on his way to continue the work.

Alfie died on January 21, 1959, the feast of Saint Agnes, appropriate for one who was known and loved as *"el corderito"*. He was buried in the vault of the Irish Christian Brothers in La Recolletta Cemetery in Buenos Aires. Each year on January 21, legionaries from all over Argentina and beyond process to his tomb, now regarded as a shrine. Following his death, many Legion members and friends of Alfie prayed that one day he might be raised to the altars. The cause for canonization was opened in Buenos Aires and in Ireland, but initially little progress was made. On March 26, 2015, the Diocesan Process of canonization in Buenos Aires was completed, and seven volumes of documentation were transported to the Dicastery for the Causes of Saints in Rome where the Roman Phase is now advancing.

As Western society is undergoing a crisis in population and civilization brought about by a real crisis in spirituality, Alfie's message for this and future generations is that, with Our Lady's help, if we listen to what God asks us to do, we can make a difference, inch by inch, and build a civilization based on recognizing human beings, not as useful or useless economic units, but as made in the image and likeness of God, brothers and sisters of Jesus Christ, and thus loved to death by the One who created us out of love. Alfie understood the importance of faith and prayer when facing the difficulties of life.

Alfie Lambe did not live to see his twenty-seventh birthday, but in that short time he accomplished extraordinary things. Young people of all times and places have ideals and dreams. The knocks and disappointments of life can turn youthful idealism into hard-hearted cynicism, resulting in older people being bitter and angry. Alfie's life encourages them; as the Scriptures say, "Harden not your hearts today, but listen to the voice of the Lord." Alfie listened to the Lord God, who encouraged him to undertake remarkable work in such a short time on the vast continent of South America—a real miracle in itself.

**Further reading:**
Firtel, Hilde. *Alfie Lambe, Legion Envoy.* Cork: Mercier Press, 1967.

# 21

# The Servant of God
# Frank Duff

## (1889–1980)

### Layperson and Founder

### *Father Eamonn McCarthy*

Frank Duff had his bicycle ready in the hallway for his weekend winter jaunt the very day he died. He never owned a car and never ventured, for the most part, farther than a short cycling distance of his home just north of the inner city of Dublin. He was very fond of this mode of transport and was in the habit, over the last thirty years of his life, of taking to the road around Ireland with a group of friends known as "The Sprockets" on annual cycling holidays. He was an avid photographer, capturing many of the beauty spots en route, and used to savor very much the Kodak slideshow "Sprocket Reunion" that would later accompany the completion of another excursion.

It was a First Friday on November 7, 1980, when the Lord called Frank, the last surviving member of his immediate family, to his reward. Likewise, it was a First Friday on the day he was born, June 7, 1889. His deathbed, which can still be visited today, is overlooked by a large portrait of the Sacred Heart of Jesus, just as the turn of the stairs in his home also commands a similar image in the form of a statue. If ever there was a soul who emulated and bore the Heart of Christ! Bearing the emblem of the Sacred Heart as part of his life-long Pioneer membership, those many laborious years were filled with a tremendous compassion toward the poor—but especially the spiritually impoverished.

In contrast to his relatively well-to-do upbringing—a maid was employed in the family home—the Dublin of Frank Duff's younger days was rife with poverty. The ill-effects of the mid-nineteenth-century famine hung over the Ireland of his day. A volatile political and economic situation led to much in the way of unemployment and desperate living conditions.

The son of two civil servants, he received a substantial education through the Jesuit-run Belvedere College for his primary schooling, followed by an equally considered grounding with the Holy Ghost Fathers in Blackrock College. Frank received several "Exhibition" scholarship awards during his teenage years and excelled in the Irish language in his Leaving Certificate. He also had a tremendous command of French and Latin. He likewise had good numerical skills that stood him well in his career in the Department of Finance and in the Land Commission.

Though eminently capable, Frank Duff never embarked on formal third-level education. His attempt to enroll as a student in 1910 was frustrated by his having to become the family breadwinner on account of his father's grave illness. This may also in part explain why he never followed a vocation to priesthood or to marriage. His care and devotion for his mother and his family ran deep. He entered the civil service and succeeded in an accomplished career, playing his part in the establishment of the new Irish State as it struggled in the years following independence. Though deprived of a higher education, among the accolades awarded Frank Duff in his later years was that of an honorary doctorate by the National University of Ireland. In the course of his ninety-one years—as his personal library will attest—he read a great deal.

It was not until the age of twenty-four that Frank began to encounter face to face the tenement squalor of the inner city. A work colleague had persuaded him to become a member of the Saint Vincent de Paul Society. This was certainly the catalyst that saw him spending the rest of his life seeing and serving Christ in the poor. The founding of the Legion of Mary would follow not long afterward on September 7, 1921. Frank Duff himself tells with relish and with characteristic humor the self-deprecating story of the "uproarious laughter" that met his prophecy at an early meeting that this organization was destined to span the world.

The Legion was founded against the background of the impoverishment of his fellow Irishmen and women, an impoverishment both material and spiritual, but also in the light of Frank's growing understanding of the role of the Blessed Virgin Mary in the life and mission of the Church. As his faith deepened, he read all he could acquire in English, Latin, and French on Our Lady. His copy of Saint Louis Marie de Montfort's *Treatise on the True Devotion to Mary*, the Father Faber translation, is retained among his effects and contains a vast number of hand-written quotations drawn from a plethora of sources. This book, which he had rebound and expanded, incorporates nearly seven hundred pages of closely spaced hand-written notes, from which he read and to which he added with great frequency, perhaps even daily, right to the end. His discovery of De Montfort in 1917, he tells us, was a pivotal moment that planted the seed for the birth of the Legion of Mary and that gives it its distinctive Marian spirituality of consecration to Jesus through Mary.

A compelling account of his heroism and that of the early Legion members, all young women, is to be found in Frank's book, *Miracles on Tap*—a gripping read. This story details the transformation from 1922 to 1925 of the former red-light district in the city of Dublin, known locally as "Monto". The fact that Frank was at this time, as a civil servant of note, embroiled in the establishment of the Free State and, by now, a recognized stalwart of the Saint Vincent de Paul Society in an impoverished and postwar state, adds to the extraordinary and dramatic telling of this tale. The setting-up by the Legion of three hostels to care for these victims of human trade and for the homeless surely measures up to the prophetic words of our Savior to Nathanael, "You shall see greater things than these" (cf. Jn 1:50). Two of these hostels, the Morning Star and Regina Coeli, are today in full operation and stand as monuments to this fearless faith. Countless thousands of souls have been and continue to be ministered to by the heroic volunteers who serve in them.

It was no small step when Frank Duff, aged forty-five, took early retirement, settling for a modest pension in order to focus his energies on the, by now, multi-national and accelerating growth of the Legion of Mary.

On a personal level, Frank was a man of deep and assiduous prayer. He prayed the full Latin Divine Office daily from 1917 until his death. Devotion to daily attendance at Holy Mass and, of course, the recitation of the Rosary were also his staples. In his work for the Church, he suffered no little opposition from within and without. His irascible nature, a common characteristic of passionate souls, was something over which he exercised great restraint, but which clearly animated his religious zeal, yielding as it did such prolific spiritual results. Adversaries toward the Legion, not excluding those in the clerical state, were met with due deference but not without determination to defend what, by its prodigious fruits, was clearly the work of the Holy Spirit.

The Legion of Mary *Handbook*, entirely Frank's work and arguably the most translated such work of any Irishman, was worked and reworked by him through at least seven revised editions from 1928 to his death in 1980. It is a masterpiece of spiritual, organizational, and apostolic counsel. Two copies of every available translation were requested for the deliberations of the Vatican Council Fathers leading up to the publication of the documents on the Church and on the laity. The standing ovation Frank Duff received from the 2,500 bishops gathered for the Council during his attendance there as a lay auditor in late 1965 was testimony to the great contribution being made by the Legion of Mary and an appreciation of his evangelical genius.

Fifty-nine years of Legion membership are borne out in a volume of correspondence that compares favorably with that of Saint John Henry Newman. Frank authored 33,000 letters, mostly by dictaphone and therefore often lengthy, addressed to all levels of hierarchy, religious, and lay Legion members the world over. It is a formidable body of thought on every conceivable topic. Notable are the long series of letters to individuals over a period of decades, sometimes running to five hundred in number, to kindred souls deeply immersed in the work of the Legion—the Austrians Hilde Firtel and Marie Victoire Zacherl, Joaquina Lucas from the Philippines, and Father Francis Ripley, a priest of the Diocese of Liverpool, to name just four. Very moving are those more personal letters accompanying souls struggling with mental affliction or moral addiction—again, often protracted over years.

His deep understanding of the doctrine of the Mystical Body of Christ shines brilliantly through the two hundred articles he published as well as his thousands of unpublished scripts. Frank Duff took with great seriousness the seeing and serving of Christ in others—based on the judgment manifesto, "as you did it to one of the least of these my brethren, you did it to me" (Mt 25:40). Who knows how many souls have been so touched and transformed by the work of millions of Legion members in the past century of its existence. To Brother Duff, as he came to be affectionately known, unapostolic Catholicism is an anomaly. All, by virtue of their Baptism, are called to share in the work of preaching the Gospel to the ends of the earth. "The ordinary person", he would say, "is capable of apostleship." This, for him, is "normal Catholicism".

In Legion of Mary membership, he sees the solution to the so-called "vocations crisis". A 1946 letter of his makes the bold claim that the Legion was contributing up to one thousand vocations to the priesthood and religious life every year—a statement that could well be true to this day. Many of the more recently professed and ordained in Ireland, including this writer, would give full credit to the value of such membership on the vocational path. Likewise, marriage and the single life are equally served by a healthy measure of the apostolic and prayer life that the Legion offers.

Frank Duff's cause was opened in 1996, and, given the length of his life, the Legion and its vast mission, his voluminous writings, published and unpublished, it has proved to be a weighty and extensive investigation. At the time of writing, the Diocesan Inquiry is continuing with the work of the Historical Commission, while other elements of the cause have been concluded and are ready in preparation for the final submission to the Dicastery of Causes in Rome.

In his earliest published work, Frank Duff asks, "Can We Be Saints?" He does not leave the question unanswered. His immensely fruitful life, lived through decades of economic, social, political, and theological upheaval, provides ample evidence in the affirmative.

Further reading:
Duff, Frank. *Miracles on Tap*. New York: Montfort Publications, 1962.
Firtel, Hilde. *A Man for Our Time*. Cork: Mercier, 1985.
Kennedy, Finola. *Frank Duff, A Life Story*. London: Burns & Oates, 2011.
Ó Broin, Leon. *Frank Duff, A Biography*. Dublin: Gill and Macmillan, 1982.

Further information:
Recommended video: Glorious Lives, Frank Duff, Shalom World TV, 2019: https://www.shalomworld.org/episode/frank-duff-glorious-lives.

# 22

# Venerable Angeline McCrory

## *(1893–1984)*

## Founder

*Sister Maria Therese Healy, O. Carm.*

Venerable Mary Angeline Teresa McCrory, founder of the Carmelite Sisters for the Aged and Infirm, was a radical in the best sense of
the word; meaning from the root, calling those who followed her
to live a deep faith. In her lifetime, she founded fifty-nine homes
for the aged and cultivated a strong healthy spirituality based on
Carmel's living out of the Gospel ideal. The aspect of Christ's mission that captured Mother's imagination was to become a vessel of
compassion, expressed in the need to make the latter years of elderly
people's lives meaningful and happy. Her relationship with God was
with an all-loving, all-merciful God who meets us where we are,
inviting us to a deeper relationship in love.

Born Bridget McCrory on January 21, 1893, in Mountjoy, Co.
Tyrone, she was the second of five children. Her parents were farmers
unable to survive on their small farm and so became part of the three
and a half million Irish who emigrated between 1851 and 1901. Her
father, Thomas, like many Irish migrants, found a job at the Clydes-
dale Steelworks outside of Glasgow. It was a hard life, but finances
improved, allowing the family to move into better housing. Tragedy
soon struck when her three-year-old sister died from pneumonia and
a few years later her beloved father was severely burned by white mol-
ten steel, living twenty-nine days in terrible pain before dying.

Through these tragedies, young Bridget developed a keen sense of responsibility and a deep compassion for humanity, which urged her to live in the service of others. She had come in contact with the Little Sisters of the Poor, who visited her home frequently, and she was impressed by them. On February 2, 1912, with the permission of her mother, she entered their community. As a young student, she excelled in French, and that helped prepare for her entrance into the novitiate at La Tour Saint Joseph in Normandy, the mother-house of the congregation. Her formation took place during World War I; as La Tour served as a hospice for wounded soldiers and refugees, the Sisters were co-opted to minister to them. On March 19, 1915, she professed first vows and was assigned to Saint Augustine Home for the Aged in Brooklyn, New York, and became known as Sister Marie Angeline de Ste Agathe.

As a Little Sister of the Poor, she spent nine years in Brooklyn, where her vivacious and kindly approach made all around her responsive to becoming more involved in the care of the elderly. She would return to France to prepare for final vows, and then returned to America. Following a year's ministry in Pittsburgh, Pennsylvania, she was named Superior of Our Lady's Home in the Bronx, New York, with eighteen Little Sisters and 230 elderly in her charge. This appointment showed the esteem of her major superiors in France. There, she began to introduce some adaptations in diet, decoration, and in furniture, as she empathized with the elderly who had left their homes. "My heart went out to these elderly folk who asked to pay a little for their own room from savings, private incomes, or pension funds and also the group whose savings had been depleted but who were accustomed to a middle class standard of living. I was even more troubled by the sight of old couples facing the threat of separation, except during visiting hours, if they accepted the established type of institutional life."[1]

When her superiors disagreed with her innovations, Mother Angeline faced the heartbreaking decision of separating from the religious order in which she had served for seventeen years. From

[1] Sister M. Bernadette de Lourdes, *Woman of Faith: Founder Mother M. Angeline Teresa, O. Carm., Carmelite Sisters for the Aged and Infirm* (New York: St. Teresa's Motherhouse, 1984), p. 382.

1927 to 1929, this inner struggle intensified, leading her to confide in her confessor, Father Edwin Sinnott, who considered it serious enough to refer her to the archbishop, Cardinal Patrick Hayes of New York, known as "the Cardinal of Charities". After two visitations by an auxiliary bishop, and with the worsening of her relationship with the Major Superiors in France, she and her companions were advised to seek dispensations. They left the Little Sisters of the Poor on August 11, 1929.

During this difficult time, many priests helped her, including Father Dionysius Flanagan, O.Carm., Commissary Provincial of the Carmelite Friars in New York. He informed her of the possibility of affiliation with a religious order. Mother recalled that when she was at a particularly low point in 1928, Father Dionysius had brought her a bouquet of roses that had been blessed on the feast of the newly canonized Saint Thérèse of the Child Jesus. She took this as a sign, asking if her little community could be affiliated with the Carmelite Order. The Prior General of the Carmelite Order, Father Elias Magennis, O.Carm., happened to be visiting from Rome at the time, and Father Dionysius introduced the Sisters to him. Mother Angeline said,

> The Sisters are most anxious to be affiliated to the Carmelite Order, as tertiaries. Our aim in seeking this affiliation is that of leaning up our work, so young and inexperienced, against one of the greatest religious families in the Church. I do not mean to withdraw from our community its special mission, nor its particular character ... but that every one of us may participate in the spiritual treasures of the order, without in any way prejudicing our duties of charity.[2]

With a speed that surprised Cardinal Hayes, the Prior General had the proper indults from the Holy See by July 16, 1931.

Against the backdrop of the Great Depression, when funds were scarce, the little community flourished. Mother Angeline's ministry then and now is one of personal, loving, family-like care; encouraging Sisters and staff to make Christ present in all their actions. "I

---

[2] Letter to Cardinal Hayes, April 15, 1931, in Jude Meade, *The Servant of God Mother Mary Angeline Teresa, O. Carm: Daughter of Carmel, Mother to the Aged* (Petersham: Saint Bede's Publications, 1990), p. 57.

cannot stress enough; be good to the residents in your homes. Try to be kinder than kindness itself. If you must fail, let it be on the side of kindness rather than harshness and neglect."[3] "Unless we use all our love and skill to make the last years golden years, our elderly can spend many lonely hours and years before God calls them to their eternal reward. Ours is a very special vocation, and we will be blessed for any little thing we did to bring happiness to the old people. As long as you did it to the least of my brothers and sisters, you did it to me, Christ tells us."[4]

Mother Angeline's Gospel narrative, like that of many other saints, is a timely reminder of how we as Christians should journey into the future. She modeled for us that the human person is always precious, even if marked by age, cultural differences, sickness, or poverty. In whatever circumstance found, each person is made in the image and likeness of God ... and is loved. She taught us to practice radical hospitality, grounded in commitment to community, understanding well that we cannot attempt this journey alone. Only with respect and care of one another can we grow and stay the course in shared commitment.

Her vision was focused first and foremost on an inner disposition of the heart, a vessel filled with spiritual fuel to live out God's plan each day. As for most of the saints, this was a daily challenge, to find the balance between prayer and ministry.

> Our holiness will be in proportion to our love and thought of God all day long. We never pray alone, of this we are sure, whenever we pray rightly. There is One dwelling in us (the Holy Ghost). He is our access to the Father. He forms the Word in our hearts. He is the Spirit in whom we pray at all times. I think the best prayer of all is just to kneel or sit quietly and let Jesus pour Himself into our souls. It is such a delight to listen, to be silent and give grace and love full liberty to act within us.[5]

The basic vision of Mother Angeline leads the Carmelite Sisters and their co-workers to continue providing twenty-four-hour

---

[3] De Lourdes, *Woman of Faith*, p. 445.
[4] Ibid., p. 462.
[5] Meade, *Daughter of Carmel*, p. 134.

holistic care, treating each person with loving kindness, becoming a vessel of God's compassion in the world, understanding the loneliness of old age, providing individual quality care, and aiding all to reach their highest potential. These ideals are both simple and profound. They do not require a high level of knowledge or skill, only a heart full of love that is willing to use one's gifts in the service of the most vulnerable of society. It is our ardent desire to continue Mother Angeline's ministry by becoming life-giving vessels of compassionate care in the places our residents now call home.

Mother Angeline died on Saturday, January 21, 1984, her ninety-first birthday, surrounded by her beloved Carmelite Sisters at the motherhouse at Germantown, New York. It had been a long life; one of serving the aged and infirm and guiding her congregation. Even in her own aging, she continued living with a great love, deep faith, a vessel making Christ present to all she encountered in real time.

In 1987, the Carmelite Sisters formed the Teresian Society, now called The Mother Angeline Society, in order to promote Mother's cause and charism. The General Council of the Congregation petitioned the Most Reverend Howard J. Hubbard, Bishop of Albany, New York, to open the cause for beatification and canonization in 1989. The Nihil Obstat was granted, and the cause was initiated. Reverend Eugene Robitaille, S.S.C.C., was the first Promoter of Mother's cause. After his death, the Reverend Jude Mead, C.P., became the first Postulator who laid the groundwork for the opening of the Diocesan Phase of the cause before his death in 1992. The new Postulator, the Very Reverend Mario Esposito, O.Carm., assisted Bishop Hubbard and the members of the Diocesan Tribunal at the opening of the Diocesan Process on August 15, 1992. By the closing of the cause on April 13, 2007, over 12,000 pages of testimony, historical information, letters, publications, and documents were gathered to testify to the reputation of holiness of life and practice of virtues by the Servant of God. Once the cause was received in Rome, Dr. Andrea Ambrosi was appointed as the Roman Postulator.

On June 28, 2012, Pope Benedict XVI approved and ordered the publication of the Decree on Heroic Virtues for the Servant of God now known as Venerable Mary Angeline Teresa (Bridget Teresa McCrory), O.Carm. The next step in the process would be beatification; for this, it must be proven that one miracle has been granted by God through her intercession. Canonization will require a second miracle.

## Further reading:

Lourdes, Sister M. Bernadette de. *Woman of Faith: Founder Mother M. Angeline Teresa, O Carm., Carmelite Sisters for the Aged and Infirm.* New York: Saint Teresa's Motherhouse, 1984.

Meade, Jude. *The Servant of God Mother Mary Angeline Teresa, O. Carm: Daughter of Carmel, Mother to the Aged.* Petersham: Saint Bede's Publications, 1990.

## Further information:

The Mother Angeline Society is dedicated to promoting the Cause for Beatification and Canonization of Venerable Mary Angeline Teresa, O.Carm., and advancing her charism in the Church. For more information on Mother Angeline, membership in the Mother Angeline Society, or to visit the Mother Angeline Heritage Center or gift shop, go to our website: motherangeline.org.

In Ireland, contact Sister Maria Therese Healy, O.Carm., Our Lady's Manor, Bulloch Castle, Dalkey, Co. Dublin. Telephone 01-2806993.

# 23

# Venerable Patrick Peyton

## (1909–1992)

## Priest

## *Father David S. Marcham and Dave Kindy*

In a small cottage in County Mayo, a poor but loving family gathered near the fireplace for its daily evening ritual: praying the Rosary as a family before a blazing turf fire. There, in the gentle foothills of the Ox Mountains, the kindhearted John and Mary Peyton raised their family to love Mary, the Mother of God, and to be strong in their Catholic faith despite their poverty. It was an important lesson for young Patrick, the sixth of nine children. He would carry this lesson from his childhood in Mayo to his life as a priest in the United States, where he became a media pioneer and one of the most influential Catholic priests of the twentieth century.

Born in 1909, Patrick lived in Ireland until he was nineteen. Despite being poor, he later remembered his childhood as an age of love and faith. He notes that there were times when the family had little or nothing to eat, but never times when they did not have a strong spirit of faith to face the difficulties and hardships of life. His parents, he said, taught him and his siblings the great truths and virtues of faith by their words, but, more importantly, by their living truth and virtues before their children's eyes. A great spirit of charity and unity dwelt in their home. Patrick and his brother Thomas emigrated to the United States in 1928. They joined three of their sisters, Beatrice, Mary, and Nellie, who had moved to Scranton, Pennsylvania, a few years earlier. Patrick found employment as a sexton at Saint Peter's Cathedral. As a result, he, who had always wanted to serve the Church, suddenly felt a renewed calling to become a priest.

In Ireland, Patrick had been discouraged from joining the priesthood because of his limited finances and education. But this dream of becoming a priest was rekindled after meeting priests from the Congregation of Holy Cross, who recommended him as a candidate for the seminary. His brother Thomas was caught up in this fervor, and he, too, decided to join the religious life.

They were welcomed as postulants, and both entered remedial programs to complete high school and become novices for one year. After completing their novitiate training, they renewed vows annually. They completed undergraduate degrees at the University of Notre Dame and then entered Holy Cross College in Washington, D.C., to study theology and eventually professed their final vows in the Congregation of Holy Cross, founded in France in 1837 by Blessed Basil Moreau.

Patrick's life took a dramatic, almost fatal, turn while completing theological studies in 1938. He began coughing up blood. At first, he tried to keep it a secret, but his condition continued to worsen. Admitted to the hospital emergency room, Patrick was finally diagnosed with advanced tuberculosis. He was sent back to the University of Notre Dame, where he battled the illness for a year with no improvement. Finally, doctors told him they could do no more and suggested he try prayer. Father Cornelius Hagerty, C.S.C., encouraged him to put his trust in the power of Mary's intercession. "You have the faith, Pat, but you're not using it", the old priest advisor said.

Patrick prayed fervently to Mary, the Blessed Mother, for a cure. The Holy Cross community also began a novena of Masses for his recovery. As Patrick was having dinner on October 31, the Eve of All Saints, he felt the darkness lifted from his soul. He knew at that moment that he had been cured. When they next examined him, the doctors were stunned; Patrick's tuberculosis was in regression. In a few weeks, it was gone, and he was completely cured.

His recovery was seen as a "miraculous healing". Patrick believed Mary, the Mother of God, had interceded on his behalf. He was also certain that his earthly mother, Mary, and sister Nellie played a part in his cure. Mary died shortly after Patrick's recovery. She had suffered two terrible strokes, but, instead of praying for herself to be saved, she prayed that God would save her son. Nellie also died a short time later, praying on her deathbed that both her brothers would become priests and "that never in their priestly lives will they commit a mortal sin".

It is not hard to imagine the impact this must have had on her brothers. Patrick was so moved by his sister's words that he devoted himself to honoring her memory. The least he could do, he once said, was to lead a life that, in its intensity of love for God and his Blessed Mother and in the totality of its concentration on God's work, would not only justify his existence, but leave a surplus to equal the good Nellie would have radiated around her had she lived. Patrick and Thomas were ordained as priests on June 15, 1941. "That day I gave my heart and soul in love to Mary", Patrick later said. He was convinced that his health had been restored so he could preach the love of Mary to the world. How he was going to do that was not something he had quite figured out yet.

His first assignment as a priest was as a chaplain for a group of Holy Cross Brothers teaching at the Vincentian Institute in Albany, New York. While attending to the Brothers, an idea began to form about how to accomplish his mission. Father Peyton began writing to bishops around the country asking for their support in organizing a Rosary campaign. He enlisted the aid of local students and the religious at the Vincentian Institute to help contact the bishops, many of whom agreed to participate in the Family Rosary Crusade.

Father Peyton set a goal of encouraging ten million people to sign pledges to pray the Family Rosary. The only way to do that was through mass media, which in those days meant radio. He convinced an executive at the Mutual Broadcasting System to give him airtime, but she had one stipulation: Father Peyton would have to find a Hollywood star to appear on the show. The young priest knew no one in show business at the time, but he approached Bing Crosby. The famous singer and actor was impressed with Father Peyton's sincerity, so he agreed.

On Mother's Day, May 13, 1945, Father Peyton took to the air nationally for the first time. Along with Crosby, the show featured Archbishop Spellman of New York and President Harry Truman, as well as the Sullivan family, who had lost five brothers in World War II when their ship was torpedoed. The show was a smashing success, and people wanted more. He reached out to other Hollywood stars beginning with Maureen O'Hara, Loretta Young, Rosalind Russell, and Jane Wyatt. They became known as "the nuns of Hollywood" for traveling with a young Irish priest persuading Hollywood stars to appear on his "Family Theater of the Air". His list of Hollywood notables also included Raymond Burr, Jimmy Stewart, Lucille Ball, Ann Blythe, Danny Thomas, and many others. In 1947, he established Family Theater Productions, which broadcast the star-studded radio programs for twenty-two years.

Over the years, the production house would also produce a series of award-winning television programs and films, including *The Triumphant Hour* and *Hill Number One*, which featured James Dean in his first movie, in 1951, and *Dawn of America*, which focused on Christopher Columbus' faith, in 1953. Father Peyton would go on to produce the acclaimed *The Life of Christ* films, which premiered as the Official Vatican Exhibit at the World's Fair in Brussels in 1958. In the 1980s, he broadcasted Christmas and Easter specials on television featuring such big-name stars as Grace Kelly, Placido Domingo, and Frank Sinatra.

In addition to radio, TV, and films, he also used billboards to spread his message far and wide. They first appeared in 1947 and featured his famous phrase: "The family that prays together stays together." His other iconic message—"A world at prayer is a world at peace"—was also part of the campaign, which would feature millions of billboards across America. Father Peyton once said that his vision for outdoor media was "Keeping before the traveling public the importance of wholesome family life as part of the American heritage."

In 1948, Father Peyton took his message of Family Rosary Prayer on the road. He first appeared in Ontario, Canada, to lead a Rosary Rally—the first of 260 such events he would hold around the world. The popularity and impact of these events was astounding, with millions of people attending the public gatherings. At one rally in Sao Paulo, Brazil, in 1964, an estimated two million faithful listened to Father Peyton spread the word of family prayer through the Rosary. "Men and women, old and young, poor and rich, shoulder to shoulder, all honored Our Lady with their presence", he said, "and gave testimony of their faith in the power of God and in prayer which should be present in all families to maintain unity."

Father Peyton continued to grow and expand his ministry over the years. Family Rosary, which was established in 1942, spread to seventeen countries: Bangladesh, Brazil, Canada, Chile, Uganda, France,

Ghana, Tanzania, Haiti, India, Ireland, Mexico, Peru, Philippines, Spain, the United States, and Uruguay.

His heavy workload, combined with advancing age, took its toll on the Rosary Priest. His health began to fail, and his heart grew weak. He died peacefully on June 3, 1992. His last words were "Mary, my Queen, my Mother".

Father Peyton's work did not end with his death. Holy Cross Family Ministries was established as the umbrella ministry with responsibility for Father Peyton's projects: Family Rosary, Family Theater Productions, and the Father Peyton Family Institutes. Each of these initiatives continues to promote the family Rosary. While radio and film remain important, other efforts include online videos, outreach through social media, family blogs such as CatholicMom.com, and the online series Catholic Central, which uses fun facts to "enterform", entertain and inform, about all-things Catholic. Father Peyton, always the media pioneer, would approve!

In 2001, the Bishop of the Diocese of Fall River, Massachusetts, opened the cause of canonization, and Father Peyton was given the title Servant of God. On December 18, 2017, Pope Francis acknowledged the holiness of life and heroic virtue of Father Peyton and decreed that he now be recognized as Venerable by the universal Church. A number of possible medical miracles are currently under investigation with a view to progressing to his beatification.

Father Peyton's messages of "The family that prays together stays together" and "A world at prayer is a world at peace" are more timely than ever before. The family is confronted with many challenges in today's culture. In particular, respect for the dignity of human life in all its stages and even the fundamental biblical understanding of the family are under assault.

The breakdown of the family leads to alienation and loneliness, addictions of all kinds, and a culture of death rather than that of life. Father Peyton's example is needed now; he used to say that he had no time to be against anyone or anything because he was so busy sharing what he was for: peace, gentleness, kindness, compassion, caring, and, above all, the unbreakable bond of family unity and love nourished by family prayer. In the prayer of the Rosary, he trusted and firmly believed that Mary would lead all families to the joy of meeting and abiding with her Son Jesus as she knew and loved him.

# 24

# The Servant of God
# Father Declan O'Toole

## (1971–2002)

### Missionary Priest and Martyr, *uti fertur*

### *Father Philip O'Halloran, M.H.M.*

On his gravestone, designed as an open book, on one side the page of text reads:

> In Loving Memory of Father Declan O'Toole (Apaulopus), M.H.M. Panyangara Parish, Kotido, Uganda, and Curramore. Who was martyred in Uganda on March 21, 2002, aged thirty-one years. Rest in peace.

On the other page is an image showing a host, as if more than half of it is raised out of a chalice, and marked on the host is a cross. The stark simplicity of the black and white stonework of the grave is noticeable; adjacent to it is a growing mountain ash tree offering some shade to the grave in the grounds of the church at Claran in Headford Parish, Co. Galway. Archbishop Michael Neary had planted the same tree to mark his ordination on June 28, 1997.

Born on February 2, 1971, in Curramore, Headford, Declan was baptized, made his first Holy Communion, received Confirmation, and was ordained a priest, all at Saint Mary's Church, Claran in Headford Parish. He grew up on the family farm with his parents, Paul and Carmel, his paternal grandmother, Julia, and two younger sisters and brother. He attended Saint Fursey's Primary School, Claran, and the Presentation College, Headford. His school principal, Sister Brid Brennan, was happy to recommend him for training for the priesthood; together with the then parish priest of Headford, Father William Clarke, she recognized the positive and helpful family background as an important factor in his formation.

In early October 1988, he was accepted by the Mill Hill Missionaries and entered formation in Dublin. First making the basic formation year, he followed this with philosophical studies at Milltown Institute from 1989 to 1991 and then to Mill Hill in London, where he continued academic studies at the Missionary Institute London. During the weekends in London, he was based at Wormwood Scrubs for pastoral placement, finding it very fulfilling. One of the prisoners there was to write a letter to the editor of a newspaper calling Declan:

A gentle giant ... a regular visitor on E-wing, which was an intimidating wing in itself when you consider that every one of the eighteen men it held was serving a life sentence. Yet Declan would not be intimidated and soon gained the respect of many with his easygoing and friendly personality. I clearly remember discussing many things with this friendly big fellow, including the fact that he knew he would be going to Uganda to spread the word of God. I clearly remember him stating that he knew it could be dangerous at times, but that this was God's will and that he lived for nothing more than to do God's will.[1]

During his formation, he undertook a two-year full-time pastoral formation placement in Saint Karoli Lwanga Parish, Mbikko, which is across the river Nile from the town of Jinja in Uganda. Learning a new language and adjusting to cross-cultural and international living, he was surrounded by chronic poverty as the parish center was in the midst of an unplanned urban slum; it was a time for greater self-awareness.

Involved with the Saint Francis Health Care Services, he worked with people with AIDS and their families in various ways. Engaging with youth, he set up an active Youth Group, while working with the Legion of Mary visiting the sick and elderly in their homes. Qualities that had been recognized from his primary and secondary

[1] Stuart McNab, Letters to the Editor: "A Prisoner Remembers Father Declan O'Toole—the 'Gentle Giant' of Wormwood Scrubs 2002" (unknown newspaper details).

school days of being reliable and trustworthy, cooperative, a conscientious worker with a positive outlook and self-discipline continued to blossom and grow in his pastoral work. The quiet shy youth was becoming more outgoing and positively extroverted with a wide range of interests, while at the same time he was also able to manifest a reflective, introverted dimension that displayed itself in a sensitivity to others, to world affairs, and to the religious side of life.

Following his ordination in Headford in 1997, he returned to Uganda, moving to the northeast of the country to Kotido Diocese. He stayed with the Comboni Missionaries while learning another new language. In early April 1998, he and two other Irish Mill Hill Missionaries opened a new parish to the southeast of Kotido town at Panyangara. Here Declan was to visit the villages and homes of the local people, walking many miles daily. The people gave him a local name, *Apaulopus*, which means "the father/owner of the blue speckled bull"; this was a term of endearment and respect. He saw people's needs in visiting their homes and did much repairing and refurbishing of the broken and spoiled water hand pumps, as "water is life" in this semi-arid and barren place. This not only helped the girls and women who drew water for their households but also the shepherds with their thirsty animals. He raised funds for a grinding mill so women did not have to use grinding stones laboriously to prepare the flour for the local foods. He encouraged lay involvement in the Church, introducing full-time instructors for women's groups and youth while encouraging more laypeople to become catechists. Many of the activities in Panyangara Parish could be seen as more developmental than religious, but Declan's motivation came from a deeply held faith.

His personal dedication to living his faith was evident as he had accepted to go to Kotido Diocese when others had declined this posting; his faith gave him courage in confronting the challenges of injustice and the local needs in the area. This was to be significant in his life as his concern for justice led to his death. He was a member of various peace-making groups and participated in peace meetings between the warring tribes of the Jie, Dodos, Bokora, Acholi, and Labwor peoples. This meant much traveling with the open back of the pickup full of elders and warriors who went to these meetings with him. In itself, it was a grueling activity, long hours and often uncoordinated. Sitting in the shade of trees, with the fine grit of the dust being blown in the hot wind, they usually had nothing to eat and drink the whole day. Many days he went hungry in the name of promoting peace. His dedication to improving people's lives earned him the respect of the elders, and sometimes he was permitted to be part of events that only the initiated like the elders and some warriors would normally be allowed to be part of.

Declan's concern for justice was rooted in the Beatitudes and in the judgment of the nations in the Gospel of Matthew, chapter 25; he sought to live it in a practical and real way. He gave food to the hungry, sated the thirsty with the repairing of broken boreholes, and made the parish a place of welcome. He clothed the naked, especially during the disarmament period as the soldiers would refuse to allow people without trousers into the town and beat them if they met them on their patrols—many of the local men wore a folded sheet as a wraparound on their lower body, in many ways like a short skirt. He cared for the sick, bringing them to the hospital, helping them with their medical fees; he drove expectant mothers from their dusty, poorly equipped homesteads to be delivered at the maternity center, and he visited the local prison.

Declan wrote frequently about the insecurity and the cruel treatment of the local people.[2] The Diocese of Kotido, and its neighbor Moroto, were well known for their well-armed warriors who swept into the neighboring tribal groups and took their animals and whatever small possessions they could take, often killing people in the process. It reached a stage that the government of Uganda began a disarmament program in 2001. Good in intention, some unscrupulous officers took advantage of it in what was an isolated area of Uganda; many miscarriages of justice were committed on both sides in the name of disarmament. Declan was a member of the sub-county disarmament task force and an observer of the Catholic Diocesan Peace Process Committee.

On March 9, 2002, he went to another part of the parish where the army was undertaking a "disarmament operation". He had had to object to the beatings of people by soldiers and their forcing pregnant

---

[2] Father Declan O'Toole, "Disarmament Process in Karamoja", in *St. Joseph's Advocate (Ireland)*, Summer 2002.

women to sit directly in the full sun for hours. While the major of the army welcomed him and gave him permission to be there, some of the junior officers, unhappy with his presence, ordered him to go away. As he went to leave, he was lashed across the back with a stick by one of the soldiers; he was more shocked by the surprise than badly beaten. Four others had their sticks ready, too, so he left to the sound of their jeering and laughter. He later reported the incident to higher authorities locally and informed the Irish Embassy in Kampala. This report was followed up with the Minister of Defense, and things calmed down somewhat in the intense disarmament operations as the task force and the Churches' peace committees had some effect. His tormentors, however, had not forgotten him.

A few weeks later, on March 21, Declan went to the Joint Diocesan Catechetical Center in the neighboring Diocese of Moroto. As he was returning that evening with other passengers, their vehicle was stopped by two soldiers; he was shot dead at point-blank range, together with the driver, Patrick Longoli, and the parish cook, Fidelis Longole, who joined them for the day out. Nothing was stolen from the car. A vehicle from the Anglican Church was behind them. Its passengers saw the soldier cocking the gun at them, and they swung out of line, driving fast to get away. One of their staff was shot in the shoulder, but they survived and were able to report the incident in Kotido. Declan had just turned thirty-one years of age on February 2; just weeks later, at the beginning of Holy Week, his body was brought back to Ireland and buried in his native parish on Holy Thursday.

Father Declan O'Toole is significant for our time in his concern for justice and his willingness to persevere in difficult circumstances. At a time of change in Ireland, he entered the priesthood to serve as a missionary, and then, taking risks, accepted to go and minister in Kotido without shirking from the challenges that faced him. His life is a reminder to people that they too can be people of extraordinary commitment and dedication, courageous faith, and heroic generosity. His willingness to live the Beatitudes and trust the will of God is countercultural with much that happens around us today: "In the end he paid the ultimate price for his commitment to peace and justice."[3]

---

[3] Fons Eppink, "Declan O'Toole MH: A Martyr for Peace and Reconciliation", *St. Joseph's Advocate (Ireland)*, Winter 2002.

In 2003, the Irish Society in Uganda invited Declan's family to attend an event in Kampala, as they wanted to honor him as "Irish person of the year". Some accepted the invitation and also visited Kotido. His sister Sharon noted what the parishioners said of her brother and later wrote: "One of the most touching moments for me was when one evening an old warrior came into the mission compound and sat on the ground crying and shouting 'Why, Why, Why?' He said, 'Apaulopus was my son, too.'"[4]

The Bishop of the Diocese of Kotido has since initiated the process of investigation into Declan's life and death with a view to, perhaps, advancing to beatification. There are already those who believe that he is a martyr, among them Stuart McNab, Declan's friend in Wormwood Scrubs. In his letter, he testifies: "I start my ninth year in prison soon, and my faith has grown immensely in that time thanks to my coming in contact with the likes of Father Declan O'Toole, that gentle giant who, by giving the Church and the world the witness of his blood, fully imitated the glorious martyrdom of Our Lord, Jesus Christ."[5]

[4] Sharon O'Toole, "A Tribute to Declan (Apaulopus)", *St Joseph's Advocate (Ireland)*, Winter 2003.
[5] McNab, "A Prisoner Remembers Fr. Declan O'Toole".

# 25

# The Servant of God
# Sister Clare Crockett

## (1982–2016)

## Consecrated Religious

### *Sister Beatriz Liaño, S.H.M.*

In Holy Week of the year 2000, at seventeen years of age, Clare Crockett arrived at a Home of the Mother Retreat in a small town in Spain. She seemed both joyful and superficial. She was looking for sun and parties in Spain, and she found herself with a group of people who were celebrating intensely the Passion, death, and Resurrection of Our Lord. That was not what she was expecting.

From her childhood, Clare had always dreamt of becoming a movie star, and she was working her way toward that dream. She knew that she had qualities: a great artistic talent, a beautiful voice, an attractive physical aspect, and an astounding personality. At the age of fifteen, she had already been contracted to host a show for young people on Channel 4—one of the biggest in the United Kingdom—and at the age of seventeen, the American channel Nickelodeon had shown interest in her.

She spent the first days of the Holy Week Encounter sunbathing and smoking. On Good Friday, someone said to her, "Clare, today you have to go into the chapel. It's Good Friday." She went into the chapel, but she stayed in the last pew. During the Good Friday liturgy, the faithful adore and kiss the Crucifix. Clare joined them. It was a simple gesture, but it was a changing point in her life. When the service was over, a Sister found her crying as she repeated, "He died for me. He loves me! Why hasn't anyone ever told me this before?" Clare had understood how much the Lord loved her and how much he had done for her and that the love the Lord asked of her meant a complete donation.

It was not easy to take the step. When she went back to Ireland, she participated as a secondary actress in the filming of *Sunday*, directed by Charles McDougall. She got caught up again in the whirlwind of superficiality and sin that the world of cinema offered her. She expressed herself in these terms, "I lived very badly; I lived in mortal sin. I drank a lot, I smoked a lot; I began to smoke drugs. I continued with my friends and my boyfriend. I continued in the same way. I didn't have the strength to break with all these things, because I didn't ask the Lord to help me."

However, the Lord insisted on "pursuing" her. One night, at a party, she overdrank once again. When she was vomiting in the bathroom, she felt that Jesus said to her, "Why do you continue to hurt me?" God's presence was so strong that she could not ignore it. Not long after, she was in her room in a Manchester hotel, reading her taping schedule for the next day. She felt such a great emptiness that she realized that her life had no meaning if she did not give it to Jesus Christ. Neither her family's pleas nor her manager's promises could stop her. On August 11, 2001, at the age of eighteen, she gave her life to God as a candidate in the Servant Sisters of the Home of the Mother.

Clare was born on November 14, 1982, in Derry, Northern Ireland, into a Catholic family. She had received the Sacraments of Christian Initiation and a Catholic upbringing, but by her teenage years she no longer frequented the church. With the bloody struggles for Northern Ireland's independence from the United Kingdom, the difficult atmosphere in Derry, her hometown, had wounded her heart deeply. As she entered the Servant Sisters, this was the first wound in need of healing. She had to change many things in her life, yet Clare had surrendered to Jesus Christ's immense love for her, and there was nothing that would stop her. She herself explained, "At first, I was tempted to look back and say, 'I want it back.' But I understood that I had found an even greater love." With the help of the Lord, she was able to overcome all obstacles and soon come to bring hope and joy to all those around her.

Following her years as a candidate and novice, she took her first vows on February 18, 2006, taking the religious name of Sister Clare Maria of the Trinity and the Heart of Mary. During the month-long spiritual exercises that she made during her novitiate, she received a grace to comprehend what the Lord had said one day to Saint Catherine of Siena: "You are the one who is not, and I am he who is." It was something that transformed her interiorly and helped her, as she matured humanly and spiritually, to put the many gifts with which she was endowed at the Lord's service.

Still very young, and with many things to learn, she arrived at her first assignment in the community at Belmonte, in Cuenca, Spain. There, the Servant Sisters of the Home of the Mother direct a residence for girls that come from families in difficulty. Sister Clare began to show her special gift to reach the souls of children and young people, teaching them the love of the Lord, guiding them to heal their interior wounds. Sister Clare would spend only a few months in that house before she was sent to a new community in the United States, in Jacksonville, Florida, in October 2006. There the Sisters had begun pastoral work at Assumption Parish and School, and Sister Clare threw herself into the work and made an impression. The parish priest, Father Fred Parke, explains: "The children picked up on the enthusiasm that she had for the Eucharist. She overflowed with enthusiasm for the Lord. Once you had been with her, you knew you had to pick up that same enthusiasm. It was so catchy."

In September 2010, she returned to Spain, where she made her perpetual profession on September 8. Afterward, she was sent to a community the Servant Sisters of the Home of the Mother were opening in Valencia, Spain. Her superior, Sister Isabel Cuesta, remembers: "There was an example that Sister Clare used a lot, which helped her to place her life in God's hands. It was the example of a 'blank cheque'. Each day she would give a blank cheque to the Lord, so that he could ask of her whatever he wanted." In Valencia, Sister Clare's main apostolate was attending to the spiritual needs of terminally ill patients in the hospital in Mislata.

In 2011, Sister Clare returned to Belmonte. This time her superior was Sister Ana Maria Lapeña, who very accurately sums up Sister Clare's spirituality in these words: "She gave everything with a great sense of humor." Sister Ana Maria admires to this day Sister Clare's obedience and affirms: "I still do not know what things she liked to do and what things were hard for her. I could never tell. And when I would ask her to do something, her answer was always, 'Of course!'"

In October of 2012, Sister Clare received a new assignment where she would be able to put into practice her potential for evangelization: Ecuador. She was sent to a recently founded community in Guayaquil. The Sisters there give classes in a few different schools in very poor areas, and they work in a parish, evangelizing youth and children. They conduct retreats, summer camps and weekly formation meetings, among other ministries. There was a lot of work to be done, and the excruciating Ecuadorian heat, in addition to the various tropical diseases she would suffer, was exhausting. Sister Clare herself talked about the disposition she had when she reached Ecuador. "When I arrived in Ecuador, we were listening to the life of John Paul II, and in one of his apostolic visits they asked him, 'Holy Father, are you tired?', and he answered, 'The truth is ... I don't know.' It was my first week here in Ecuador, and I wanted to use that quote from John Paul II as my way of life here. Sometimes you get tired, of course! But even though I am tired, I hope to not feel sorry for myself and to keep giving."

Two years later, Sister Clare was sent to another community in Ecuador: Playa Prieta. There the Servant Sisters run a school where poor children can receive a high quality, Catholic education, thanks to the sponsorship of many benefactors. After the intense school day is over and the extracurricular activities have finished, the Sisters find time to work in the parish and to attend to many poor families. Under the scorching sun or in the torrential rains, the Sisters visit the impoverished houses in the rural area to evaluate the basic needs of each family and thus be able to give them Jesus Christ and the hope of Eternal Life, together with food baskets, medicine, and many other solutions to their material problems. Everyone always remembers Sister Clare with a guitar in her hand, her great companion in evangelization. They remember her singing and singing, even to the point of losing her voice, and, even then, she continued to sing, in spite of the heat, fatigue, and migraines. Her way of singing reflected the way she lived. Sister Kelly Maria Pezo recalls, "When she sang, she kept nothing back. And when she lived, she kept nothing back." Despite the hustle and bustle and joy that always surrounded her, as the years passed by, Sister Clare's need for silence and moments to be alone with the Lord increased. It was evident to the Sisters to what extent Sister Clare was giving of herself. To her, nothing seemed enough for Christ.

The earthquake that put an end to Sister Clare's life, and those of five other young aspirants, began at 6:58 P.M. on Saturday, April 16, 2016. Due to the strong floods that in the previous days had devastated Playa Prieta, the Sisters had lived a very difficult week. Just two weeks before the start of a new school year, they found themselves with a school that was in a state of total disaster. All of the classrooms were flooded; the recently painted walls, chairs, tables, doors, and a large quantity of teaching materials were destroyed by the water. For that reason, as soon as the water level began to recede, the Sisters got busy cleaning. They worked with joy and generosity. The work was hard, because, as the water subsided, it left several layers of mud. They were also worried about the many poor families in the area that had lost everything, or almost everything, as a result of the floods.

In the face of an extreme situation, they reacted with total donation. Contemplating the events in hindsight, it seemed as though the Lord was preparing them. The earthquake began shortly after they had come back from Mass at the village's parish. It was already dark. Sister Clare and a group of young women were on the first floor. They had had guitar class and were about to pray the Rosary with the rest of the Sisters and girls. The heavy quake caused the building to collapse, with four Sisters and seven girls inside. Only five were rescued alive. Curiously enough, they had been talking about death during lunch that very day. Very convinced, Sister Clare had said: "Why should I be afraid of death, if I'm going to go with the One I have longed to be with my whole life?"

We now entrust her and the other five young girls to the Lord's mercy and have the firm hope that she, who only desired to love him and serve him in this world, may now be praising him eternally in the next.

Further reading:
Gardner, S.H.M., Sister Kristen. *Sister Clare Crockett: Alone with Christ Alone.* Cantabria: Agencia, 2020.

Further information:
See www.sisterclare.com to learn more about Sister Clare and the five girls who died with her.

Part 2

# Irish Men and Women
# with a Reputation for Holiness

# 26

# Bishop William Walsh

*(ca. 1512–1577)*

Religious, Bishop of Meath and Martyr, *uti fertur*

*Father John S. Hogan*

It may have reminded the bishop of the kindness of the Philippian jailer to Saint Paul, that through the connivance of his jailer in Dublin Castle, he was secreted out to freedom after thirteen years of suffering for the Catholic Faith, seven of them in a prison cell. Bishop William Walsh fled Ireland at Christmas 1552, making his way to France, where more hardship awaited him, and then to Alcalá in Spain, where he would end his days marked with the scars of a confessor. He had defended the Faith heroically and had been, in the words of the then Protestant Archbishop of Armagh, Adam Loftus, "of great credit amongst his countrymen, and upon whom (as touching causes of religion) they wholly depend". Loftus was complaining, but the Catholics of Meath and the Pale were not: William had proven himself to be a heroic shepherd and a man of eminent virtue and holiness in a time of great strife and suffering; as a Cistercian historian described him, "one of the outstanding confessors of the Catholic Faith in the country during the early Elizabethan period".[1]

William Walsh was born in Dunboyne, Co. Meath, around the year 1512. At some point in his youth, he entered the Cistercian

[1] Flannan Hogan, "William Walsh, Bishop of Meath, 1554–1577", in *Riocht na Midhe: Records of Meath Archaeological and Historical Society* (1977), p. 3.

Abbey at Bective, was professed and ordained a priest. During that time, he was sent to Oxford, where it is believed he took a doctorate in Divinity. In 1536, following Henry VIII's break with Rome, William returned to Bective, but the following year the abbey was suppressed and the community scattered. He found a home at Saint Mary's Abbey in Dublin, but his time there was short as it, too, was suppressed in 1539. As he was expelled from the abbey, he was granted a pension of £2 ($2.50) per year in the hope that, like the rest of the community, he would fade into secular life and leave the question of religion to the reformers. William was not inclined to such retirement, and he made his way to Rome, where he met Reginald Pole, the son of Blessed Margaret Pole, Countess of Salisbury. Pole was in self-imposed exile following his own dispute with Henry over the marriage to Anne Boleyn. Henry had tried to bribe him to gain his support, but Reginald resisted. While still only a deacon in 1536, Pole was created cardinal by Pope Paul III and appointed papal legate to England, charged with organizing help for the Pilgrimage of Grace, a Catholic rebellion against Henry in the North of England. William was engaged as Pole's chaplain during this time.

Remaining in Rome until the accession of Queen Mary Tudor, it has been argued that at some point William was dispensed from his vows as a Cistercian and entered the Canons Regular of Saint Augustine. In his capacity as an Augustinian, he was appointed prior to the Augustinian communities of Duleek and Colpe in Meath and rector of Loxeudy (Ballymore) in Westmeath. The historian Flannan Hogan suggests that he remained a Cistercian but was given some form of canonical association with the Augustinians to allow him to take up the appointments. In the service of Cardinal Pole, William accompanied him in his various missions, including that of papal legate at the Council of Trent in 1549, which William would most likely have attended. In the Conclave of 1549–1550, Pole was almost elected pope. William used his years in Rome to good effect and may have been teaching theology.

When Edward VI died and Mary I ascended the throne, Pole and Walsh made their way to England. Given his faithful service, his orthodoxy, and his opposition to the reforms of Henry VIII and Edward, William was considered a worthy candidate for promotion within the Church. Sent to Ireland in 1554 to depose Matthew

Staples, the Bishop of Meath who had embraced Henry's reforms and taken a wife, William was chosen as Bishop of Meath himself. Elected by the clergy of the diocese, the decision was affirmed by Rome, and he was consecrated bishop.

William proved to be a zealous and evangelical bishop. The diocese and clergy had suffered much, and many abuses had crept in thanks to Bishop Staples' apostasy. Given the religious disorder of the past number of years, people were confused, many had abandoned the Faith, and discipline was lax; the diocese was also impoverished. William understood that there were many spiritual wounds to be healed and realized he had not only to restore order to the Diocese of Meath, but renew its clergy, tend to the souls of the faithful, and attempt to win back those who had left the Faith. It was an onerous task, but William embraced it with extraordinary energy. As if ecclesiastical matters were not enough, he was also charged with various tasks by the government. The Diocese of Meath was regarded as if it were an English diocese, second only to Dublin in terms of importance in Ireland; this meant the Bishop of Meath was also an important government official. In this capacity, he was appointed to various commissions including those for the governance of Meath and Westmeath.

As he worked among them, the clergy and people of Meath witnessed the virtues of their bishop. While he was in the thick of Church affairs and the political life of the kingdom, an acquaintance of cardinals and monarchs, it was noted that he was virtuous—he possessed an obvious purity that would lead some to say that he never had sinned seriously in his life. William's reputation for holiness emerged in these years as the people of Meath were convinced that their bishop was a saint.

In 1558, Queen Mary died and was succeeded by her half-sister, Elizabeth. Initially it seemed little would change. William continued his work for the Church and state in Ireland, but after about a year, it was obvious that the new queen would not uphold her sister's program of renewal, but would rather direct her efforts to reinstating the reformation of her father and brother. Elizabeth reintroduced the *Book of Common Prayer*, directing its use at religious ceremonies. In the Irish parliament, the Crown's representative, the Earl of Sussex, had a number of enactments passed that criminalized clergy's refusal to use the *Book of Common Prayer* and outlawed the Mass. Fines and imprisonment were enshrined for those who disobeyed these new laws.

On February 4, 1560, having been called to Dublin, William was presented with the Oath of Supremacy, which declared the monarch the Head of the Church; he refused to take it. At this stage, it was already known that he would put up virulent resistance to the new order. He initially continued his episcopal ministry in his diocese, but on one Sunday he took to the pulpit in his cathedral in Trim and preached against the *Book of Common Prayer* and its imposition. He was taken into custody and deprived of his office and assets. Sir James Ware, in his *Annals* for 1560, noted that the bishop was "zealous for the Romish Church". In his study of the Reformation in Ireland, the historian Henry Jefferies suggests that William "may have been involved in organizing a Catholic pastoral network across the Pale".[2] The Bishop of Meath was a maverick who had to be dealt with. On October 21, 1563, Elizabeth deposed him and appointed Hugh Brady as bishop.

After about a year to eighteen months imprisonment, William was released; he immediately appealed the queen's deprivation of his office to Rome. In 1564, Rome found in his favor, declared his deposition invalid, and confirmed him as Bishop of Meath. Interestingly, during the time of his imprisonment, his name had been submitted to Rome for consideration as Archbishop of Armagh: he was held in great esteem in Church circles. On July 13, 1565, the authorities rearrested him, and he was committed to Dublin Castle at the queen's pleasure until he took the oath. Once again, William refused to take the oath and was committed to prison indefinitely. It was around this time that Adam Loftus of Armagh had expressed serious concerns about William's ministry and recusancy and advised that he be taken out of Ireland: he was too dangerous.

The conditions of his imprisonment were bleak. It is said that he was chained much of the time and left in solitary confinement with few visitors allowed. The food was coarse. Not allowed any diversions to ease the tedium, he spent a great deal of time in prayer: it is said he

[2] Henry A. Jefferies, "The English Reformation in Dublin", in *Reformation & Renaissance Review*, vol. 18, no. 3 (2016): 233–53.

would often pray whole days and nights. Spiritually, it is believed he
received many consolations, and one biographer maintained that his
cell was transformed into "a paradise of delights".[3] Somehow he managed to devise a rough entertainment to occupy himself: he acquired a
bed made of twisted cords, and when he needed diversion, proceeded
to untie the cords and retie them.

Around Christmas 1572, through the kindness of a jailer and help
from his friends, William escaped captivity. Taking a ship to Brittany,
the voyage was difficult. Thanks to violent storms, it took sixteen
days for the ship to make it to Nantes; some sources say the vessel was
in fact shipwrecked on the coast. With no resources and his health
seriously undermined by his sufferings, he lived for six months in
destitution in Nantes. Finally receiving financial aid from the papal
nuncio to France, William made his way to Paris, but it was in the
middle of the Wars of Religion, and though he and others had tried
to find something for him, the impoverished bishop could find little
help there. He decided to make for Spain and arrived in Alcalá in
September 1574. William appears to have been living on alms at this
time, and his health was seriously impaired and not improving. He
was first assisted by a Spanish noblewoman and then found lodging
with the Cistercian community at Alcalá and received a pension from
King Philip II.

Some sources maintain that he returned to Ireland and took up a
hidden pastoral ministry in Meath. A brief was issued from Rome
in 1575 authorizing him to return and act for the then imprisoned
Archbishop of Armagh, Richard Creagh.[4] However, there seems to
be no evidence he ever returned to Ireland. He tried to arrange a
return to Brittany; he found the climate in Spain too much to bear,
and he wanted to be closer to Ireland to take up the care of his flock
again, but it never materialized. For the time that was left to him, he
served either as an auxiliary bishop or coadjutor to the Archbishop
of Toledo; he occupied that office for eight months before his death.
His health never recovered from the years of imprisonment and suffering, and he died in Alcalá on January 4, 1577. He was buried in

[3] Patrick Francis Moran, *History of the Catholic Archbishops of Dublin since the Reformation*
(Dublin: J. Duffy, 1864), p. 131.
[4] See chapter 2, "The Martyrs of Ireland".

the Collegiate Church of Saint Secundinus (the Irish Saint Seachnall of Dunshaughlin) in Alcalá, and a testimony commissioned by the Bishop of Granada was placed over his tomb. That church no longer exists, and today his tomb lies beneath a military barracks.

During his lifetime, William was renowned, not only among Catholics, but also among Protestant reformers, government officials, and even monarchs—Mary I and Elizabeth I—as a man who was zealous for the Catholic Faith and resisted every effort to impose the new religious dispensation. In death, he was revered as a martyr, one who bore the marks of the suffering and hardships that he had endured in prison—suffering that eventually claimed his life. As he was held in great veneration for his heroism, fidelity, and holiness, when the list of the Irish martyrs was being compiled, he was included, and the cause for his beatification was introduced with 256 others in 1915. Of those candidates, seventeen have been beatified and a further forty-two are now advancing; Bishop William Walsh's cause remains to be examined at a later date.

# 27

# Father Andrew Mullen

## *(1790–1818)*

### Priest

*Father John McEvoy*

In the New Testament, Saint Paul frequently addressed the Christian community as "the saints" (Eph 1:1; Phil 1:1; Col 1:2 *et passim*). The injunction to "be holy as God is holy" is a universal invitation. The Second Vatican Council brought to the modern era a renewed sense of the universal call to holiness that applies to all the baptized. "The classes and duties of life are many, but holiness is one—that sanctity which is cultivated by all who are moved by the Spirit of God, and who obey the voice of the Father and worship God the Father in spirit and in truth. These people follow the poor Christ the humble and cross-bearing Christ in order to be worthy of being sharers in His glory" (*Lumen Gentium*, 41). At the conclusion of chapter 5 of the Vatican II Dogmatic Constitution on the Church, we read: "all the faithful of Christ are invited to strive for the holiness and perfection of their own proper state" (*Lumen Gentium*, 42).

No doubt every century has seen people from the Diocese of Kildare and Leighlin live saintly lives. Like all other Irish dioceses, it is rich in the number of early saints who are revered in certain localities: the better-known Saints Brigid, Conleth, Laserian, Fintan, and Moling and the lesser-known Saints Fiacc, Coca, Abban, Manman, Faolán, Tegan, Auxilius, Senchall, and many others. Several of them are only remembered in association with a single parish or a small territory. Martyrs are in evidence, too. In the period of the Penal Laws, several priests, monks, and laypeople gave their lives for the Faith.

Daingean in Co. Offaly, previously called Philipstown in King's County, is the place of origin of our subject: Father Andrew Mullen. Apart from the fact that he was born around the year 1790, little is known of Andrew's early years or his family. His mother is believed to have been a Delahoide. The Mullens were local shopkeepers; his father is said to have been a baker and may also have run a public house and grocery, as the two were often combined. He was educated in a local school, most likely mixed Catholic and Protestant. Andrew lived with his mother, Catherine, and younger brother, Peter, on the Main Street of the town. It is known that the local curate, Father Matthew Reilly, played a major formative role in the life of the young man. As was frequently the case in those times, this priest provided Andrew with his pre-seminary education and assisted him further during his more formal studies in Carlow and Maynooth.

At the time of Andrew Mullen's birth, apart from Kilkenny, no seminary for priestly training existed in Ireland. Most candidates were required to travel to the European mainland to any of the many Irish Colleges dotting France, Spain, Italy, and elsewhere. In his childhood years, two ecclesiastical colleges began their educational activity: Carlow College, founded in 1782, was opened as a seminary and a lay college on October 1, 1793; and Maynooth College, founded for the education of Irish clergy in 1795. Father Mullen was among the first students at Carlow College.

Records show that Andrew spent the academic year 1809–1810 in Carlow. A letter, which he wrote to his mother, still exists from this time; it is the only surviving document written in his hand. In the course of this letter, he expresses his delight at solemn liturgical celebrations in Carlow on special feasts. He refers to the decorations for Adoration and Benediction. He also is pleased that Philipstown (Daingean) will soon have Benediction in the parish church. He sends his regards to the Confraternity members in Philipstown and Kilclonfert (another district of his home parish) and to the Dominican Third Order members. This letter reveals the presence of a strong devotion to the Blessed Sacrament in his life.

In September 1810, he matriculated into theology in Maynooth College. The date and place of his priestly ordination are uncertain. Maynooth records show that he received tonsure and minor orders on Friday, May 22, 1812, and subdiaconate on the following day. In 1813, he was one of the first six students to enter Dunboyne Establishment for postgraduate studies; as students were already ordained priests, it can be assumed that 1813 was the year of his ordination. It is feasible to presume that Father Andrew Mullen may have been ordained deacon and priest by Bishop Daniel Delany in a private ceremony as other priests at that time had been. He remained for a further two years in Maynooth pursuing deeper courses in theology and related studies.

Following his studies, Father Andrew received his appointment to the parish of Clonmore, situated in both Counties Carlow and Wicklow. He seems to have spent three years and some months there before his death. He lived in the priest's residence in Killinure, since demolished. His short ministry appears to have had a large emphasis on healing and comforting the afflicted. He is therefore a great exponent of evangelical mercy. He made great personal sacrifices to care for his people, often going without a fire in the house and giving away his food and clothing. His dedication to the corporal works of mercy may well have led to his demise. The tradition suggests that he had given his coat to a poor person and may, as a result, have picked up a chest infection leading to a rapid death.

Father Andrew died on December 17, 1818, in his twenty-eighth year.[1] The cause of his death "after a short illness" was described in the *Carlow Morning Post* as "bilious fever combined with jaundice". The announcement continues, "In the death of this young Champion of Christ, a bright ornament of the Catholic Church, Religion and the lovers of virtue have lost a true and steady friend in the way of Salvation." His burial took place in Clonmore Church grounds. However, he was to have a second burial as his remains were removed about five weeks later from the Clonmore grave by people from Daingean and

---

[1] The date of Father Andrew's death on his grave is inscribed as "*Ad Kal XV* Jan 1818", i.e., on the 15th day before the Kalends of January 1818. Meanwhile, a report in the *Carlow Morning Post* of January 7, 1819, refers to the death of the Reverend Andrew Mullen at Killenure, Co. Wicklow, "a few days since". Both point to a December date of death. It is now accepted that the true date of death was December 17, 1818.

transported by night, back to his native people. After being waked again in Daingean Church, his remains were interred in Killaderry Cemetery on the Croghan Road.

While knowledge of Father Andrew prior to his death was confined to a limited number, his reputation spread widely afterward, and his grave became a place of pilgrimage. Many flocked to the grave in search of answers to prayer, seeking intercession for difficult situations and illnesses. One further burial took place in the same grave plot in 1825, when Father Andrew's mentor, Father Reilly, died in Holy Week. In subsequent years, throngs of people made visits to the grave on Good Friday, the anniversary of Father Reilly's death. This tradition of devotees visiting Father Andrew's grave on Good Friday, rather than in January or February, which would correspond to his date of death and second burial, continued for many years. The grave remains a place of pilgrimage to the present time.

An elegy printed in his memory soon after his death paints Father Andrew as a zealous pastoral worker who poured himself out for the flock entrusted to him.[2] A sample stanza from the elegy notes:

> Those that were afflicted he instantly cured,
> He fed the weak and hungry that went from door to door.
> Those that were blind for many years their sight he did restore
> That wander through this nation, enquiring for Clonmore.

In his book, *The Story of Father Andrew Mullen*, Father Edward Kinsella records graphically the devotion that was developing and the mementos left at his grave by so many pilgrims; the crippled and infirm sought cures for sciatica, rheumatism, headaches, and other ills, and many mementos such as crutches, walking sticks, rosaries, medals, and coins were left behind.[3]

A brief flavor of Father Andrew's life and reputation is given by a poem composed by Father Edward Kinsella:[4]

---

[2] An extended poem of nine stanzas, included in a volume entitled *The Light Brigade*, published in Limerick ca. 1820 by S.B. Goggin (publisher).

[3] Father Edward Kinsella, *The Story of Father Andrew Mullen* (London, 1992), a reprint of an earlier publication.

[4] Ibid., p. 4.

## The Story of Father Andrew Mullen

Native of Philipstown County Offaly
where he was born A.D. 1790
Curate in Clonmore County Carlow
where he died A.D. 1818
in the 28th year of his age.

Legend has woven such a fragrant garland
around the brief life span of this
saintly young priest of a past age
that his memory is revered
and his grave is regarded as a
hallowed spot and place of pilgrimage.

Given the young priest's reputation for holiness and the consistent devotion to him, another priest from County Offaly, Father William Dempsey, who was a priest of Westminster diocese, put huge energy into the promotion of Father Andrew's cause, working tirelessly for many years before his death on October 31, 2008. He had lived for some years in retirement in Daingean and had been fulfilling the role of postulator for the cause. He was encouraged in his efforts by Bishops Laurence Ryan and James Moriarty.

While advice on the cause has been sought from personnel in the Dicastery for the Causes of Saints and the *Nihil Obstat* has been granted,[5] the process has not proceeded beyond diocesan level. Bishop James Moriarty formally opened the Cause of the Servant of God, Andrew Mullen, priest of Kildare and Leighlin diocese, and invited the faithful to report to the Bishop's House in Carlow any healings or favors granted through his intercession. This declaration was published in Carlow Cathedral's weekly bulletin on March 30, 2003. A Historical Commission was established and reported in 2004. A Diocesan Tribunal considered that report and other information in 2006 and judged that there was insufficient indication of heroic virtue to proceed with the cause—much more information and evidence needed to be brought to light. Nonetheless, strong local devotion

---

[5] The official letter granting *Nihil Obstat* is dated April 21, 1995, and signed by the Prefect of the Dicastery of the Causes of Saints, Cardinal Angelo Felici.

remains to Father Andrew, with many continuing to visit his grave seeking his intercession.

## Further reading:

Dempsey, M.A., Rev. William. *A Light from the Grave. Father Andrew Mullen 1790–1818*. (Published privately, 2000). This publication (186 pp.) is essentially the Master of Arts thesis presented in Durham University by the author. Copies are available through the Dempsey family.

# 28

# Father Luigi Gentili

## (1801–1848)

### Priest and Missionary

*Father Joseph O'Reilly, I.C.*

An Italian called Luigi Gentili hardly seems a likely candidate for a book dedicated to holy Irish men and women. In truth he did not even spend much time in Ireland. However, his presence in the country had an enormous impact, and devotion to him continues to grow even 170 years after his death.

Luigi Gentili was born in Rome in 1801, the eldest of ten children. Luigi's father was a lawyer, and his son followed him, qualifying at the age of sixteen to study law at the university. By the time he was twenty-one, he had a double doctorate in civil and canon law. The road ahead seemed clearly mapped out for him. This immediately brings us to one of the great themes in the life of Gentili—expectation, disappointment, and transformation. As was the custom at that time, Luigi had attached himself to an eminent person who would guide him in his new profession. In this case, the eminent person was Cardinal Consalvi, the most powerful man in Rome, who had the power to open and close doors for a young ambitious lawyer. Unfortunately for Luigi, Cardinal Consalvi died suddenly. Luigi was thrown into confusion, so much so that he decided to abandon his profession.

In the following months, he confined himself to his room and turned all his efforts toward learning new languages, including Spanish and English. Rome at that time was a city awash with wealthy foreigners who sought learning, culture, and a warmer climate. Among these foreigners were many English people. Luigi took to teaching them Italian and to performing at social gatherings as he had a rich baritone voice. This brought him social success, and soon he was in great demand. In the following two years, he was able to put away some £2,000 ($2525)—a very handsome income. Not for the first time in his life when things were going very well for Luigi, suddenly everything changed. Luigi was on the crest of a wave and proposed marriage to a young English lady, Anna de Mendoza. His proposal was twice rejected by her guardians, and the young lady was returned to England. Luigi was devastated and withdrew entirely from all his former work and social activities. In an interesting twist of fate or Providence, Luigi met the young lady again many years later, just five months before he died, when he visited her and her husband, Sir Patrick Bellew, at Barmeath Castle near Dunleer in Co. Louth. But by this time he understood how the Lord can be present in the great "disappointments" of life.

This second turning point in his life provided the opportunity to explore his deepest desires. He had always been a man of faith, and he quickly decided to develop it fully. His decision to study for the priesthood was mixed with a desire to become a missionary in England. During his days as a socialite, he had often engaged with English Catholics, and they discussed the prospects for the growth of "the old religion" in England in the aftermath of the recently achieved Catholic Emancipation. He was convinced he had something to offer.

Another unexpected development happened when Luigi met Blessed Antonio Rosmini, who had recently formed a new religious congregation, the Institute of Charity. Gentili and Rosmini had little in common as personalities. Gentili was tall and handsome, a striking character who was charismatic and full of energy and enthusiasm. Rosmini was much more reserved, but Gentili observed in Rosmini a depth of personality and holiness that he desired and respected. Rosmini was an excellent listener, and Gentili a fluent speaker. Rosmini undertook to sponsor Gentili to finish his studies and arranged for him to attend the newly reopened Irish College where he could perfect his English. It was a truly providential decision. At the Irish

College, Gentili became acquainted with many Irish students who would become lifelong friends. He also heard, for the first time, of the sufferings of Ireland, and that seed of compassion began to ripen in him.

On September 18, 1830, Gentili was ordained to the priesthood. He soon moved to the north of Italy where Rosmini's Institute of Charity was based and began to plan with Rosmini for his mission to England. The requests to Rosmini to provide missionaries to work in England were coming quick and fast. Eventually it was decided to take up the request of Bishop Baines, who was determined to establish Prior Park College at Bath. Gentili and two companions arrived in England on June 16, 1835, but he was less than impressed by London. Writing to Rosmini, Gentili described the city: "We seemed to be entering the very city of Pluto; black houses, black ships, dirty sailors ... the waters of the Thames were a dirty yellow and emitted a highly offensive stench. On land, all was noise and confusion; in short, the devil is here seen enthroned, exercising his tyrannical sway over wretched mortals."

The England that Gentili sailed to was truly missionary territory. Before the Reformation, England had been among the most Catholic of European countries, but by the beginning of the nineteenth century, the number of English Catholics had dwindled to a few tens of thousands. Those who had remained Catholic knew that in order to survive they had to keep their heads down. Although the "Roman Catholic Relief Act" had been passed in 1829, removing many of the remaining substantial restrictions on Catholics, nevertheless the atmosphere in the country was still openly hostile to Catholics. Furthermore, those Catholics, especially the wealthier ones, were extremely timid in their faith, wishing to avoid anti-Catholic sentiment—an understandable attitude given the many years of opposition and derision. In the course of his thirteen years in England, Gentili experienced many incidents of open, public aggression and ridicule. His effigy was burned on bonfires, and he was frequently told to return to his country. But he was a determined man and had prepared himself for years for the opposition he knew would await him. By his perseverance, he won over many to the Catholic Faith.

One of those who was "converted" was William Lockhart, who was one of Saint John Henry Newman's closest companions. At this time, Anglicanism was in turmoil. Newman and others formed part of the Oxford Movement, which tried to steer a path between Anglicanism and Catholicism. Lockhart found Gentili a compelling man and was not only received into the Catholic Church by him, but also joined the Rosminians. Newman was deeply affected by the conversion of his friend and shortly afterward preached his last sermon as an Anglican on "The Parting of Friends" before he himself was received into the Catholic Church.

Gentili spent almost all of the rest of his life in England. For several years, he worked with Bishop Baines at Prior Park to establish a seminary and a college for Catholic laity. Then he moved into the East Midlands, where he was much happier undertaking pastoral work. From the early 1840s, he concentrated on parish ministry, and this experience transformed him. Up to now most of his experience in England was in Catholic education and small rural parishes. Once he moved into Loughborough, he began to experience firsthand the plight of ordinary people who were cogs in the wheel of the industrial revolution. He also saw the price they had to pay for their adherence to Catholicism or for joining it. If Gentili had been a man of conviction up to now, he soon became a man of passion. In 1845 alone, he preached nineteen missions, gave ten retreats, and somehow found time to fit in a large number of other charity sermons and talks in places as far apart as Dublin, Manchester, and London.

The Irish connection was no small coincidence. From the time of his studies when he stayed in the Irish College in Rome, he had maintained contact with a number of well-placed Irish clergy who had introduced him to the pitiful suffering of Ireland. When Irish people started arriving in their thousands, and then in their tens of thousands, in the cities of England during the 1840s, Gentili saw firsthand the dire circumstances of these people. He also experienced for himself their deep faith and their receptiveness to the spirituality he was offering. As the leader of a small group of dedicated missionaries, including the Passionist priest Blessed Dominic Barbieri, Gentili was largely responsible for the introduction of parish missions, May devotions, Forty Hours Exposition, daily Communion, the wearing of the clerical collar in public, and public procession of the Blessed Sacrament—a deep shock to anti-Catholics. The Irish who arrived in England and Wales were ready for a man who was full of energy and conviction and who recognized their dignity, despite their pitiful state. While he had little or nothing to offer in terms of material help, he offered the gift of his presence, his life, and his faith, and these he gave in abundance.

Gentili spent the last years of his life giving himself completely to parish missions and talks. In the last sixteen months of his life, he preached no less than eight hundred full-length sermons, aided providentially by the breakthrough of rail travel in England. Thousands came to hear him preach with the Italian accent he never lost. He spent hours in the confessional, often well into the night. He was a man who lived a very austere life-style, never eating meat and surviving on a few hours of sleep each night. Five times in all he traveled from England to Ireland. Having traveled from Dublin to Waterford in September 1846 to preach for the Christian Brothers, he wrote of having never seen such unparalleled wretchedness. He wrote to his companions in England, pleading with them to "go through England begging for alms". He wrote in similar terms to Rosmini in Italy, who himself wrote to all his wealthy friends and put notices in the press and made public appeals in various Italian cities.

The last five months of his life were spent in Ireland. When he arrived in Dublin on April 29, 1848, he was already a man exhausted. Throughout the month of May, he preached a mission in Saint Audeon's Church. In June, the Rathmines Mission opened, and he introduced the Blue Scapular and promoted a scheme of consecrating Ireland to the Immaculate Heart of Mary; there were 40,000 communions. In August he gave several retreats to seminarians at Clonliffe College and to the Sisters of Mercy in Birr. At the beginning of September, he began his last mission at Saint John's Augustinian Church in John's Lane Dublin. It proved too much for him, or perhaps it was just enough. He had been warned about cholera in that area of the city and had been advised not to give the retreat as it would kill him. His answer was typical: "not at all, and anyway are there not souls to save in the slums as well as in favored areas." Overcome with exhaustion, he withdrew from the mission and died on September 28, 1848.

Extraordinary scenes were witnessed at his funeral, immense crowds followed the funeral procession to Glasnevin cemetery, where he was buried in the O'Connell Circle. Many years later, in 1938, his body was transferred to Saint Michael's in Omeath, Co. Louth, where it lies today. In 2014, a new oratory was constructed at the Calvary in Omeath to house his remains, and every day pilgrims come to his tomb to pray and to seek his intercession.

The prospect of Gentili's canonization cause has not been very actively promoted, largely out of respect for the cause of Rosmini, Gentili's superior and spiritual father. Now that Antonio Rosmini has been declared Blessed, perhaps the time is right to consider Gentili's cause in recognition for his apostolic zeal, his holiness, and his self-sacrifice.

# 29

# Father Paul Mary Pakenham

## (1821–1857)

### Passionist Priest

*Father Paul Francis Spencer, C.P.*

As he lay semi-conscious in a room of the farmhouse-turned-monastery at Mount Argus in Dublin, doctors tried to spoon a few drops of champagne into the mouth of Father Paul Mary Pakenham, thinking to provide some nourishment for him in his last illness, now that he could no longer swallow. Becoming aware of his surroundings for a moment, he realized what was going on and said with surprise, "This is a nice way for a religious to die!"

Born into a world of champagne and silver spoons, Charles Reginald Pakenham, known to us as Father Paul Mary, first saw the light of day on September 21, 1821, at 10 Rutland Square (now Parnell Square), Dublin, the town house of his father, the Earl of Longford. Most of his early years, however, were spent in County Westmeath at Pakenham Hall (Tullynally Castle), near Castlepollard. His schooling at Winchester was followed by officer training at the Royal Military Academy Sandhurst. During his years in the British army, he rose to the rank of Captain in the Grenadier Guards. But behind this outward career path, an inner journey was leading him closer to Christ crucified.

In spite of his telling us that he led a "wild and dissipated life" while in the army, we know that he was during those years following the development of the Tractarian movement in the Anglican

Church. His copy of John Henry Newman's *Parochial and Plain Sermons* was well read and annotated, with penciled notes in the margins and lines marking significant passages such as this one: "How is it that we are so contented with things as they are—that we are so willing to be let alone, and to enjoy this life—that we make such excuses if anyone presses on us the necessity of something higher, the duty of bearing the Cross, if we would earn the Crown of the Lord Jesus Christ?" "It was Newman", he would say later in life, "who taught me the beauty of religion."

It was during this time that Captain Pakenham, still an Anglican, began fasting, practicing meditation, and seeing a spiritual director. *The Imitation of Christ* became his spiritual reading of choice as he set out on the "Royal Road of the Holy Cross".[1] His hope of finding peace within his own church communion was shaken, however, when he saw Newman leave the Church of England and seek admission into what he called "the one true Fold of the Redeemer". Charles was further stirred by a little book given to him by his spiritual director, the Reverend Upton Richards of Margaret Chapel, London; this was *The Spirit of Saint Alphonsus Liguori, A Selection from His Shorter Spiritual Treatises*. The more he read Saint Alphonsus, the more certain he became that his own true home would be found in the Catholic Church.

On the Feast of the Assumption, August 15, 1850, the twenty-eight-year-old Charles Pakenham was received into the Catholic Church by the future Cardinal Nicholas Wiseman. He later said to a friend, "It was a hard fight, because the spirit of irreligion had sunk so very deeply into society in England that I stood quite alone. I met no sympathy anywhere.... It was a hard struggle."[2]

His family were shocked at his decision to become a Catholic and thought only of the shame this would bring on them. He found refuge from turmoil at the home of his uncle and former superior officer, General Lygon, at Spring Hill in Worcestershire. The nearest Catholic Church was Saint Saviour's in Broadway, attached to a Passionist monastery and novitiate. Here he came to Mass on Sundays and was impressed by what he called the "joyful countenances

[1] Thomas à Kempis, *The Imitation of Christ*, II, 12 (ca. 1418–1427).
[2] Joseph Smith, *Paul Mary Pakenham, Passionist* (Dublin: M. H. Gill, 1915), p. 32.

and unaffected simplicity" of the novices. Charles would probably have already heard of the Passionists, whose first superior in England, Blessed Dominic Barberi, had received John Henry Newman into the Catholic Church. Intrigued by the joy that their life of prayer, poverty, and penance seemed to produce, he asked permission to make a retreat at the monastery and, at the end of the retreat, requested entry into the novitiate.

The rector, Father Vincent Grotti, was reluctant to admit one whose health was delicate and whose life had been lived in wealth and comfort, but he did not succeed in dampening Charles' enthusiasm. After several conversations, Father Vincent was won over, and he agreed to accept Captain Pakenham as a novice. After breaking the news to General Lygon, Charles went to London to sell his officer's commission (as was the practice at that time), dispose of his property by giving his money to various charitable causes, and try to explain his decision to his family. One of his sisters, thinking of Father Ignatius Spencer, a son of Earl Spencer, who had become a Catholic and joined the Passionists, said to a friend: "I wish he were dead, but the worst of it is we shall be like the Spencers, who have not only the sorrow of losing their near relative, but the shame of seeing him go about barefoot, like a dirty, mad mendicant, begging prayers for the conversion of England."[3]

For Charles Reginald Pakenham, who would be known in the Passionists as Paul Mary of Saint Michael the Archangel, the entry into religious life was not an easy transition. His first weeks in the monastery were marked by doubts and questions; he found the monotony of the way of life particularly uninspiring. Finally, after weeks of struggling in darkness, he came to a place of light and peace and experienced the joy and consolation that would be his strength in the years ahead.

Father Vincent had hesitated to admit Paul Mary as a novice because of his health. This fear was not unfounded: a childhood bout of rheumatic fever had left him with a weak heart. He also suffered from rheumatism, which, although he was only in his early thirties, sometimes led to him having to walk with two sticks. None of this deterred him from the prayer, fasting, manual work, and study that formed the daily routine of the monastery. Nor was he one to welcome special

[3] Ibid., p. 40.

treatment or dispensations even when these were offered. "What does it matter?" he used to say, "You know I cannot live very long at best, and if I take notice of every little ailment I shall end up by doing nothing at all for my time in the world."

The joy and simplicity that had drawn him to the Passionists became the hallmarks of his own religious life. In a *Memoir* of Paul Mary written by his novice master, Father Salvian Nardocci, we read:

> On one occasion, during his stay at The Hyde [an early Passionist monastery near London], two noble men called to see him. When they arrived, Paul with the rest of the community happened to be at recreation, and for the sake of amusement as well as to be usefully employed, they were engaged in shelling peas. When the two gentlemen were shown in, Paul received them with the greatest cordiality and after exchanging the usual compliments, sat down and without the least embarrassment continued his occupation. His two friends, far from being in any way disconcerted, enjoyed the circumstance very much and, having asked and obtained permission, assisted him with the peas during the remainder of their visit.[4]

After his ordination to the priesthood, Paul Mary was asked to go to Rome to accompany a group of English Passionist students who were being sent to the Passionist Retreat of Saints John and Paul for courses in theology. He stayed with them for about nine months, living in the house where the founder of the Passionists, Saint Paul of the Cross, had spent the last years of his life, after which Paul Mary was appointed as the first superior of the new Passionist foundation at Mount Argus, Dublin. He celebrated the first Mass at Mount Argus on the Feast of the Assumption, August 15, 1856, exactly six years after his reception into the Catholic Church.

Father Paul Mary was to live at Mount Argus for just over six months. In that time, he became an example of holiness both to his Passionist community and to the people who came to the little church he built at Mount Argus. In some ways, he was extreme in his practice of poverty, reducing the food allowance for himself and his brothers to the bare minimum. He would walk in his habit, with a basket on

[4] Salvian Nardocci, *Memoir of the Late Father Paul Mary of St. Michael, Passionist*, unpublished manuscript in the archives of the Passionist community of Mount Argus, Dublin, p. 74.

his arm, to the markets around Patrick Street to buy the cheapest food from the small shops frequented by the poor of Dublin. What his uncle, Henry Pakenham, who was at that time the Anglican Dean of Saint Patrick's Cathedral, thought of his nephew wandering around like this outside his cathedral is not recorded.

Day by day, during those hours not spent in community or personal prayer, he was to be found "in the confessional helping the fallen in their effort to return to God, or counselling and consoling those who came to seek aid and advice in the difficulties and trials that beset their paths."[5] In November, he took part in a mission given by the Passionists in the local parish at Rathmines. Halfway through the mission, an attack of heart trouble left him unable to continue, and he had to return to Mount Argus.

His health continued to deteriorate, and in February 1857, his weak heart and poor circulation brought on other complications. Liver disease was "accompanied by a violent and continuous nausea and retching which compelled him to take to his bed".[6] Sir Dominic Corrigan, an eminent cardiologist, examined him and pronounced his condition to be "hopeless". The following day, Father Vincent, who was now Provincial, gave him the Sacrament of the Sick, after which Paul Mary, with a painful effort, spoke to his Passionist brothers. He began by thanking God for the grace of dying in the Passionist Congregation. He thanked the community for all the kindness they had shown him and asked their forgiveness for anything he had done that had hurt them or been a bad example to them. He then asked them to remember him in their prayers.

After this, he drifted in and out of consciousness for about a week, sometimes crying out in pain when the delirium caused his mask of self-control to slip. It was during this time that the doctors tried to ease his suffering and give him some small nourishment with a few drops of champagne.

Finally, early on the morning of March 1, 1857, he peacefully gave his soul back to God. It was a Sunday, and he had been due to preach a charity sermon that day at the Jesuit Church in Gardiner Street on behalf of Saint Clare's Orphanage in Harold's Cross. Instead, it was

---

[5] Smith, *Paul Mary Pakenham*, pp. 106ff.
[6] Ibid., p. 111.

Father Ignatius Spencer who stood in the pulpit of the Church of Saint Francis Xavier and announced that Father Paul Mary Pakenham was dead. He was just thirty-five years old.

What did the life and death of this young man mean to the crowds who came to see him laid out in the little church at Mount Argus? A newspaper of the time, *The Nation*, summed it up in these words: "Of all the thousands and thousands who gazed on the shell of a soul so holy, there was not one who did not seem to feel that a saint had gone home to the House of God."

For us today, he is someone who put Christ before career or comfort, who was faithful in sickness and in health to the vows he had made, and who, in the words of Saint Paul, was content with the loss of everything if only he could have Christ.[7] He also shows us that holiness need never be devoid of good humor and that gentleness and joy have the power to draw people into the life of the Church.

When the coffin of Father Paul Mary was moved to the new cemetery at Mount Argus thirty-seven years after his death, his body was found to be (in the words of an eyewitness) "perfectly intact and incorrupt, and the face wore a most lifelike expression as of one who lay in a peaceful slumber".[8] May his example inspire us with a living faith in Jesus Christ, crucified and risen.

**Further information:**

Smith, C.P., Joseph. *Paul Mary Pakenham, Passionist.* London and Edinburgh: Sands & Co., 1915.

Warren, G.P. *An Account of the Life, Conversion and Holy Death of the Hon. and Rev. Chas. Reginald Pakenham, in Religion Father Paul Mary of Saint Michael, Superior of Blessed Paul's Retreat of the Passionists, Harold's Cross.* Revised by Ven. Ignatius Spencer, C.P. Dublin: G.P. Warren, 1857.

---

[7] Philippians 3:8.
[8] Smith, *Paul Mary Pakenham*, p. 117.

30

# Father Henry Young

## *(1786–1869)*

### Priest

### *Dr. Patrick Kenny*

The soldier must be at his post, the sentinel in his sentry-box; so must I be on my watch-tower. Officials must be at their respective posts, otherwise they will not be rewarded. I do attend with satisfaction to all my duties, and hope to persevere till the Lord God will call me into Eternity.[1]

This faithful "soldier" was the Dublin priest Father Henry Young, who vigilantly watched over his parishes with such zeal and care that he was regarded during his lifetime as a living saint and after his death was known as "the Curé d'Ars of Dublin".

Henry Young was born in 1786 in the Liberties in Dublin, the third of eleven children. The Young family was extremely pious—of the eight children who survived to adulthood, three became priests of the Dublin diocese, a fourth son became a Jesuit, and three sisters entered the convent.

Henry was distinguished by his personal piety from an early age. His family knew him as "The Saint", and he was often to be found praying or reading devout books by candlelight in the cellar. He

---

[1] Fullerton, Lady Georgina (1874), *A Sketch of the Life of the Late Father Henry Young of Dublin* (London: Burns and Oates), p. 41.

saved up his pocket money and various sweets and cakes to distribute to the poor. Around the age of fourteen, he was sent to boarding school in Balbriggan, where he encouraged his classmates to join him in the Sodality of the Blessed Virgin. Several of these classmates became priests, and they attributed their vocations to the example of the "little apostle of Balbriggan", as they affectionately nicknamed him.

It was no surprise, then, that he felt the call to the priesthood. At the young age of sixteen, he left Dublin for Rome, enrolling as a student in the Propaganda College. His stay in Rome seems to have had a profound impact on him. According to testimony from one of his sisters, it was while praying in a church in Rome that he felt inspired to follow a life of great austerity and self-denial, a calling to which he adhered for the rest of his life. Around this time, one of his student friends was dying, and Henry requested that, when he got to Heaven, he would pray that Henry would acquire the grace of only ever being occupied with God and his service, to the exclusion of all else. It is a grace that he seems to have received—Henry's complete dedication to his duties as a priest, and indifference to all else, was the keynote of his priestly ministry.

Henry was ordained in 1810, at the age of twenty-four, and spent the first four years of his priesthood as a missionary priest with the Vincentian Fathers in Rome. He arrived back in Dublin on Christmas Day, 1814. On disembarking from his ship, he went straight to the Augustinian chapel in John's Lane, where he offered the three traditional Christmas Day Masses, only after which time he returned to see the family he had left twelve years previously.

Much of Father Henry's remaining sixty years were spent as a curate in parishes in Dublin city center, interspersed with periods as a roving missionary priest in more distant parts of north and west Dublin and parts of Wicklow. An incident that occurred soon after he became curate in Saint Michan's, his first parish, captures the detachment and charity that characterized his entire life. His mother had arranged for his small room in the presbytery to be comfortably furnished and carpeted for him. On visiting him a few days later, she found him sitting in the cold, without a fire, most of the furniture already given away, and her son in the process of cutting the new carpet into smaller segments for distribution to the poor.

Working tirelessly at every task entrusted to him, Father Henry placed himself entirely at the service of God and his parishioners. He visited every house in whatever parish he was working in. He provided the sacraments at times that were convenient for his flock. For example, when he was stationed in Harold's Cross, he made it easier for local mill workers to attend Mass by offering it at 5 A.M. each morning (he himself was often in the church praying from 4 A.M.). He held night prayers in the church, often walking through the village ringing a bell and encouraging people to come with him to church to pray. He built and developed the infrastructure of the Church wherever he was stationed, helping to establish chapels and schools where they were needed.

He was also a social reformer, most notably working in the temperance movement to combat alcoholism among workers, a problem that led to spiritual, emotional, and economic ruin for so many in Ireland. He set up a booth during fairs and festivals from which he distributed free coffee and buttermilk as an alternative to the temptation to enter public houses. He also published a booklet that argued against the strange practice of the time whereby workers had to gather in a pub to receive their weekly wages. His zeal was not without opposition—on more than one occasion, he was physically attacked by Protestant proselytizers for his efforts to preserve and promote the Catholic Faith.

Especially devoted to the ministry of the confessional, he was constantly available to provide the sacrament for penitents, while he personally availed of it once a week himself. He placed a sign in his window stating that he was available at any time for confession. As he aged, some friends expressed concern about the amount of time he spent in his confessional in cold, unheated churches. His reply was simple: "When I feel very cold, I have a fire at which to warm myself—the Blessed Sacrament."

It is mistakenly perceived that lay Catholics of the nineteenth century were passive and that their function was to pray, pay, and obey. But Father Henry's ministry encouraged a high degree of holiness among the laity. He worked with several confraternities, guiding them and writing their rule of life. Some of these involved significant spiritual commitments with important and novel apostolates. For example, the rule of life he wrote for the Purgatorian Society specifies that members should teach the poor, visit the sick and dying to prepare them for the Last Rites and for death, and to officiate at wakes by praying the Office for the Dead. The confraternities that he directed lived the universal call to holiness more than a century before the Second Vatican Council.

Father Henry's pastoral zeal was accompanied by great personal austerity. For many years he ate only once per day, and it was not unusual for him to survive on only bread, water, and porridge. He slept little, often using only boards and a wooden stool for a pillow. He hid many of his personal mortifications, but there were clues for the observant. After his death, an old woman testified, "We had a saint one time in our parish, his name was Father Henry Young. He wore something made of bristles; I saw it once myself through an opening in his waistcoat." Father Peter Kenney, S.J., who reestablished the Jesuits in Ireland following their suppression in 1773, was a close friend of Father Henry, and he declared that he was the only person that he had known or heard of in his own time who practiced the same austerity as the ancient saints.

These mortifications bore fruit in his personal charity and detachment from material things. He could often be seen walking through the city with bundles of clothing or bedding straw for the poor. Concerned with the misuse of money, especially because of alcoholism, he devised a scheme whereby he opened accounts in several shops and distributed tickets that could be redeemed in store for food and other necessities. He was known to visit the houses of those who had suddenly fallen on hard times. He would leave some money with the family, requesting that they prepare a good supper for him that evening, which, of course, he never returned to share. In this delicate way, he provided a good meal for those who needed it and were too proud to ask for help.

Father Henry was also detached from his own life and safety. During the dangerous cholera epidemic of 1832, he spent many nights in the cholera hospital assisting the dying, hearing their confession, and anointing them, risking his own life in the process.

Like many of the canonized saints, Father Henry was known to give away even his own clothing if he met a shivering beggar who needed it. On one occasion though, he went a little bit farther. A visiting priest had left some wet clothes to dry in Father Henry's room, they were soon distributed to a beggar who called at the door. When the priest asked what had happened to his apparel, Father Henry reminded him that naked we came into the world and naked we will leave it. History has not recorded whether his priest reacted with the same degree of detachment!

At the age of seventy, Father Henry "retired" to the position of chaplain of Saint Joseph's Asylum in Portland Row.[2] Apart from a few months spent as a chaplain to a Carmelite monastery in Clondalkin, he stayed there until his death thirteen years later. He lived a semi-monastic life right to the very end. He had a room built for himself beside the chapel where he spent hours each day praying, commencing at 4 A.M.; he remained available to the many Dubliners who sought him out in his confessional. He continued practicing the same austerity with which he had always lived—sleeping on boards and having one daily meal of bread and water.

Father Henry died on November 17, 1869. Father Russell, the superior of the Dominicans, was with him when he died, and he declared, "A saint has passed to Heaven, it is now our turn to ask his intercession for us." He was buried in the vaults of the Pro-Cathedral; before death he had declared, "my ardent wish is for my poor remains to be near daily Masses and the Tabernacle." Those who knew him believed him to have been a saint. As he was waked, thousands of ordinary people queued for hours to catch a glimpse of his body and to touch it with their Rosaries or holy pictures.

Father Henry was viewed as a living saint by those who knew him. Even in his younger days in Rome, there were some who declared that, if they outlived him, they expected to be called upon to testify in his canonization process. Ordinary Dubliners revered him, especially the poor and the workers, who sometimes knelt in the street to ask his blessing as he passed by. Devotion to Father Henry continued long after his death—the demand for relics around the world was so great that his clothing was soon all exhausted. There were many reports of alleged miracles and healings through his intercession, and even some alleged miracles during his lifetime. One woman even

[2] Saint Joseph's Asylum was a retirement home for older single ladies who had lived charitable and pious lives but were now unable to support themselves. Many of the members were Carmelite, Franciscan, or Dominican tertiaries, and they formed a quasi-monastic community there.

claimed to see him, near the end of his life, lifted three or four feet in the air while he prayed.

For unknown reasons, and despite the very real popular devotion to him, Father Henry's canonization cause was never initiated, and devotion to him seems to have dwindled over time. But his example of fidelity to duty remains relevant and inspiring to all, especially to priests who face an increasingly secular and hostile culture.

# 31

# Father John Spratt

## *(1796–1871)*

### Priest

## *Professor Fergus A. D'Arcy*


In an age of remarkable priests, few were as remarkable and yet as forgotten as the Carmelite friar John Spratt of Whitefriar Street. When he died in 1871, his funeral was one of the largest ever seen in Dublin, with a procession of some 30,000 following his remains to Glasnevin Cemetery. It was, perhaps, second only to that of his hero and friend, Daniel O'Connell. He deserves to be remembered, not least as the Peter McVerry of nineteenth-century Dublin, as the great provider of shelter and support for the homeless, the orphan, the blind, and the deaf. For these alone, his outstanding work should be remembered, but his commitments and achievements were far wider still, from church and school-building, through famine relief, ecumenical social reform, and charitable endeavors, and on to the causes of full political and religious liberties.

A Dubliner through and through, John Spratt was born in Cork Street, beside the Liberties and the Coombe. Apart from his priestly formation years in Cordoba, Spain (1816–1820), some months on a visit to Rome (1835–1836), and a few days on a temperance mission in Belfast, London, and Liverpool in the 1850s and 1860s, he spent all his years in the city of his birth and died in the sacristy of the church of Our Lady of Mount Carmel, which he himself had built. John's family were tanners of Cork Street, his father having been in the business of tanning and parchment making there from the early nineteenth century, if not before. The business must have been prosperous enough to see two of its three boys become priests, John the Carmelite and his younger brother, James, the Augustinian, and one of its three daughters, Catherine, become a Carmelite nun. The oldest boy, Michael, succeeded their father in the tanning business until trade depression in the later 1830s led to his bankruptcy and the loss of the family home and business in Cork Street.

John's mother, Esther Elizabeth, was a devout Catholic who worshipped at the Calced Carmelite church in Ash Street, in the Liberties. It was doubtless her influence that led John to his priestly vocation. He was accepted into the Carmelites and left Dublin for Cordoba, Spain, in 1816. Upon his ordination, he returned to Ireland at the start of the 1820s and was assigned to the Calced Carmelite community of French Street (now Mercer Street), where they had moved in 1809 from Ash Street.

He rose quickly in the ranks and became prior at the age of twenty-seven in 1823. He set about the purchase of the original medieval site of their Dublin foundation and built the Church of Mount Carmel and the community house at Whitefriar Street. It was a very great achievement for which he was not thanked by all of his confreres since it involved taking on a large expense, on top of the nearby primary schools that he also built. A devoted antiquarian with a passionate interest in Dublin and Irish history, it was John who rediscovered the famous statue of the Virgin of Dublin, had it restored, and then installed it in a shrine that still graces this church today. A decade later, on a visit to Rome in 1835–1836, he was gifted by Pope Gregory XVI with the relics of Saint Valentine, which in turn became the focal point of the famous Whitefriar Street shrine that is still much visited to this day.

In the course of the 1820s and 1830s, he founded and managed the nearby Catholic primary schools, and in addition he became very actively involved in three great charities, Saint Peter's Orphan Society, the Cholera Orphan Society, and the interdenominational Sick and Indigent Roomkeepers' Society of which he was joint secretary (with the Church of Ireland clergyman, Reverend Thomas Shore) for close on forty years. During the 1840s, and again in the 1860s, he became a leading figure in national famine relief, relentlessly raising financial aid and persisting with this even when other individuals and organizations had given up and left the field. Concurrent with all of these endeavors, the 1840s saw this uniquely ecumenical priest join forces with the Unitarian social reformer James Haughton in their long-enduring campaign for temperance and teetotalism. Spratt became an iconic figure in this, long after Father Mathew had gone, and worked tirelessly for temperance until literally his dying day: he died within minutes of having administered the pledge to two local parishioners.

During the deeply troubled 1840s, with the disastrous split between the O'Connellites and the Young Irelanders, the Carmelite friar became the leading protagonist in the eventually abortive cause of reconciliation and reunion of the nationalist factions. Yet, for all his own frenetic activity in multiple public causes, he found time to produce a significant body of writing as his contribution to the devotional revolution. There is no question that, in this regard, he proved the most prolific of writers in the Carmelite apostolate in Ireland, up to the time of his own death, and perhaps beyond that. He did so at a time when Catholic devotional literature in Ireland was only in its post penal-age infancy. His contributions were generally directed to a popular lay readership. As befitted a Carmelite, he cultivated a particular commitment to Our Lady, his very first publication being *A Novena, or Nine Days' Devotion to the Ever Glorious and Blessed Virgin Mary of Mount Carmel*, produced in 1824. He returned to this theme in 1835 with *An Eulogium on the Ever Blessed Virgin Mary of Mount Carmel*, a substantial work of prayer, followed two years later by *The Sincere Christian's Manual of Devotion*. His most substantial contribution, exceeding 500 pages, was *The Carmelite Manual: Containing a Selection of Beautiful Prayers and Various Practices of Piety*, first published in 1846 but reprinted in many editions, some even after his death. It had an extensive appeal and served its readership for a very long period. Critically, it supplied a domestic devotional spiritual literature that had been scant up to his day and at a time when there was a growing lay demand for Catholic devotional works. We may surmise from his writings on Our Lady that Father Spratt had a particular personal devotion to Mary.

Although he was a friar, living in community, John Spratt was extraordinarily socially and politically active: he was unquestionably one of the most political priests of his age, and this was despite episcopal and papal admonitions against clerical participation in politics. Learning his political trade in O'Connell's Catholic Association,

Spratt was unique among Dublin conventual and diocesan priests in fighting to secure the voter registration of himself, his confreres, and the wider Catholic and liberal public of Dublin. He was persistent in this from the 1830s through to the end of the 1860s. He was also one of the most prominent public figures, whether lay or clerical, in pursuing clemency for state prisoners, from the men of '48 to the Fenians of '67. Indeed, he himself was the founder of the amnesty movement for Fenian prisoners in the 1860s: even when he was attacked by the Fenian press. This did not prevent him from securing a place in Saint Peter's Orphanage for the children of executed Fenians, including the son of the Manchester Martyr, Michael Larkin, and the two sons of the Dublin Fenian, William Sheedy. At the same time, his devotion to the memory of Daniel O'Connell saw Spratt become one of the leading figures in trying to secure the great O'Connell Monument in the city center. Although he did not live to see its final unveiling, he himself was accorded the privilege of being buried within the august O'Connell Circle in Glasnevin Cemetery.

A devoted Dubliner, John Spratt was actively committed to social and environmental improvement. He was a leading supporter of Sir John Gray's campaign for a clean city water supply; he was equally active with his friend James Haughton in securing the opening to the public of the Botanic Gardens on Sundays, and, toward the end of his days, he was closely involved in the campaign for securing the opening of Saint Stephen's Green as a public amenity for the citizens of his native city. However, his towering achievement was one of the last in the long line of his contributions. This one was entirely of his own initiative, namely, the foundation and management of the Night Refuge for Homeless Women and Children. He began this initiative in 1859 and opened the doors of his new foundation in February 1861, almost across the road from where he had been born, at Brickfield Lane, opposite Cork Street. Initially he secured the renting of this remarkable property and its reconstruction into a hostel. Originally it had been built as the Stove Tenter House, a gift to the weavers of the Liberties from the philanthropist Thomas Pleasants, designed for the purpose of enabling them to dry out their woven cloths. With the collapse of the weaving trade by the 1840s, it became at one point an auxiliary workhouse for the South Dublin Union and then was abandoned. John converted it into a night hostel, and before his death he had managed to secure the right to purchase the property outright. Here, over the ten years 1861 to 1871, he provided night shelter for large numbers of the homeless. The figures of those relieved are arresting: from over 960 per week in early April 1861 to over 1,140 a week in March 1862; over its first year, it sheltered close on 30,000 destitutes, and that figure had little changed in the final year of Spratt's life.

It was not only his most remarkable achievement, it was also his most long-lasting; one hundred years later, it was still sheltering homeless women and children until, at the beginning of the present century, it evolved into its present mission as the Sophia Housing Association project of the Daughters of Wisdom.

His legendary kindness was not confined to mankind, as he was also a champion in the campaign against cruelty to animals and wrote on that subject as on so many others. It was hardly a surprise then that Friar John was mourned by Dubliners in their tens of thousands and was at the time of his funeral remembered not only as a great charity worker but as a priest who, uniquely for the age, crossed the sectarian divisions of Dublin to work with Quakers, Unitarians, Methodists, and Anglicans. Perhaps the greatest tribute paid to him was that by the Church of Ireland priest of nearby Saint Bride's, Reverend William Carroll, who said that despite the differences of their denominations, Father Spratt was a shining light among them.

Similarly, Archdeacon Redmond of Arklow recalled that he had never known a more simple, humble, or more dignified man who was emphatically unselfish and animated with goodwill to all men. According to Archdeacon Redmond, his work for the Night Refuge alone would be enough to immortalize him.

One of the most significant tributes was that from a pseudonymous writer who suggested that it was the women of Dublin who would most feel the death of Father Spratt, for it was they who best knew the wide expanse of his charity. Yet, by their descendants and fellow citizens, John Spratt, Carmelite, has been forgotten and today is remembered only by his own confreres of the Carmelite Order. He deserved better from Dublin City and from Catholic Ireland.

## Further reading:

D'Arcy, Fergus A. *Raising Dublin, Raising Ireland: A Friar's Campaigns— Father John Spratt, O.Carm. (1796–1871)*. Dublin: Carmelite Publications, 2018.

# 32

# Archdeacon Bartholomew Cavanagh

## *(1821–1897)*

## Priest

## *Tom Neary*

The centenary of the death of Archdeacon Bartholomew Cavanagh, the parish priest of Knock at the time of the apparitions, was marked in special ceremonies in Knock Basilica on Sunday, September 7, 1997, attended by the West of Ireland bishops, the Kavanagh Clan from the U.S., and thousands of pilgrims. Afterward, a bronze bust of the archdeacon by artist Rick Lewis was unveiled on the excavated site of his cottage by his grandniece from the U.S., Peggy Cavanagh-Knoell, and blessed by Archbishop Michael Neary of Tuam. Since his death, numerous people have remarked on the many similarities between the archdeacon's life and that of the Curé of Ars, Saint John Vianney, the patron saint of parish priests, most especially in both priests' work for the poor and the long hours they spent in the confessional.

Bartholomew was born in 1821 in Annaghadown, which is situated on the southeast shore of Lough Corrib in Co. Galway. The Cavanaghs were an old Catholic family, originally living in Co. Carlow, where they owned much land, but they lost it in Cromwellian times and had to settle in Connaught. His parents, John and Kate, whose maiden name was Browne, had thirteen children: eight girls and five boys. Bartholomew got his early education in Galway city, traveling there on horseback. After that, as he felt that he had a vocation to the priesthood, he went to Saint Jarlath's College in Tuam before moving on to Saint Patrick's College, Maynooth. While there, he cultivated a special devotion to the Blessed Virgin Mary. He was ordained a priest in 1846.

Father Cavanagh's first appointment was to Westport, Co. Mayo, as curate. At that time, the Great Famine was gaining momentum, and he was confronted with the most awful scenes of poverty; hunger-stricken people like walking skeletons, utter desolation and misery everywhere. He often had to anoint forty dying parishioners before his own meager breakfast. Throughout the Great Famine years, he did everything he could to help his suffering and starving people. His love and kindness for them and his outstanding charity were heroic. He gave everything he had to help the poor, even his personal possessions. He raffled his horse and even his watch, using the money to enable girls who were in the workhouse to emigrate. He managed to have a home erected to provide work for young orphan girls. He never had a bank account and was usually in debt himself.

Having labored for twenty-one years in Westport, where the people today still speak of his spirituality and charity, Father Cavanagh was appointed parish priest of Knock-Aghamore in 1867. Moving into the village, he was given a small thatched, three-roomed cottage with whitewashed walls; as he was a tall man, he had to bend down to enter the doorway. His ministry in Knock-Aghamore was onerous as it extended over a large area; in reality, it was two parishes in one, but he continued his good work as in Westport.

From 1867 to 1897, he lived through the most trying period of Irish history, marked by hardship, hunger, evictions due to landlordism, risings, reprisals, secret societies, proselytism, which was rampant, and the Land War. He was strongly opposed to all kinds of violence and warfare. He did everything in his power to provide an adequate supply of schools and teachers for the youth of the parish so that a good and sound Christian education was available to all. He was opposed to the *modus operandi* of the secret societies. He regarded them as deceitful and dangerous, and he spoke out strongly against them. Threats were made against him, and his ears were to be cut off as a punishment. Luckily, when the Apparition occurred, everything changed, even their mindset, and the threatened tragedy was averted. In 1875, the honor of Archdeacon was conferred on him by the Archbishop of Tuam, John MacHale.

He was a man of deep faith and prayer. His special devotion to the Blessed Virgin Mary was most evident when he preached his sermons. His best ones were always on Our Lady, whom he referred to as the "Ever Immaculate Mother of God". In addition to his many devotions, he also did penances; when he died, it was discovered that he had been wearing a hairshirt. In 1880, he was described by journalist T.D. Sullivan: "He towers over men of average height.... His forehead is lofty, his face long and full of healthy color, his features regular and firm, his eyes blue, full and expressive; his whole air denoting gentleness and benevolence.... He speaks with an easy fluency.... He is good looking, strong of constitution ... energetic, active, cheerful."

In August 1879, everything changed for the archdeacon. In the hundred days before it, he had set himself the mission of offering one hundred Masses for the Holy Souls. He had a great devotion to the Eucharist, and when he learned that his parishioners could not afford to have Masses offered for their deceased ones, out of the goodness of his heart and his own wonderful devotion to the Holy Souls, he offered these one hundred Masses for them, depriving himself of a stipend for that period of time. He offered the last Mass shortly before August 21. At 8 P.M. on that night, as rain was falling heavily, some of his parishioners were suddenly confronted with an extraordinary sight at the gable wall of their church. For two hours, they gazed at an apparition of the Mother of God, Saint Joseph, and Saint John the Apostle, with angels hovering around an altar on which stood the Lamb of God; behind the Lamb, a large cross stood upright on the altar, dominating the entire scene. The archdeacon was in his cottage. His housekeeper, Mary McLoughlin, arrived and told him to come up to the church to see the apparition, which she had already seen herself when passing by the church with Mary Byrne. He was not inclined to believe her; he would regret this for the rest of his life.

The next morning the people of the parish and surrounding area were speaking of what had happened; knowing his parishioners well, he realized they were telling the truth. From the beginning he believed and placed his whole ministry at the service of Our Lady and the apparition. He worked very hard to facilitate pilgrims and the sick who visited Knock Shrine. He participated in the ceremonies, spent long hours in the confessional, and received countless visitors in his humble residence. All of this work was in addition to his parish duties, which were many; he had just one curate to help him though the work was increasing significantly. He kept a "Diary of Cures" that took place at Knock, and it was also time-consuming. In it are hundreds of extraordinary healings, especially in the years immediately after the heavenly event.

Following the apparition, he became known, not only in Ireland, but all over the world, and this would add to the burden of his office. He received correspondence from every quarter, and many of the letters he received were published in the Irish, British, and foreign press in 1880 and in the following years. Dealing with the huge volumes of mail meant much extra work for him.

The archdeacon died shortly after midnight on the Solemnity of the Immaculate Conception, December 8, 1897, worn out by a lifetime of faithful ministry. His obsequies were attended by Archbishop McEvilly of Tuam, numerous priests, religious, and a vast concourse of people. He was laid to rest in the right-hand side aisle of the parish church, in front of Our Lady's altar.

Many people believed that it was the Holy Souls that obtained the unique Apocalyptic Apparition for Knock, and they couple with that, as another reason, the spirituality, saintliness, and charity of the archdeacon. The people of the parish erected a memorial to their venerated pastor, and it is attached to the church wall above his burial place. It is in Latin, and it is a glowing tribute to a pastor they dearly loved. They also cherished a rumor that seemed to come from those who tended to the archdeacon in his last hours. Though he had not been present at the apparition on that night in 1879, as he lay dying, the Lady of the Apparition came for him: before he closed his eyes, he saw her.

The archdeacon's life should be studied today as much can be learned from it by many, such as students studying to become priests, priests already in ministry, and the general public. They will be inspired by his faith and spirituality, the extraordinary sanctity of his life, his many fine personal qualities, his devotion to the Eucharist, the Mother of God, and the Holy Souls, his outstanding works of piety and charity, his love of the poor, and his tireless work in the confessional. There is no doubt that the archdeacon's life is the stuff out of which saints are made, and perhaps, one day, he may be canonized. In the meantime, let us pray for that intention.

# 33

# Father Thomas Nicholas Burke

## *(1830–1883)*

## Priest

## *Father Terence Crotty, O.P.*


Hundreds of delighted faces broke into laughter as the preacher, with dancing eyes, recalled his mother in his youth—young, beautiful, devout, but oh, so strict! "When I saw my mother enter the room, make the Sign of the Cross, and solemnly invoke the light of the Holy Ghost to direct her, I knew I could expect no mercy; I never got such a beating as that one—directed by the Holy Spirit!"[1] Little Nicholas Burke had been caught as he cavorted out of control around the streets of Galway. It was a different world, when the preacher was just a boy and the Catholic Church in Ireland did not yet recognize the religious revival that followed emancipation. But now this same man, the Dominican, Father Tom Burke, was playing one of the major roles in the revival of the Church in Ireland. He was, in the words of the "Lion of the West", Archbishop McHale of Tuam, "one of the most extraordinary men of the nineteenth century".

Nicholas Burke was born in Galway in 1830, an only child. His mother was a member of the Dominican Third Order. To his mother's fiery youth and beauty was attached his more elderly father, who, nevertheless, shared more closely the humor of their child. The young boy's spontaneous one-man theatricals and his capacity as a

---

[1] James Cassidy, *The Great Father Tom Burke* (Dublin: Gill, 1947), p. 12.

mimic delighted his school friends. One of these later wrote how, when he began to entertain, "the very shape of his features wholly changed and we forgot in the contemplation of those mature portraits the fragile figure which produced them."[2]

The Liberator, Daniel O'Connell, then at the height of his political power, affected young Nicholas greatly. "Amongst the things that made a deep impression on me as a boy, was when I stood in the chapel of Galway to see the great O'Connell coming to eight o'clock Mass in the morning, kneeling amongst us and receiving Holy Communion, to watch him absorbed in prayer." And he added, "He contributed largely to make a priest of me."[3] Burke witnessed the Famine—"the terrible sights which I then beheld",[4] and saw at first-hand as well the dedication of the people to their Catholic Faith in the face of Protestant missionary attempts.[5] At the end of "Black '47", he left Ireland for Italy, to enter the novitiate of the Dominicans in Perugia, taking the name "Brother Thomas".

A revival was underway. Father Alexandre Vincent Jandel was a man whom Pope Pius IX called "the holiest man in Rome". In the "year of revolutions", 1848, the pope personally named him to the role of "Master of the Dominican Order". In the following twenty-four years, Jandel furthered the spirit of renewal that had already sprung up independently in France, in England, and in Ireland. Young Brother Thomas Burke caught his eye, and, even before he was ordained a priest, Father Jandel made him responsible for the training of a new generation, in the newly founded Dominican novitiate in England.

Sleeping rough, begging for money, and depending on food from a kindly railway porter, Brother Tom finally arrived as master of novices in Woodchester in the Cotswolds. He took time to learn his task and was more feared than loved by his first class of novices. He was ordained a priest in 1853, and almost immediately his reputation as a preacher began to grow. His fame was hard-earned. A novice from that time records that "he wrote out carefully, word for word, his sermons and took great pains in getting them up. In his early days

[2] Ibid., p. 5.
[3] Ibid., p. 14.
[4] Gerald Joyce, "Fr. Tom Burke OP" in *Dominicana Journal*, vol. 16, no. 3 (1931): 225.
[5] Daphne Pochin Mould, *The Irish Dominicans* (Dublin: Dominican Publications, 1957), p. 209.

he would rehearse before his two companions and ask them what to amend or alter; and with quite childlike docility, he took their advice, though they were much his juniors."[6] The theatrical bent he had shown as a child was to stand him in good stead as he "mounted the pulpit" in churches across the world.

From his work in the English Province, Father Jandel called Father Tom back to Ireland in 1855, to found a novitiate in rural Tallaght, Co. Dublin. Tallaght became the place most associated with him in the future, and it was from here that his fame began to grow.

In that era of religious revival, nobody was more dedicated to the ascetical life than Father Tom, and yet he left his brothers wide-eyed with his humor. His preaching also changed in these years: his early Victorian penchant for rhetoric of a baroque quality grew simpler. After a sermon he gave in Fairview, Dublin, in 1858, one of his listeners wrote, "It was no mere effort of polished rhetoric we heard on that occasion. It was the full flow of an apostolic soul that came down on the congregation and swept everything away on its irresistible tide. The chapel was small and his voice never rose above a whisper, but every whisper thrilled the nerves of his hearers."[7]

Saint John Henry Newman asked Father Tom to give a series of lectures in the newly founded Catholic University in Dublin where he had the chance to display his brilliant learning. And one sermon in Sheffield, on the last night of a mission, on the Apostles' Creed, lasted no less than three and a quarter hours. He was not for the fainthearted.

For his part, Father Tom loved the faithful who came to hear him, and when he was briefly assigned to Rome in 1864, and often had no public Sunday Mass and no sermon, he felt like a fish out of water. "Someday I'm going to climb into the pulpit when the church is closed", he said, "and bawl out 'Auld Lang Syne!'" Nevertheless, it was while he was giving a series of Lenten sermons in Rome that he heard that Pope Pius IX was calling him "the Prince of Preachers".

He was able to repay the debt to Daniel O'Connell when, now famous as an orator, he was invited to give the address when O'Connell's remains were returned from Rome for internment in Glasnevin Cemetery in Dublin. The oration lasted two hours in the presence of

50,000 people. Far from being an empty eulogy, Father Tom turned the listeners' attention to themselves, remembering that O'Connell knew that the first battle to be fought was a spiritual battle, and only then political. In memory of O'Connell's devotion, he reminded them, "Our wrestling is not against flesh and blood, but against principalities and powers: Put on [yourselves] the whole armor of God" (Eph 6:10–11).

Father Tom's greatest fame lay ahead, and it was in 1872–1873, during his visit to the United States, that he broke all the records he would ever break. One lecture he gave in Boston, to 40,000 people, was to the largest paying audience ever recorded in the country. Over eighteen months he gave four hundred lectures—not counting continuous sermons in churches—and the proceeds for charity that he received from these amounted to $400,000. If he wanted to make money, he could have been a millionaire, but it all went to charity. Despite receiving constant invitations, despite being the most entertaining of guests, Father Tom stuck rigidly to the fasts which his religious life asked of him. When he left the U.S. after a year of unlimited success, he left with a box little bigger than a rucksack. Unspoiled by fame, there was little "self" in his sermons. A friend who often heard him preach in Tallaght, if he offered a compliment to his sermons, would hear the reply, "I suppose I'm becoming a talking machine", and the subject would quickly be changed. He finished 1873 by preaching at the consecration of Saint Patrick's Cathedral in Armagh.

The visit to the U.S., however, broke his health. The volume of speeches to vast crowds, when nobody had dreamed of a microphone, left his lungs damaged and bleeding. For the next ten years, until his death at the age of fifty-three, his health frequently slowed him down. A Spanish crucifix in his room, still in the priory in Tallaght today, gave him consolation. "When the pain is very bad on me," he once said to a priest, "I crawl down here and stand before it and say to myself, 'what are my sufferings compared to His?'" But when he was good, he was still very good. The Irish patriot Charles Gavan Duffy wrote on one of Burke's sermons on Saint Ignatius of Loyola, delivered in London in 1880, "The subject had been exhausted by a hundred predecessors in the pulpit; it had, perhaps, special difficulties for a Dominican, and his health was known to be failing fast. But it stands out in my memory as one of the three or four greatest orations I have heard ... lucid as the waters of the Mediterranean."[8]

The Catholic revival in nineteenth-century Ireland had many facets and was led by people of charity, educators, political leaders, contemplatives, artists, and more. But it is faith in Christ that motivates everything. In Father Tom Burke, the revival met a man of the preached word that reveals to the nations "the unsearchable riches of Christ", as Saint Paul wrote (Eph 3:8). After all, without the wonder of Jesus Christ and without faith, nothing makes sense. No Catholic education or social teaching or any liturgy has real meaning without those whom the First Eucharistic Prayer names as "holding to the truth, handing on the Catholic and apostolic Faith". But "faith comes from what is heard", says Saint Paul elsewhere (Rom 10:17), and Father Tom opened the minds and hearts of people to Jesus himself and to the treasure of faith that alone gives life to Christian life and Catholic identity. Father Tom could exhort and entertain, or leave his listeners laughing and pensive at the same time, but he brought them back to the essential, "the full flow of an apostolic soul that came down on the congregation and swept everything away on its irresistible tide".

In our own time of religious confusion and scandal, the memory of Father Tom is the powerful memory of what a selfless and holy priest can do for tens of thousands of people in his priestly work and life: in preaching and example and zeal.

Father Burke died in Tallaght in 1883, having just returned from another major sermon delivered in the midst of sickness, in Gardiner Street in Dublin. A beautiful church was erected in his memory in the priory in Tallaght, but changes in the 1970s have closed off public access to the very fine tomb erected for him. This memorial church witnessed the great cult that followed him in life and in death, but there was never an official cause for his canonization. The Dominicans of his day saw more pressing needs elsewhere, not least in furthering the cause of the Irish martyrs, in which several of them were then involved. I once asked a now-deceased Dominican historian about the possibilities of canonization of Father Tom Burke, and he gently smiled, saying, "Poor Father Tom would laugh at the idea

[8] Ibid., p. 87.

that he was a saint." This is certainly true. After his death, Cardinal
Manning of Westminster wrote, "We shall no more hear that eloquent voice, eloquent because so simple, for in all he spoke for God.
He remembered God and forgot himself; it was the eloquence of the
great soul speaking of God and for God. The whole man spoke and
yet, in the pathos and beauty and light of what he spoke, we never
remembered the speaker."[9]

## Further reading:

Cassidy, James. *The Great Father Tom Burke*. Dublin: Gill, 1947.

Joyce, Gerald. "Father Tom Burke, O.P.", *Dominicana Journal*, vol. 16,
no. 3 (available free online at www.dominicanajournal.org).

Mould, Daphne Pochin. *The Irish Dominicans*. Dublin: Dominican Publications, 1957.

[9] Joyce, "Fr. Tom Burke OP", p. 230.

# 34

# Ellen Organ
# (Little Nellie of Holy God)

## (1903–1908)

## Child

### John Donovan

Technology has made the world a smaller place. But 100 years ago, Rome and Ireland were places very distant from each other. All the more remarkable, then, that in 1910, Pope Saint Pius X issued a papal decree reducing the age for First Holy Communion and cited the example of a recently deceased four and a half year old Irish girl as his inspiration.

Ellen "Nellie" Organ was born on August 24, 1903, in Waterford City. Her father, William, was a soldier and a native of Dungarvan. Her mother was Mary Hearne from Portlaw, Co. Waterford. Nellie was the youngest of four children, the others being Thomas, Mary, and David. Already by the age of two, Nellie displayed a precocious spirituality rarely seen in one so young. While walking to Mass holding her father's hand, she would constantly talk about "Holy God". Nellie spent much time at the bedside of her ill mother, where she was fascinated to learn all she could about God and prayer.

By 1906, Mary Organ became very ill with tuberculosis, and the family moved to the barracks at Spike Island in Cork Harbor in the hope that the fresh sea air would bring relief from TB. It was not to be, and Mary died in January 1907 with Nellie by her side. Nellie was just three and a half years old.

William Organ was now left with four motherless children. It was not common at that time for a widowed father to look after little children himself, so Thomas was sent to the Christian Brothers; David to the Sisters of Mercy, and Mary and Nellie to the Good Shepherd Sisters in Sunday's Well, Cork City. They arrived there on May 11, 1907. The nuns treated them kindly. Nellie was happy to call all of the Sisters "Mothers".

On arrival at the convent, both of the girls were ill, so they were sent at once to the Mercy Hospital in Cork. After two months, the girls returned from the hospital, but Nellie was still frail. The nuns saw that the regulation shoes were too heavy for her, so they gave her a fine pair of slipper shoes. Nellie's appearance was very striking because her coloring was quite unusual; her fair hair framed a face set, not with blue eyes as one might expect, but with great, luminous, solemn, dark eyes. "She looked like a little angel", said a companion.

A young girl caring for Nellie reported that, despite her obvious physical distresses, Nellie never complained, but they heard her crying and coughing during the night. She told the Sisters, and Nellie was moved to the school infirmary. Upon examination, it was discovered that Nellie had a crooked spine (scoliosis). Sitting up was very painful for the child, and sitting still for any length of time caused her great pain. Though her hip and her back were out of joint, she stoically tried to hide her pain and offer it up for God. All the Sisters could do was make the child as comfortable as possible.

Nellie astonished the nuns with her insight and knowledge of the Catholic Faith. The Sisters and others that cared for her believed without reservation that the child was spiritually gifted. Nellie loved to visit the chapel, which she called "the House of Holy God".

Before long, the sad discovery was made that, just like her mother, Nellie had advanced tuberculosis. The doctor told the Sisters there was no hope for recovery and gave Nellie only a few months to live. She was now moved back into the main convent to Nurse Hall's room, where she was to spend the rest of her short life.

Nellie loved the Holy Eucharist deeply. She would ask the Sisters to kiss her when they were coming back from Communion so she could share in the Holy Presence of their Holy Communion. She desperately wanted to receive her First Communion, but she was far too young;

the normal age for receiving Communion at that time was around twelve years old.

There was a statue of the Infant of Prague in the Infirmary, and Nellie at first took it for a doll. When she was told it was Holy God as a child, she became interested. She embraced the statue and put it on the ground and said, "Now, little Jesus, dance for me." Nellie took her little trumpet, began blowing, and called out enraptured, "Look, look, see how he dances." Another girl came, but they saw nothing except Nellie, sparkling eyes and cheeks aglow. When she was not able to blow the trumpet anymore, she called on the girl to "blow more music." In a few moments she called out, "He has stopped", and her face regained its usual calm. One of the Sisters, hearing of this incident, said, "Dear Lord, if you really did dance for Nellie, give us money for a bake house which we badly need." A few days later, a letter arrived containing £300 ($380) from an anonymous lady marked "for a bake house".

Nurse Hall carried Nellie down to the chapel during Exposition of the Blessed Sacrament. Nellie had never before actually seen the Sacred Host exposed, and she exclaimed to Nurse Hall: "Mother, there he is, there is Holy God now", and with her little hand she pointed to the monstrance, after which she never once took her eyes off the Host. From that day onward, she always knew when there was Exposition at the convent.

During the last days of September, Nellie had grown so weak they feared she would die. Bishop O'Callaghan said that if any children were in danger of death, he would confirm them. He agreed to confirm Nellie, so Sister Mary Immaculata was busy preparing Nellie for the sacrament, but Nellie already knew what the nun intended to teach her. Nellie was confirmed on October 8, 1907. She declared to all who came to see her on that day, "I am now a soldier of Holy God."

All this time, TB was wasting away her tiny frame. Not only were her lungs affected, but her jawbone had also begun to crumble away. In the end, it came away in pieces, and the odor from it was extremely unpleasant—at times unbearable. The devoted nurse syringed it with disinfectants. Following her Confirmation, Nellie never resisted this. When the pain was sharpest, she would take a crucifix and, kissing it, would sigh with tears, "Poor Holy God! Oh, Poor Holy God! What is my pain compared with what he suffered on the Cross for me?"

For several days, she remained preoccupied. When asked if she wanted anything, she would answer, "No, mother, I was only thinking of Holy God." Father Bury, S.J., during a retreat at the convent, often went to visit Nellie. He asked her, "Now tell me, what is Holy Communion?" Nellie answered, "It is Holy God. It is he who makes the nuns and everyone else holy." Father Bury heard Nellie's confession and gave her unconditional absolution, showing he fully believed she had come to the use of reason. He wrote to that effect to the bishop, also saying she was endowed with ardent love of God in an exceptional way and desired to be united to him in Holy Communion. The bishop agreed. When Nellie heard of the bishop's consent, she kept repeating, "Oh, I will have Holy God in my heart, I will have Holy God in my heart." Night brought little rest. She kept Nurse Hall awake all night long asking, "Is it not time to rise yet? The stars are gone, Mother, surely it is time to get up now."

The morning of December 6, 1907, dawned at last. It was the First Friday. Dressed all in white, she was carried down and placed in an easy chair before the sanctuary. The community Mass had just ended. Nellie remained silent and motionless with her head bowed down in prayer and adoration. When Father Bury approached to bring Nellie her First Communion, she lifted her eager face. "The child", writes Father Bury, "literally hungered for her God, and received him from my hands in a transport of love." So all her yearnings were satisfied. Holy God had come into her heart at last. Still Nellie sat there motionless, insensible to things of earth, in silent, loving conference with the Savior, her radiant countenance reflecting the Eternal Light that dwelt within her.

On December 9, she was anointed. Little Nellie had now received all the sacraments except Holy Orders and Matrimony. Yet Nellie did not die. On Christmas Eve, Nellie was to receive the Infant Jesus at Midnight Mass. She had tried to rest early in the evening, but long before the hour for Holy Communion had arrived, Nellie was making her preparation. "Do not speak to me before Mass," she said, "I want to keep thinking of Holy God."

The New Year 1908 dawned, but it brought no hope to those who loved Little Nellie. It was a wonder to all how she continued to exist. The tiny frame was quite exhausted. She could retain nothing, not even a spoonful of broth. She seemed to live on the

Blessed Sacrament alone. On February 2, 1908, Nellie flew to Holy God whom she had loved so faithfully. She was just four years, five months, and eight days old. A couple of days later, Nellie's remains were buried in Saint Joseph's cemetery.

Nellie's story began to spread, and soon people congregated at her grave, sometimes to such an extent the civil authorities were concerned. The resting place of this little child became celebrated throughout the country, and it became more practical to move her body back to the convent cemetery. Eighteen months after her death, Nellie's grave was opened, it was found that the body was incorrupt. Generations of people have come to visit Nellie's grave over the years. Unfortunately, today the grave is not easily accessed, but it is hoped that this will change in the future.

Nellie's story spread and quickly reached the ear of Pope Pius X himself. It was providential because when Pius X read the documents about "Little Nellie of Holy God", he took this as a sign to lower the age at which children throughout the world could receive Holy Communion. He personally requested a relic of Little Nellie, and he promulgated a decree, *Quam Singulari*, thereby reducing the age of receiving First Holy Communion from twelve years old to age seven.

Much progress was made for Little Nellie's cause in the decade after her death. Both Bishop O'Callaghan (Cork) and Pope Pius X encouraged this, and material furthering her cause was gathered and sent to the Vatican where it is still held. With regard to Nellie, Pope Pius wrote:

> May God enrich with every blessing ... all who recommend frequent Communion to little boys and girls, proposing Nellie as their model.... It is certain that Little Nellie practiced virtue to a heroic degree. She was a little angel. Her patience was admirable, her resignation in suffering perfect. Moreover, she showed a superior intelligence in supernatural matters. As for her innocence, it is beyond a doubt ... she was an angel, living with angels.

The impetus for the cause, however, was lost due to the untimely deaths of both Bishop O'Callaghan in 1916 and Pope Pius in 1914. Today, however, the "Little Nellie Foundation" is gathering details of any favors granted that people attribute to Nellie's intervention. It is hoped that the cause for Little Nellie may progress in the future.

**Further information:**
For further details, please contact John Donovan and The Little Nellie Foundation at 15 Bayview, Dungarvan, Co. Waterford. Email: johnjm donovan@gmail.com. Telephone: 087-2782825.

# 35

# Olivia Mary Taaffe

## *(1832–1918)*

### Layperson
### Founder of Saint Joseph's Young Priests Society

## *Dominic Dowling*

The leading note in her character was directness and simplicity, illuminated by strong faith in God and the Catholic Church. Her devotion was neither emotional nor obtrusive. It was all centered in the Mass, but especially as an offering for departed souls. Saint Joseph, patron of a holy death and universal provider for the people of God, living and dead, was to her something intensely real and almost everpresent to her mind. He was her protector, model, companion and friend. She took it for granted that he knew everything and was both able and willing to do everything that was necessary or right. Hence she never worried about trifles, and found it easy to cultivate a spirit of comfortable and joyful trustfulness. There was in her a brightness and vivacity combined with a playful humour which was found to be irresistible.... She was proud to be a Celt and at times showed almost a fiery disposition if any anti-complimentary remarks were made regarding her countrymen, and more particularly regarding those of her native county, of which she was extremely proud.

So wrote Father Henry Brown, S.J., the editor of *Saint Joseph's Sheaf* magazine, of Olivia Mary Taaffe, founder of Saint Joseph's Young Priests Society.

Olivia was born near Tuam, Co. Galway, into the Blake family of Brooklodge and Ballyglunin on June 24, 1832. Her place of birth was Annagh House, the seat of another Galway family, the Bodkins, her mother Elizabeth's family. Elizabeth had returned to her family home for the birth of her daughter, but tragically she died a few months after Olivia was born, so the child remained at Annagh House, where she and her older sister Harriet were raised by her Bodkin grandmother and aunts. When her uncle Robert Bodkin married in 1842, the two Blake girls, Olivia and Harriet, were taken by the Bodkins to live in Monkstown, Co. Dublin. In return visits to Annagh House in the late 1840s, Olivia witnessed the ravages of the Famine, and this left an impact on her. In 1852, Olivia and her sister moved to Dun Laoghaire.

Olivia received a private education, mainly from French governesses, and later, in her twenties, she went to live in Paris, where she completed her education; this French influence, which increased over the years, was to leave a mark on her life and work. In France, she was particularly impressed by widespread devotions in honor of the Blessed Sacrament, such as day-long Adoration in some churches. On feast days, she saw processions with great pomp and ceremony ending with Benediction of the Blessed Sacrament.

Returning to Dun Laoghaire, Olivia and Harriet were introduced into society, and for four years they participated in a constant round of social events and charity functions. Harriet's decision in 1861 to enter the Presentation Sisters in Midleton in Cork left Olivia alone. While Harriet entered a life of teaching as Sister Mary Ignatius, her sister cared for their father until he died four years later. On his death, Olivia found herself a wealthy woman. She inherited Brooklodge House and lands, as well as the Garbally estate near Banagher in Offaly. These properties gave her a considerable income. She was also in line to inherit the Bodkin lands and Annagh House as her uncle Robert Bodkin had no children.

As a wealthy heiress, and being quite attractive, she had a number of offers of marriage, but only one interested her in the end; that of John Joseph Taaffe of Smarmore Castle, Ardee, Co. Louth. John was a member of a well-known and respected family. The Taaffes had remained true to the Catholic Faith through centuries of persecution, and John himself was a pious man, sharing with Olivia a devotion to Saint Joseph and an interest in the Jesuits. When John proposed, Olivia suggested they make a novena to Saint Joseph to discern if this was the will of God. On May 29, 1867, Olivia and John were married in Saint Michael's Church, Dun Laoghaire; the couple would make their home in Smarmore Castle. The castle was actually owned by John's brother, Myles, who also lived there together with their mother and their five sisters.

For their honeymoon, the couple traveled around Europe; the trip lasted several months. On the itinerary was a pilgrimage to the Shrine of Saint Joseph at Maranville in France. There they met Abbé Joseph Léon Roy. This meeting would prove to be providential; Abbé Roy had been the founder of the Archconfraternity of Saint Joseph, and Olivia became a member and benefactor; the Abbé would play an important part of her life and mission in the years to come. From France, the couple traveled to Rome, where they stayed for a month and had a private audience with Pope Pius IX: the pontiff and Olivia enjoyed a conversation in French. A tour of the north of Italy brought them into Germany, and from there they returned to Ireland.

On returning home, Olivia settled down at Smarmore Castle. A son was born to the couple in 1872, Robert George. From his birth they had hoped he would become a Jesuit, if it was God's will, but suffering from tuberculosis, the boy was delicate all his life. Apart from her duties toward her husband and family, Olivia was active in Catholic affairs. In her local church, Saint Catherine's in Ballapousta, she set up a shrine in honor of Saint Joseph. For the feast of Corpus Christi, with the help of the priests and other parishioners, she organized a public procession of the Blessed Sacrament, French style, with some children dressed up as saints, and others enacting scenes from the life of Christ—an event unknown in Ireland at that time. After the death of Myles Taaffe in 1872 and of old Mrs. Taaffe that same year, Olivia established herself as the mistress of Smarmore. She helped her husband in running the estate, caring especially for widows and orphans during the famine years of 1879 and 1880. Olivia later said that her twenty-seven years at Smarmore were the happiest of her life.

On April 23, 1890, John Taaffe died, succumbing to tuberculosis; George Robert's health was not stable, either. Newly widowed, Olivia found herself trying to save her son's life. His parents had provided him with the best education, studying at different Jesuit schools and at university, but this was often interrupted by illness. In the winter of 1893–1894, Olivia took him to Switzerland to help alleviate his condition, but on January 5, 1894, Robert George died at Davos Platz at the age of twenty-three. Both father and son were buried at Ballapousta.

At the beginning of 1894, Olivia was left widowed and childless. She had to vacate Smarmore Castle as, being entailed, it passed to a nephew of her husband. Moving back to Dublin, she lived first with the Presentation Sisters in Lucan, before moving to Dun Laoghaire and then to Killiney in 1898. She devoted herself to propagating Abbé Roy's Archconfraternity of Saint Joseph; tireless in promoting this devotion, she became the administrator of an Irish branch. She secured the approval of the Archbishops of Armagh and Tuam for her work. Meanwhile in France, where Abbé Roy was now engaged in teaching Latin to boys in preparation for the seminary, he had set up an institution to help poor boys realize their vocation to become priests. He often secured the support of benefactors for their education, and Olivia helped in this work. She soon decided that if this could be done for French boys, it could also be done for deserving Irish boys. But for such a work to be placed on a sound footing, it would have to be assured of continuance for the future. As an instrument toward this end, she decided to start an English language version of *La Gerbe*, the publication of the French branch of Saint Joseph's Archconfraternity. She enlisted the help of a Jesuit convert, Father Joseph Darlington, S.J., who had known her son at University College Dublin, and together they founded *Saint Joseph's Sheaf* early in 1895.

This was the beginning of what would become Saint Joseph's Young Priests Society, a charity to help young men toward ordination. Among the devotional articles in the *Tallapoosa Sheaf*, Olivia inserted an appeal for funds to support a young altar boy from a family of slender means in Dun Laoghaire who wanted to become a priest. The appeal was successful. Soon afterward, when Father Henry Browne, S.J., took over the editorship of *The Sheaf* in 1896, he saw possibilities for promoting and supporting vocations and suggested to Olivia that the appeal be widened. As a result, at the end of the second year, the readers were contributing to the support of ten students for the priesthood. In the publication's second year, she announced that "Henceforth, *Saint Joseph's Sheaf* will be entirely devoted to fostering and helping vocations.... Already we have done something by

Saint Joseph's Burse, but we hope and intend to do far more in the future." From this emerged a society in which members dedicated themselves to assisting vocations to the priesthood.

In 1907, Olivia moved from Killiney to Donnybrook to be closer to Dublin city and the various apostolates she was involved in. The society was expanding and so, too, the number of seminarians it was supporting in Ireland and around the world. Since that first appeal in 1895, over 4,800 priests for ministry in all five continents have been assisted to their ordination by the prayers, encouragement, and financial support of the members and benefactors of the society she founded. By 1917, *The Sheaf* no longer carried the masthead of the Archconfraternity of Maranville, but had that of Saint Joseph's Young Priests Society.

When Olivia turned eighty on June 24, 1912, it was a turning point, as her health began to fail. She died on May 3, 1918. Following a Requiem Mass celebrated by Canon Patrick Lyons, parish priest of Ardee, in the presence of the Taaffe family and an overflow congregation, she was laid to rest beside her husband and son at Ballapousta. The notice of her death published in *The Irish Catholic* on May 11, 1918, recalled "her innate goodness of heart and ... gift of vivacity and quiet humor which never failed her, even when frustrated by weakness". As she was buried near a side wall of Ballapousta Church, Canon Lyons noted "She awaits the glorious resurrection when her sons will rise up and bless her."

Olivia Mary Taaffe was a woman before her time in understanding what the Second Vatican Council was to emphasize some fifty years later—that the Church is not just the clergy but all the People of God. Hence the twin objectives of the society she founded—to promote priestly vocations and the role of the laity. Today the readers of *The Sheaf* and the members of the society she established to carry on her work, Saint Joseph's Young Priests Society, are now contributing to the support of hundreds of clerical students worldwide each year. The credit for the truly remarkable development of the society over the last 125 years must go, in the first place, to Olivia, who started the organization in Dun Laoghaire, at sixty-three years of age. She worked tirelessly for priestly vocations, but in effect she was working for eternity, and it is only in eternity that the work she started and passed on can be appreciated.

# 36

# Father James E. Coyle

## (1873–1921)

### Priest and Martyr, *uti fertur*

### James Pinto

Father James Edwin Coyle was truly a man after God's own heart. His dedication to Christ, the Church, and all of humanity was well known to the people of his generation and is being rediscovered in ever growing numbers in our day.

Born on March 23, 1873, in Drum, near Athlone, Co. Roscommon, he attended the Jesuit-run Mungret College in Limerick, and from there went to the North American College in Rome to study for the priesthood. Ordained on May 26, 1896, at the Basilica of Saint John Lateran by Lucido Cardinal Parocchi, he was sent as a missionary priest for the Diocese of Mobile, Alabama, in the U.S., and was assigned to the Cathedral of the Immaculate Conception. He later became rector and then director of the McGill Institute for boys in Mobile. In 1904, he was appointed rector of the prominent parish of Saint Paul's in Birmingham, Alabama. Birmingham was a burgeoning city both in its industries—coal and steel—and population, as people from various lands were drawn to the many employment opportunities; many of them were Catholic. Among the vision-casting words of his inaugural sermon to the congregation of Saint Paul were these: "I appeal then to you, my new friends, to beg Our Lord during this Mass for the graces and blessings and help you and I need in the great work before us in extending God's Kingdom, and make the spiritual keep pace with the material progress of this great city in winning all hearts to it."[1]

In tandem with the growth and variety of ethnic and religious groups seeking opportunity in the city, various associations like the Ku Klux Klan and so-called patriotic associations like the "True Americans" targeted the various immigrant and religious groups for discrimination and violence. The intensity of the bigotry, and in particular an anti-Catholic bigotry, intensified during Father Coyle's years of ministry. He was an outspoken apologist for the Catholic Faith and the dignity of every human person. With accuracy and eloquence from the pulpit, in newspapers and on the streets, Father Coyle was the face of Catholicism and the voice for human equality in the midst of systemic and physical threats against ethnic and religious minorities. He would serve for seventeen years in Saint Paul's.

In 1915, twelve-year-old Ruth Stephenson visited Father Coyle on his porch to discuss the Catholic Faith with which she had become enamored. Ruth's father was a Methodist minister and Klansman, E. R. Stephenson, who earnestly warned Ruth that if she ever spoke with Father Coyle again, he would do violence to him and the parish. Despite the threat, Ruth was eventually received into the Church. Six years after that first visit and months after her conversion, she asked Father Coyle to perform her wedding; she had become engaged to a dark-skinned Puerto Rican Catholic by the name of Pedro Gussman. Father Coyle was happy to do so, and he married the couple at Saint Paul's at 5:30 P.M. on August 11, 1921. During the ceremony, anticipating the possibility of danger, he asked the two witnesses to stand a safe distance from the altar. Indeed, earlier in the day he had predicted that if he presided over the wedding there would be trouble: "I suppose old man Stephenson will shoot me or something!" he said.[2] When Rev. Stephenson learned of the marriage, he was irate and paced up and down in front of the church grounds plotting to kill the priest.

It was Father Coyle's custom to say his evening prayers sitting on the rectory porch swing; August 11, 1921, it would be no different. At 6:30 P.M., while he was reading his breviary, Rev. Stephenson

---

[1] James Pinto, *Killed in the Line of Duty* (Birmingham, AL: Fr James E. Coyle Memorial Project, 2011), p. 35.

[2] "Letter Proves that Fr. Coyle Had Premonition of His Death", *Daily American Tribune* (Dubuque, Iowa), November 16, 1921.

entered the front gate of the rectory grounds and shot three times at Father Coyle; one bullet fatally entered his left temple and exited the back of his skull. He was found lying on the front porch by his beloved and devoted sister, Marcella, who also confronted the murderer as he walked away from the scene. Father Coyle was rushed to the local hospital, Saint Vincent's, where he received the Last Rites of the Church just before he died at 7:43 P.M.

Following the shooting, Stephenson walked into the County Courthouse, almost adjacent to the rectory, with the smoking gun in his hand and confessed, "I just shot the priest." Thus began an agonizing yet faith-filled process of grief for the family, friends, and diocese. The murder would also lead to a tortuous and prejudicial trial.

Father Coyle's body lay in state the next afternoon, a Friday, until his funeral on Sunday, August 14. Thousands of mourners paid their respects, and it was said that his funeral service was the largest in the history of Birmingham, with crowds spilling out from the church to the street outside. Bishop Edward Allen, Bishop of Mobile, celebrated the Requiem Mass. Visibly moved, numerous times his speech faltered with overwhelming grief and compassion as he spoke of the priest. Among his poignant reflections, he stated: "Father Coyle was a zealous and devoted missionary.... He labored and preached the word of God in season and out of season, visiting the sick, instructing the little ones of the poor and needy and afflicted. He especially labored to bring the people to the Holy Sacrifice of the Mass."[3]

Moving thoughts and reflections also poured forth from parishioners and community leaders. One parishioner said:

They have killed all they could kill of Father Coyle, and God has already comforted us with a vision of how little that really is. His tragic taking off has only underscored the simple Gospel he was always expounding by word and example. If the words were written in fire they could not be burned more indelibly into the hearts of the Catholics of the district: "Blessed are ye when men shall revile you and persecute you and shall say all manner of evil against you, falsely, for my sake; rejoice and be exceedingly glad for great is your reward in heaven."[4]

[3] L. T. Beecher, "The Passing of Father Coyle", in *The Catholic Monthly*, September 1921, vol. 12; *Killed in the Line of Duty*, p. 15.
[4] Ibid., p. 12.

Reverend Stephenson was a known Klansman; as his trial approached, funds were raised by that association to gather the best defense team including attorney Hugo Black, who would later join the Klan, become a U.S. Senator, and later a Justice of the U.S. Supreme Court. The trial was followed closely not only locally, but nationally, including detailed coverage by the *New York Times*. Stephenson's defense claimed that he was not guilty by reason of insanity; however, in the preliminary hearing, his daughter Ruth testified that her father had often made threats against Father Coyle's life. The minister also claimed that the priest had attacked him and the killing was in self-defense—other witnesses claimed that when they thought they heard the shots, there had been no raised voices or audible indication that there was a scuffle. Both judge and jury had strong Klan and anti-Catholic representatives, and in the end the Rev. Stephenson was found "Not guilty and not guilty by reason of temporary insanity".[5] Stephenson was given his gun back and resumed his ministry as the "marrying parson" in the county courthouse.

Father James Coyle was a priest who knew his faith, lived what he believed, and freely imitated his Lord unto death. He was a priest who sought to make a full donation of his life each day and was killed in the line of duty. As his bishop and friend, Edward Allen, so clearly stated shortly after the murder: "Father Coyle was a martyr to duty.... He married a couple. The man was Catholic by birth. The woman was taken into the Catholic Faith several months ago. The marriage ceremony was performed before God's altar and then Father Coyle was shot down with no one near to defend him."[6]

Well before his murder, Father Coyle's life was under sincere threat. These threats were confirmed by the Federal Bureau of Investigation and shared with diocesan authorities.[7] In the face of multiple threats over a number of years, and at the risk of his own life, he courageously chose to remain faithful to God, the Church, and respect for the dignity of the human person.

[5] Rose Gibbons Lovett, *Catholic Church in the Deep South* (Diocese of Birmingham, AL: 1981), p. 60.

[6] Beecher, "The Passing of Father Coyle", p. 6.

[7] Sharon Davies, *Rising Road. A True Tale of Love and Religion in America* (Oxford: Oxford University Press, 2010), p. 46.

On Ash Wednesday, February 22, 2012, almost ninety years after the murder, Methodist Bishop William Willimon of the North Alabama Conference, prayed a Prayer of Confession and Reconciliation that included words specific to the Father Coyle tragedy:

> Forgive us if we have been guilty of treating baptized sisters and brothers as if they were our enemies. More specifically this night, we ask forgiveness for the indifference of the Methodist Church in the unjust death of Father James E. Coyle, a servant of God among us, whose ministry was tragically ended. Heal us, we pray, of dissention and hatred for brothers and sisters of other faiths.

Father Coyle's life and legacy grow in reverence throughout the United States and especially in Birmingham, Alabama, the city where he gave his life. "The Father James E. Coyle Memorial Mass and Reception" is celebrated yearly in the Cathedral of Saint Paul, on the very grounds where he ministered and was slain. *The Father James E. Coyle Memorial Project* is an ongoing multifaceted project promoting the life and legacy of Father Coyle to foster respect, justice, and peace. The world-renowned *Civil Rights Institute of Birmingham* hosts an exhibit on Father Coyle's sacrifice on behalf of human and civil rights. A film on Father Coyle entitled *Pursuit of Justice* has been produced, based on the book, *Rising Road: A True Tale of Love, Race and Religion in America*, by former Ohio State University law professor Sharon Davies.

Many emulate Father Coyle's sacrificial life as articulated in the last words he penned in the *Church Notice Book* shortly before the giving of his precious life: "Give. Give until it hurts, then and only then is there sacrifice."

# 37

# Father James Cullen

## *(1841–1921)*

### Priest

*Father Bernard McGuckian, S.J.*

To the distinguished Jesuit, Father Cullen, the great Apostle of Temperance, more than to any single individual must be given the honor of spreading this devotion throughout the length and breadth of Ireland. A man of the highest spirituality himself, thoroughly convinced of the efficacy of this devotion to effect a spiritual revolution and gifted with wonderful powers of organization, he threw himself with ardor into the work once he had been appointed Director of the Apostleship of Prayer.

Speaking at the Eucharistic Congress in Dublin 1932, Monsignor James MacCaffrey, the President of Saint Patrick's College, Maynooth, praised the remarkable work of the late Father James Cullen, S.J., who had died a decade previously. His work, especially that of combating alcohol abuse and encouraging temperance, lives on a century after his death, with tens of thousands of dedicated Pioneers around the world offering their prayers and sacrifices for those who struggle with addictions.

James Cullen was born in New Ross, Co. Wexford, the fourth of eight children. Being born in 1841, twelve years after the passing of the Catholic Emancipation Act, meant that he was spared direct experience of the rigors of the iniquitous penal legislation that had proscribed the practice of Catholicism for so long. His pious parents made the most of their newfound religious freedom. James and his siblings embraced the values of their parents with enthusiasm. His father was a prosperous merchant in the town, and the Cullens raised their children with the solid, traditional piety of that time—the family Rosary and devotion to Mary and Saint Joseph were strongly encouraged within the family. James was an exceptionally intelligent child, and he excelled academically at the Christian Brothers school in New Ross and later in Clongowes Wood College, operated by the Jesuits. It was while attending Mass one morning in Clongowes that he discerned his call to the priesthood. However, despite being in a Jesuit school, his primary attraction was to the diocesan priesthood. At that time, he had little understanding of the Jesuit vocation, misperceiving them as mainly teachers, and he felt that his pastoral zeal would be more suited to the life of an ordinary priest in a parish.

James began his studies for the priesthood in Carlow College in 1861 and was regarded by all as an outstanding student, not just academically, but also in terms of his piety and the example it set for other students, as well as for his musical abilities and his contribution to the social life of the seminary.

Ordained in 1864, the young Father Cullen was initially stationed as curate in Rowe Street, Wexford. He had great scope for his zeal here, being called upon to preach with growing frequency. It was here that he developed his remarkable capacity for organization, founding various sodalities and confraternities in the town. He had a constant care for the poor and urged the more well-off to fulfill their obligations to the needy. He could be demanding at times. One wealthy young lady of his acquaintance thought she was performing great acts of charity by bringing nice cakes to a destitute crippled girl, but for Father Cullen this was not enough—"you must bring her each day exactly the kind of dinner you get yourself", he told her.

In 1857, the new Bishop of Ferns recognized the need for regular parish missions in his diocese. At that time there were not enough religious orders engaged in the work of parish missions to meet the demand, so in 1866 the bishop founded the Missioners of the Blessed Sacrament in his diocese, comprised of four diocesan priests following a simple common life and dedicated to conducting missions in the parishes of Wexford. Father Cullen was chosen to be one of these priests, and he dedicated himself to this task for fifteen years. He was in high demand as a preacher and retreat master, and of course he did not neglect the demands of social justice, involving himself in raising funds for the construction of a considerable number of houses for workers. It was at this time that he came into contact with sailors moving merchandise between Wexford and Enniscorthy and saw firsthand the problems created by alcohol. The seeds of his work for temperance were planted at this time and would come to fruition in the decades ahead.

It was while working with the Missioners of the Blessed Sacrament that Father Cullen felt the call to his "second vocation" as a Jesuit. It was his study of the *Spiritual Exercises* of Saint Ignatius that allowed him to see aspects of the life and spirit of the Jesuits that were unknown to him twenty years earlier when he opted for the life of a diocesan priest. It was finally in 1881, after several requests, that his bishop approved his entry into the Jesuits, and he made his profession in the congregation two years later. His time as a parish curate and as a diocesan missionary priest had honed his pastoral and organizational skills and would bear remarkable fruit in a range of Jesuit apostolates.

He had his finger in an endless variety of apostolic pies and is mainly remembered as the founder of the *Messenger* magazine in 1888 and, a decade later, of the Pioneer Association. Both of these initiatives are still a feature of Church life in Ireland and abroad more than a century later. There is a story that when he approached his rector with the suggestion of founding the *Messenger*, he was given a room and one pound. But for a man of his faith and skill, this was enough—he raised the rest of the money and almost single-handedly wrote the leading articles, acted as editor, and managed the logistical operations of the enterprise. Launched in 1888, it had a circulation of 9,000 by the end of that year, and 73,000 when he retired from the role in 1904. The *Messenger* remains one of the most popular religious publications in the country and is the flagship in Ireland of what is now the pope's Worldwide Prayer Network.

However, the founding of the Pioneer Association of the Sacred Heart is the work with which Father Cullen is most associated. He commenced his work for temperance with the sailors of Wexford, but it was as a Jesuit that the work was to take on national, and later on international, dimensions. Initially the work was aimed toward moderation and temporary abstinence from alcohol, but over time Father Cullen discerned a role for those who would make the heroic offering of complete self-denial, a life-long pledge to abstain from alcohol, offering this in reparation to the Sacred Heart. By 1905, there were 43,000 Pioneers; fourteen years later there were over a quarter of a million, and by the 1950s, almost one in every three Irish adults was a member of the association. Perhaps one of the most famous Pioneers was the Venerable Matt Talbot, whose pledge to abstain for life, while utterly addicted to alcohol, was truly heroic. Others profiled in this book were also involved in the association, including the Venerable Edel Quinn, the Servant of God Frank Duff, and Blessed John Sullivan. Interestingly, the Servant of God Father Willie Doyle was also a Pioneer and served on its central council; Father Cullen had earmarked him as his successor as leader of the Pioneers, but his death on the battlefield of Passchendaele frustrated that wish.

Father Cullen was not satisfied in merely encouraging people to give up alcohol—he knew that positive entertainment was needed. He urged priests to acknowledge the "intolerable dullness of life weighing upon our rural districts and country towns". In 1908, he established the Saint Francis Xavier's Hall near Gardiner Street Church; this was a venue for the Pioneers in Dublin to gather for social events, singing, dances, and tea parties, and it ultimately led to the development of a variety of sports and social clubs for Pioneers.

Father Cullen was no mere activist. Fueling all of his initiatives was a deep spiritual life, and we know much about this aspect of his life because, like many Jesuits of the era, he kept detailed spiritual notes in his diaries. From these notes it is clear that he knew that the value of all of his work depended on prayer: "my work must be soaked in prayer", as he once noted in his diary. He had a profound devotion to the Eucharist; when he died, many people said that their most vivid recollection of him was a kind of transfiguration that came across his face when he held the monstrance or ciborium. Closely connected to this was his devotion to the Sacred Heart—it was this great love of his that fueled his work for the *Messenger* magazine and for the Pioneers. He noted in his diary: "O sweet, adorable Heart of My Savior, my only desire is to love Thee. O sweet Jesus, take this icy heart of mine from out of my bosom and fill it with Thy burning love. Give me the heart of a true priest of Thine that I may convert the whole world to Thee and to Thy love."

In addition to his lifelong devotion to Mary, he had a special devotion to three saints—Joseph, Ignatius Loyola, and Patrick, the Apostle of Ireland. In his prayer he seems to have returned to Saint Patrick again and again, viewing him as a model for the apostolic life in Ireland and seeking his help in his own ministry. One of his prayers to Saint Patrick ran as follows: "I am one of thy children. Like thee, I am a priest … ordained to minister to the Irish. Make me resemble thee in thy kindness, charity, tact, perseverance, prudence, and self-sacrifice.… Make me like thee in thy missionary life, thy love of souls—of every Irish soul."

His spirituality seems to have been characterized by the traditional Ignatian approach of that time—a strong emphasis on self-discipline based on an understanding of his own weakness and limitations, and a deep trust in God's goodness and mercy to help him progress toward holiness. "I have no trust in myself at all", as he often noted in his diaries, "but there is no limit to my trust in God." But his diaries were not entirely introspective. One interesting feature is how he constantly noted anniversaries—not just those in his own life, but the key dates and anniversaries in the lives of family and friends, and these dates are always accompanied by prayers for them on those special days.

On November 19, 1921, at the age of eighty, as a result of heart problems, he left his community at Saint Francis Xavier's, Gardiner Street, Dublin, for the last time and went by taxi to the Linden Nursing Home in south Dublin. A friend said to him: "Father Cullen, you have done a good work in your day." He answered, "Well, I think I can honestly say I have tried to do my best." On the morning of December 6, when the newspapers arrived, he was told that the Anglo-Irish Peace treaty had been signed during the night; he replied, "Thank God. I have lived to see Ireland free." A few hours afterward, he said to the nun attending him, "I am going into port", and he breathed his last peacefully about 12 o'clock. His funeral procession was one of the largest ever seen at Saint Francis Xavier's; spectators lined the streets as 1,000 Pioneers accompanied his coffin to Glasnevin cemetery.

Despite his evident holiness of life and the enormous legacy he left behind, it seems that there has been no groundswell toward a canonization cause. Nonetheless, Father James Cullen, S.J., remains one of the most important Catholics, and Irishmen, of the last two centuries.

# 38

# John McGuinness

## *(1900–1947)*

## Layperson

## *Dr. Patrick Kenny*

Matthew, the tax collector, was transformed when he met Jesus Christ. He surely never expected that he would end up as an apostle, evangelist, and eventual martyr when he "left everything, and rose and followed him" (Lk 5:28). Some 1,900 years later, the Dublin tax official, John McGuinness, also encountered Jesus Christ, this time on a weekend retreat. Like Matthew, he followed Christ without delay. His zeal unleashed a whirlwind of charitable activities in the slums of Dublin. He could never have imagined that he would spend himself so much in the service of the poor that it would cause him to die of malnutrition at the early age of forty-six.

John Anthony McGuinness was born in Clontarf, Dublin, on August 16, 1900. He was the seventh child in a family of eleven. His father was a traveling salesman, and the family moved a lot, eventually settling in Dalkey, Co. Dublin. John entered the civil service as a boy clerk in the Revenue Commissioners in 1916, moving to the Inland Revenue in London in 1919. By the time he returned to the Revenue Commissioners in Dublin Castle in 1920, he was respected by colleagues as a hard worker with a bright future.

In February 1924, a colleague invited John to a weekend retreat with the Jesuits in Milltown. Someone else had dropped out, and they needed an extra person. John was not really the type to go on an enclosed retreat. He was an average Catholic who fulfilled the minimum, but not much else. Besides, he had a golf match that weekend, and golfing was his passion. He had a handicap of nine, and he had recently won a local tournament. There was some speculation that he might even have a future as an international golfer. But John responded to the encouragement of his friend, cancelled his golf appointment, and went on the retreat. He seems to have received the grace of a radical and permanent change of life. The retreat master, Father Michael McGrath, S.J., urged the retreatants to join the Saint Vincent de Paul Society. The very next Monday, John signed up. He was a civil servant by profession, but from that moment on he voluntarily became the servant of the poor.

It is impossible to know the full extent of John's charity work. He was discreet and rarely talked about himself, but the testimony of those who worked with him gives us some insight into his activities. He could often be seen cycling or walking around Dublin in the evenings with a worn haversack on his back, bringing clothes and provisions to the poor. He gathered useful items for them wherever he could and wasted nothing that could be of use. He collected old matchboxes and devised a way in which they could be transformed into firelighters with the help of used candle butts. He also pestered people for their used toothpaste tubes—he knew a scrap metal dealer who would give him good money for the lead they contained. He would take annual leave to sing Christmas carols on the street to raise money and also organized flag days, raffles, and tea dances to raise funds. He did not just bring money or clothes to the poor. He knew everyone in their families and offered personal advice in their difficulties. He encouraged them to pray the family Rosary together, giving them Rosary beads, scapulars, and other religious items.

He was the founder of Saint Kieran's Lodging House Guild whose members visited hostels for down and out men. Some of these men were in desperate straits. It was not unusual to find them without the minimum of decent clothing; once they found a man dressed in a newspaper. Often, they found men lying in squalor and close to death. John was not afraid to get his hands dirty, and on more than one occasion it was his hands-on care for these men that finally opened their hearts and made them willing to receive the priest. He prayed and sacrificed for them, especially those who were stubborn and hostile. Worried about one hard case, he told a colleague that when he was next tempted to have an extra slice of cake, he should withdraw his hand and offer it up for the man because such sacrifices have great effect in Heaven.

John also founded a club for unemployed men in High Street and spent as much time as he could there, chatting with the men, but also cleaning the entire building, including the toilets. He was involved in the Seamen's Institute and the Night Shelter for Destitute Men as well as being an active member of the Legion of Mary, organizing activities and retreats for residents of the Morning Star hostel. As this took a lot of time, John abandoned his time-consuming passion for golf and sold his golf clubs, the proceeds going to the needy.

John's care for the poor sprang from his understanding that they were his brothers and sisters in the Mystical Body of Christ. This sense of Christian fraternity found an outlet in the other great love of his life: the foreign missions. Over the years he established special funds to build churches or to educate priests in China. This economic help for missions was accompanied by a close friendship with the missionaries themselves. He wrote regular friendly letters of encouragement to them, always accompanied by significant donations. One of his regular correspondents was Mother Kevina.[1] Sadly the letters he wrote no longer exist, but we can imagine what they meant to the missionaries by reading their grateful replies to him. To take only one example from a Spiritan missionary: "I thought I was quite alone and quite forgotten. You may imagine then what a real tonic it was to get your letter. Though I was very tired I seemed to get new energy. I felt no longer alone." He also established a circle of volunteers to assist him in raising funds for the missions. Until relatively recently, almost every shop in Ireland had collection boxes for the missions beside the till. In his day, John personally constructed these boxes and coordinated their distribution and collection.

This vast range of activity was the overflow of a vibrant spiritual life. The retreat of 1924 was the starting point, but his interior life deepened over the years, especially after the Eucharistic Congress in 1932. He had a tremendous devotion to Matt Talbot, and a plank from Matt's bed, given to him by Matt's sister, was one of the few personal possessions in his room when he died. He explicitly modeled his life on Matt, even following in his footsteps in becoming a

---

[1] See chapter 19.

Third Order Franciscan at Merchant's Quay in 1934. Like Matt, he arose before 5:30 A.M. every morning to attend two Masses prior to attending work in Dublin Castle. He prayed the Stations of the Cross every day of the year for the souls in Purgatory and was seen to pray constantly as he walked through the city going about his business. He organized pilgrimages, particularly to the shrine of Oliver Plunkett in Drogheda, a saint to whom he had special devotion.

When he died, he left behind some simple diaries, but they do not reveal any introspective reflections on his spiritual life. What his notes do reveal is the stunning reality of his belief in the Communion of Saints. Each and every day he lists the saints of the day—both famous and obscure—greeting them as brothers and sisters. For example, on July 22, 1941, the feast of Saint Mary Magdalene, his diary opens with "Hail, my dear, dear Sister! Hail, oh Hail, pray for me, for I was worse than thee." And on the feast of the Guardian Angels that same year: "Hail, dear brother of mine! Hail Shining Warrior! Thanks be to God for thee, Brother."

He was intelligent and well informed about the Faith. He was a regular at the Central Catholic Library, where his favorite reading was the lives of the saints. He also enthusiastically studied every papal document, but avoided all controversies and religious arguments, stating that in all such matters he preferred to remain as simple as a child. He never wanted to be a priest, recognizing that he could be holy as a working man in the world, just like his model, Matt Talbot.

At work, John remained the consummate professional, steadily advancing in his career and being promoted to the rank of Assistant Principal Officer when he was forty-one. He never wasted time at work, declining to accept any personal phone calls and avoiding casual conversations.

Despite his austere personal habits, those who knew him said that he was the happiest person they knew—always gentle and radiating peace. He remained strong and virile right to the very end. He always dressed in a manner befitting his position as a senior civil servant. He had the respect of his colleagues, with one recalling that he was so easy to be with that they often forgot how extraordinary he really was. Another observed, "during the last ten years of his life we sensed that a saint in the making was working in our midst."

At the time of his death, he was in receipt of a salary of approximately £1,000 ($1300) per annum, a significant sum in those days.

As a bachelor, he could have lived a life of great ease. But he denied himself all comforts, living in a single room on Upper Mount Street, eating very little, and practically giving everything away. When he died, he had £50 ($63) put away for his funeral, and £69 ($87) in cash. But alongside the cash was a remarkable slip of paper on which he had planned how that £69 was to be disbursed—numerous names and causes are listed beside the relevant amount, with "self" appearing at the end of the list after everyone else, to receive only the tiny amount that was left over.

In late 1946, he started to age rapidly and suffer from fatigue. He was finally prevailed upon to visit the doctor, who was alarmed at his low weight and exhaustion. John had no idea up to that point that his life-style was undermining his health. He acted on doctor's orders, taking himself off to a hotel to rest and feed himself up on four-course meals—he acknowledged to others that he had a duty to his employer to be fit for work. However, he refused to cut back on his charitable visits; when told by a colleague to quit them and put himself first, he responded, "You mustn't say that. I couldn't do enough for God no matter what I did. Nobody could."

The medical intervention was too little, too late. He collapsed at home on February 8, 1947, and was removed to Saint Michael's Hospital in Dun Laoghaire, where, with a smile on his face, he died five days later. The certified cause of death was pellagra—a vitamin deficiency caused by malnutrition. John McGuinness literally died of love for the poor.

He was buried in Glasnevin cemetery with a friar announcing at the funeral that "we have buried a second Matt Talbot today." Within weeks, his example was being preached from the pulpits of Dublin. A man who suffered with TB for many years, and for whom John prayed daily in life, was allegedly inexplicably cured on the day of John's death. Within a few years, articles started appearing in religious magazines and newspapers, even as far away as the U.S., declaring him to be a serious candidate for canonization. Sadly, no steps were taken in that direction, although as recently as 1997 a Mass attended by the papal nuncio was offered for him in Dublin on the fiftieth anniversary of his death. We can only hope that devotion to him is rekindled—his example of manly holiness in the midst of a successful professional career is needed in Ireland today.

# 39

# Monsignor Hugh O'Flaherty

## (1898–1963)

## Priest

## *Fiorella De Maria*

In the most iconic scene of *The Scarlet and the Black,* Monsignor Hugh O'Flaherty is seen through the gun sights of his archenemy, Obersturmbannfuhrer Herbert Kappler. Having been warned in a previous scene not to stray out of Vatican territory, a smiling O'Flaherty deliberately taunts Kappler, walking along the famous white line separating the Vatican from the rest of Rome. Kappler's fingers tremble on the trigger, desperate to fire, but the wily Irish priest gives him the slip, and he vanishes from sight.

The scene almost certainly never occurred; Hugh O'Flaherty was far too shrewd and intelligent to have deliberately provoked a man as dangerous as the head of the Gestapo in Rome. Nevertheless, the scene vividly depicts the intensely personal battle that took place between a devoutly Catholic priest and a fanatical Nazi during the German occupation of Rome.

Hugh was born in Kiskeam, North Cork, in February 1898. He was the eldest of four children and spent what appears to have been an idyllic childhood in Killarney. His father was a policeman with the Royal Irish Constabulary, but James O'Flaherty felt called to resign his position and took up the post of steward at the Old Killarney Golf Club. This decision had a profound influence on the young Hugh, as he was to be a keen golfer all his life, winning amateur championships and—most importantly—forging friendships and alliances during the war years in Rome that would prove crucial to his work with the Escape Line.

Like his brothers, Jim and Neil, Hugh was educated by the Presentation Brothers, but, unlike them, he felt called to the priesthood from a very young age. Hugh was fortunate in that he was supported in his decision for the priesthood by his father, who declared that he would be prepared to sell everything he owned to make his son a priest, but the road to ordination proved to be very hard. At fifteen, Hugh enrolled to train as a teacher only for his studies to be disrupted by ill health. He was twenty—two years above the age limit—when he was finally able to enter the Jesuit College at Mungret, Co. Limerick, in the summer of 1918. Despite the awkwardness of being older than most of the students and never having studied Latin, Hugh thrived, spiritually and intellectually, in the highly disciplined academic environment at Mungret.

Adopted as a candidate for priesthood by the Diocese of Cape Town, Hugh was sent to complete his studies in Rome in 1922, the year Mussolini rose to power, and was ordained in 1925. Like many young priests of his generation, Hugh dreamed of being sent to Africa as a missionary, to his new diocese in Cape Town, but God had other plans. His intellectual and diplomatic skills were noted, and he worked for the Vatican in Czechoslovakia, Egypt, San Domingo, and Haiti, before being appointed to the Holy Office.

Hugh's travels helped hone skills that would prove valuable during the dangerous years of the war. Ironically for a fierce Irish nationalist who made no secret of his anti-British sentiments, Hugh's early war work involved ministering to British prisoners of war (POWs). He was so horrified by the brutal conditions of the camps that he became a champion of the POWs, smuggling messages home and demanding better treatment in accordance with the Geneva Convention. Hugh was such a passionate advocate that senior German figures eventually forced his resignation.

Hugh's work had barely begun, however, and when the Nazis occupied Rome, his ministry took an altogether more dangerous turn. Hundreds of Allied POWs were escaping the camps and fleeing to Rome, where they hoped to find sanctuary in the neutral Vatican. Hugh found them hiding places, but the task soon snowballed. An

Escape Line was formed, run by Hugh and a group of friends, tasked with the care and protection of hundreds of enemies of the Nazis, not just POWs but also Jews and anti-fascist dissidents. Hugh's group was made up of a motley selection of individuals—a Maltese widow named Henrietta (Chetta) Chevalier, a Dutch Augustinian priest, Father Anselmus Musters (nicknamed Dutchpa), Sam Derry, a British army officer, John May, the British ambassador's Cockney butler, and many others. It is hard to imagine a more varied team, in terms of both their nationalities and their skill sets, but they showed exceptional courage and tenacity. The penalties for resisting the Nazis were well known, and not all of Hugh's helpers survived unscathed; Father Anselmus was arrested and severely tortured by the Gestapo before escaping from a train bound for the concentration camps; John Armstrong, one of Hugh's British helpers, was taken as a hostage by the retreating Germans and shot at a roadside; others were arrested and killed, including five who perished in the Ardeatine Caves Massacre.

Hugh himself was the target of multiple kidnap and murder attempts. Herbert Kappler quickly identified Hugh as the brains behind the Escape Line and made it his personal mission to bring him down. Hugh was repeatedly urged to lie low, but he refused to hide when innocent lives remained at risk. Ironically, when the Germans were finally forced out of Rome, one of Hugh's greatest enemies came to him for help. Pietro Koch, chief of the Fascist Police, was a man so bloodthirsty that even Mussolini had found him too violent. He was responsible for the deaths of countless men and women, but Hugh never hesitated to help save the man's innocent mother and wife, though the women refused his help and disappeared into the chaos that overtook Italy in the final stages of the occupation.

Hugh spent the years following the war working hard to help the survivors. He ministered to a refugee community which had taken up residence in the ruins of a church, converting the community to Catholicism and rebuilding the church. The act that undoubtedly caused the biggest shock, however, was Hugh's decision to visit Herbert Kappler in prison. Kappler had fallen into Allied hands soon after the liberation of Rome, but it was some years before he was called to account for his many crimes in a dramatic public trial, at the end of which Kappler was sentenced to life imprisonment. Hugh befriended his old enemy and eventually baptized Kappler in a quiet ceremony behind closed doors. Hugh's readiness to forgive Kappler confused and horrified some. This was, after all, a man who had deported Jews to the death camps, organized the worst single act of bloodshed on Italian soil, arrested and killed some of Hugh's closest friends, and tried repeatedly to kill Hugh himself. In the aftermath of the war, there were reprisals across Italy and much of Europe, with suspected Nazi collaborators falling victim to rough justice. Against this background, Hugh's willingness to forgive was a powerful act of witness.

Hugh's health never recovered from the stresses and privations of life in Nazi-occupied Rome, and he never did fulfill his dream to work in Africa. After suffering a stroke in 1960, Hugh returned home to Ireland and lived quietly in County Kerry in his sister's home. He died on October 30, 1963.

Hugh O'Flaherty is believed to have saved the lives of 6,500 Jews, anti-fascist Italians, British and American servicemen. He became known as "The Scarlet Pimpernel of the Vatican", receiving awards from all over the world including a CBE (Commander of the British Empire) and the U.S. Medal of Freedom. What remains more of a mystery is why Hugh O'Flaherty's cause has never been seriously considered. During his lifetime, Hugh was regarded as a "living saint", a title he would have found very embarrassing, yet following his death, his cause has not been opened. While he is revered as a hero and has been the subject of films, books, articles, and documentaries, with websites devoted to his memory, there has never been popular devotion associated with him. His cause may have been hindered by the lack of a spiritual "paper trail" to shed light on his inner life—he never wrote a memoir, keeping a detailed diary while working against the Nazis would have been extremely risky—but it may also be that the perception of saintliness at the time worked against him. It is possible that his love of the golf course and a good party (though he was a lifelong teetotaler) was not in keeping with the accepted image of a saint, but this is an assessment that should surely be reconsidered today.

Hugh O'Flaherty's heroic witness during the darkest chapter of the twentieth century remains an example of the Christian duty to protect the oppressed and to witness to the Truth even at the risk of suffering and death. Though not called to martyrdom, Hugh worked selflessly and courageously, knowing what awaited him at Gestapo Headquarters in Rome if he were captured. He demonstrated an absolute trust in God and a willingness to lay down his life, if necessary, to protect others. The call to saintly heroism in the face of evil never dies, nor does the need for saints who strive for reconciliation and healing in a divided world. Ultimately, this proud son of Ireland lived by the motto: "God has no country."

**Further reading:**

De Maria, Fiorella. *Hugh O'Flaherty: The Irish Priest Who Resisted the Nazis.* San Francisco: Ignatius Press, 2022.

Fleming, Brian. *The Vatican Pimpernel.* Wilton, Cork: Collins Press, 2014.

Walker, Stephen. *Hide and Seek.* Collins, 2011.

Walsh, Alison. *Hugh O'Flaherty; His Wartime Adventures.* Cork: Collins Press, 2010.

# 40

# Mother Mary Martin

## *(1892–1975)*

## Founder

## *Sister Isabelle Smyth, M.M.M.*

As she wrote the Constitutions of the Medical Missionaries of Mary, grafting it onto the Rule of Saint Benedict, Mother Mary Martin reflected deeply on the charism she had been given by God and then invited the members of her new congregation to "Reflect on the signs of the times ... allow the Spirit to unfold the charism that is given you as MMM. In hope and love, be ready to walk in paths that are new."[1] It was to be the dynamic of her life and the legacy she gifted to her religious family and the Church.

Born on April 25, 1892, Marie Helena Martin was the second of twelve children. The Martin household had a resident staff of seven people including a German-born tutor. In this comfortable home, each season was marked with a round of social events. When Marie was fifteen years old, her father died tragically when her mother was pregnant with her twelfth child. Marie—always close to her mother—became a reliable helper in managing the large household.

Marie loved to travel. But loneliness for home led her to plead with her mother to let her leave a boarding school run by the Sisters of Mercy in Scotland, and later from the Holy Child Sisters' school at Harrowgate in England, and a finishing school in Germany. At

---

[1] Constitutions of the Medical Missionaries of Mary, 2.6.

the age of nineteen, she was invited to accompany a widowed uncle on a cruise to the Caribbean. Her world view was shaped by what she learned on her travels. When she looked out of the upstairs windows at home, she could see the busy Dun Laoghaire harbor. As she watched the ferries come and go, she subconsciously absorbed the fact that the sea voyage led to a bigger world to which she belonged.

The social scene changed dramatically with the outbreak of World War I. Marie's brothers, Tommy and Charlie, interrupted their education to train at the Curragh. Marie's boyfriend, Gerald Gartlan, also signed up for service. As the young men prepared to sail to the warfront, Marie and her sister Ethel trained as nurses with the Voluntary Aid Detachment.

Charlie was already serving at Gallipoli and Tommy at Alexandria when Marie sailed for Malta aboard the Hospital Ship *Oxfordshire*, arriving in Valletta on October 23, 1915. Marie threw herself into the work at Saint George's Military Hospital with heart and soul. Much of this experience is detailed in her letters home.[2] Just after Christmas, worrying news arrived that Charlie was missing. During her remaining months in Malta, all Marie's free time was devoted to seeking information about what happened, hoping Charlie would arrive at Valletta on one of the hospital ships—never daring to believe that he might not be alive.

Following her six months in Malta, Marie was called up again in June 1916 and assigned to France, where she nursed soldiers badly wounded at the Battle of the Somme. When she came off duty on July 2, she received the news that Charlie had been confirmed dead. He had died shortly after being wounded on December 8, 1915. War was radically changing the world view of the young socialite, transforming her into the woman whose concern for human suffering became the dominant driver of her life. As the world witnessed the first use of chemical warfare, Marie became expert in the painstaking care of young men whose lungs were melted by mustard gas. When she was transferred to caring for men with appalling skin diseases, her patience was honed to an extraordinary degree. This firsthand experience of the power of healing through medicine and nursing initiated a deep sense of calling within.

---

[2] Marie's letters from France can be read at http://letters1916.maynoothuniversity.ie/.

Back in Dublin in 1917, while at prayer in her parish church, Saint Patrick's in Monkstown, Marie became aware that God had some special life's work for her to do. She dressed up in her new navy suit and white spats and went to meet her boyfriend to tell him "marriage is not for me." She was not yet clear as to what her calling might be. With guidance from her spiritual director, she had begun to study sacred Scripture and the writings of Dom Columba Marmion.[3] She grasped the global mission of the Church. As her relationship with God deepened, the mysteries of the Incarnation and Mary's Visitation to Elizabeth began to shape her call. The next twenty years would relentlessly test this. For Marie, accepting God's will was all that mattered. "If God wants the work, God will show the way", she would often say.

When the great epidemic of influenza swept across Europe in 1918, Marie's nursing skills were well used by her local doctor in Monkstown. In 1920, she went to the National Maternity Hospital in Holles Street to train as a midwife. Bishop Joseph Shanahan,[4] who became a lifelong friend, supported her desire to establish a religious congregation of medical missionary Sisters. At his invitation, she sailed to Nigeria in 1921. Working as a lay missionary, she hoped to offer some health service among the women of Calabar. On arrival, she discovered that the bishop had been obliged to confine the work in that area to education—a very difficult situation for her. He still envisaged the founding of a medical missionary Sisterhood in Africa. However, in 1924, he changed his plans and established the Missionary Sisters of the Holy Rosary in Ireland, a congregation where Marie felt the provision of education was likely to put at risk her calling to provide medical missionaries. Following Bishop Shanahan's direction, Marie completed her novitiate, but she knew that was not her calling.

Each setback to her plans would lead her to take a new approach. She was advised to meet Father Thomas Agius, S.J., founder of a Glasgow-based society of medical missionaries known as *Institutum Deiparae*. After a year's experience, she felt that endeavor was lacking in essential spiritual formation. With difficulty, she withdrew in very poor health.[5] From her sickbed, she became greatly involved in the

---

[3] See chapter 12, above.
[4] See chapter 15.
[5] The *Institutum Deiparae* was later dissolved by the Archbishop of Glasgow.

establishment of the Apostolic Workers' Society in Dublin.[6] Now in her late thirties, she maintained contact with a large network of men and women whose friendship and interests she shared. She realized that great endeavors are not achieved single-handedly. Her vision and determination attracted the interest of other women of her age, as well as that of great Church leaders in Ireland and Africa.[7]

Marie believed the Church's ban on women religious practicing obstetrics and surgery did not respond to the needs of the times. She prayed for an end to this ruling, and her spiritual advisors assured her that the question was under discussion. When the ban was lifted in February 1936,[8] she lost no time. With two of her aspirants, she returned to Nigeria at the invitation of Monsignor (later Bishop) James Moynagh, who was responsible for the Vicariate of Southern Nigeria. Many saw it as "the last straw" when Marie succumbed to malaria in March 1937. She was admitted to the government-run hospital in Port Harcourt. In his memoirs, the late Bishop Thomas McGettrick—then a priest at Anua—acknowledged that he discreetly had a coffin made during her critical illness.[9]

Many were skeptical when Marie pronounced her religious vows on her sickbed on April 4, 1937. Preparations were made for her to sail back to Ireland, leaving her would-be novices behind. For Marie, it was all "a wonderful little story and all arranged by God". With her religious profession, she established the Medical Missionaries of Mary and became known as Mother Mary Martin.

World War II presented enormous challenges. Nonetheless, back in Ireland, she embarked on a building program in Drogheda and sent young missionary Sisters to Nigeria on ships that had to travel in convoy. Before the war had ended, she had contacted a leading London filmmaker, Andrew Buchanan, about sending a crew to Nigeria to capture the healing charism in the film *Visitation*. In

---

[6] Records in the Archives of the Archdiocese of Dublin contain meticulous reports from the early 1930s.

[7] As well as Bishop Joseph Shanahan and Bishop James Moynagh, Marie counted on great support from Archbishop Paschal Robinson, Apostolic Nuncio to Ireland, Archbishop Antonio Riberi, Apostolic Delegate with responsibility for East and West Africa, and later from Joseph Cardinal MacRory of Armagh.

[8] *Constans ac Sedula* was issued by the Sacred Congregation of Propaganda Fide on February 11, 1936.

[9] Thomas McGettrick, *Memoirs* (Nigeria: Diocese of Abakaliki, 1988).

this way she would mark the achievements of the first decade of the
Medical Missionaries of Mary.[10] Mother Mary grasped an important aspect of missiology; in order to understand the culture of other
people, the missionary must first look closely at her own. So Andrew
Buchanan was asked to make a second film entitled *The Bridge of the
Ford* depicting the vocation of Saint Patrick and the story of the town
of Drogheda. Today, these films still receive the attention of historians and producers of moving images.

Through her business sense, Mother Mary saw that film was the
way to make this vocation and ministry known. As well as attracting
vocations, her venture depended on crowd funding, and through
these films she engaged a large cohort of supporters in Ireland, the
U.K., and U.S.

She saw new inventions as tools for mission. In December 1946,
she recorded in detail her first flight to Africa—a journey with ten
stops between London and Lagos. While 150 miles east of the Canary
Islands, flying at an average of 7,000 feet with a speed of 172 miles
per hour, she foresaw that "Someday God will give us our own plane
and pilot, perhaps even a sister of our own." And indeed, this dream
came to reality during the great famine in Kenya's Turkana Desert in
the 1960s. She would instill this forward-looking vision in those who
embraced her charism.

By the end of the second decade, Mother Mary was receiving
many requests for Medical Missionaries of Mary. She embarked on
a fact-finding tour that took her to twenty-two countries over a
period of seven months. It led to decisions to send Sisters to several
new countries. By now Sisters were specializing in many particular
branches of medicine and other healthcare professions. She attended
the open sessions of Vatican II and ensured its documents were studied by her communities. She collaborated with Leo-Jozef Cardinal
Suenens, author of *The Nun in the World*. She wrote "it was for this
challenge we were founded." Medical Missionaries of Mary are to be
contemplatives who are active in the world.

Not all Mother Mary's ventures ended in success. As she grew
older, she referred often to her personal failings. But, as in her younger

[10] Andrew Buchanan also wrote a book about the making of *Visitation* (Medical Missionaries of Mary, 1948).

days, she bore the disappointments with fortitude. She did not let the pain of loss of family members and of great missionary friends deter her in working toward her goal. Nigeria's civil war brought great sorrow, as missionaries supported the people who suffered on both sides of the conflict.

By this time Mother Mary was growing old. In 1968 she became confined by an illness that lasted for seven years of isolation. Her death came quietly, in the small hours of January 27, 1975. She was granted the equivalent of a state funeral. Tributes and messages of condolence flowed in from Church leaders and politicians of many countries, as well as professional bodies, simple grateful patients, and marginalized people.

At her funeral Mass, William Cardinal Conway recalled Mother Mary's "quite remarkable gift of clear vision, a capacity to see the total picture of what she was about and where in that picture were the vital things that she had to do, the peaks she had to climb. Her faith and almost childlike confidence in God gave her courage, a daring almost, to climb those peaks with gaiety and then to move briskly on to her next range." Her inspiration echoes through time. Facing today's challenges, the Sisters and associates of the Medical Missionaries of Mary believe the high hills that contain that echo are theirs to climb.

# 41

# Tom Doyle

## *(1905–1992)*

## Layperson, Legionary of Mary

### *Liam Hayden*

During his lifetime, Tom Doyle was unknown outside Legion of Mary circles, and today his name is only slightly known among the current crop of legionaries. This would not have been of the slightest concern to this most humble of men; however, to this writer, Tom was a giant of the spiritual order, and to those who knew him, he left a legacy of holiness in the truest sense of the word.

Tom was born on August 31, 1905, at Carrigeen, Baltinglass, Co. Wicklow, the fourth of six children born to Patrick and Mary Doyle. The Doyles were of farming stock with a small holding at Carrigeen. Tragedy struck in 1910 when TB claimed the lives of his father in June 1910, then his mother in September of the same year. The same disease had claimed the life of his sister Rose, who died seven months after her, and, in later years, his sister Mary at the age twenty-two. Following the deaths of his parents, Tom and his brothers Patrick and James were sent to Saint Vincent's school and orphanage at Glasnevin in Dublin, while their sisters Mary and Julia were admitted as boarders to the Holy Faith convent school, also in Glasnevin. The family was eventually reunited under the care of their uncle, who farmed at Rathvilly, Co. Carlow.

After schooling at Rathvilly, Tom completed his education at the Patrician Brothers School at Tullow, where he was a contemporary of Kevin Barry. He then returned to work on his uncle's farm for two years before moving to Dublin, where he was employed by Messrs. Shiels of Moore Street as a grocer's apprentice. He was not lonely for company as his Aunt Sissy was Matron of Cork Street Fever Hospital, and his uncle Denis Doyle, to whom Tom was very close, ran a successful business in Camden Street.

As often happens in extraordinary spiritual lives, a purely chance meeting was to alter the direction of Tom's life. In 1923, while sheltering from the rain under a bridge at North Strand with his friend Michael Murphy, a mutual acquaintance, who was sheltering with them, told them he had to leave as he had to go to his Saint Vincent de Paul meeting that evening. Tom enquired as to the location and time of the meeting and resolved to "give it a try" the following week. He followed his intuition and turned up at Myra House, Francis Street, where, as Providence would have it, Frank Duff was a member of one of the conferences meeting there.

The Legion of Mary's Morning Star hostel opened its doors to the city's poorest in March 1927, and, while still a member of the Saint Vincent de Paul Society, Tom was invited to visit. He helped with the general chores there until 1930, when he decided to throw in his lot with the fledgling Legion and give his undivided spare time to the hostel. This momentous decision to volunteer as a full-time indoor Brother was described by Frank Duff as "the best news I've heard in a long time". In later years, Tom divulged to his sister-in-law Vena Doyle that "Our Lady had shown me the way I should go."

At this time, the indoor staff was comprised of two elderly men, so this young twenty-six-year-old was a gift to the infant Legion; it allowed Frank Duff to give his undivided attention to the development of the Legion. Shortly after becoming full time in the hostel, Tom was appointed manager, a position he occupied up to his retirement in 1986. By 1936, the number of men staying at the Morning Star had risen to 200, fifty men in each of the hostel's four dormitories. Indoor staff numbered four, and these were supplemented by three vibrant praesidia with almost sixty brothers in total. Tom founded one of these praesidia, Stella Maris, and served two six-year terms as president. This praesidium would in turn start five new praesidia.

Tom's daily life soon assumed a regular pattern. He began his day with Mass. Brother Kevin Crowley of the Capuchin community at

Saint Mary of the Angels, Church Street, clearly remembers Tom waiting to enter the gate at Bow Street each morning for the 6 A.M. Mass, which he served each day; sometimes he served a second Mass at 6:30 A.M. After Mass, Tom returned to the hostel and prepared the residents' breakfast having a light repast himself. He then organized the duties for the indoor staff. Having dealt with the post, and any other matters demanding his personal attention, he donned Wellington boots, rubber gloves, and set about cleaning the toilets. He reserved this duty for himself, and one can only assume that his humility dictated the most menial jobs should be done by him.

After one o'clock lunch, Tom went to his room, which was separated from the oratory altar by a thin wooden partition. He was resolute in being as close as possible to Jesus at all times, and he placed enormous value in being that close to the Blessed Sacrament during his private time. After a short nap, he was back at hostel duties; he remained at his post until late evening. The afternoon period was always punctuated by prayer in the hostel oratory whenever his busy schedule allowed. He retired to bed at 10:30 P.M. It is worth mentioning here that Tom did not allow himself the luxury of a decent mattress but had only a very thin one. Michael Murphy, an indoor Brother, recalls being asked to sleep in Tom's room while Tom was on holiday. He was so happy to revert to his own room on Tom's return, as sleeping on that bed was akin to sleeping on boards.

Sid Quinn, who served as an indoor Brother for forty-two years, maintained that Tom experienced mystical prayer as he was almost incommunicado during his private time in the oratory. On one such occasion, Sid, who, by nature, was not a person of emotion, said that he perceived the odor of roses. When questioned later about this, he was adamant about his perception. Frank Duff was also known to comment on how he often discovered Tom in the oratory in a state of what seemed to be mystical prayer. As a devotee of Our Lady, Tom practiced the True Devotion to Mary throughout his life. He stressed his utter reliance on Our Lady to intercede with her Son for the many graces needed to manage the hostel, especially in the many crises that occurred. In the same spirit, he was completely detached from material things. The Capuchins, who sent many seminarians to the Morning Star during the summer months, noted that all of them reported the extraordinary effect Tom Doyle had on them. Several orders and congregations did likewise, and the students reported to their superiors the holiness evident in the manager of the hostel.

It is important when speaking of Tom Doyle to know that his life encompassed more than the hostel. He regularly visited Mountjoy prison to comfort residents incarcerated there, and the prison authorities were so impressed by him that they petitioned him to counsel other prisoners. His heavy Legion workload precluded him from acceding to this request, however he was instrumental in founding a praesidium to tackle this much needed work. He was very much involved with the development of the Legion at home and abroad. He initiated discussion groups in the Morning Star to help the men know more about their Catholic Faith, and this grew into a wider Legion activity called "The Patricians". Tom was by no means a prolific letter writer, and his Legion correspondence was confined to his role as a Concilium correspondent. Reading his letters to Madras, now renamed Chennai, in India, one could not but be impressed by the eloquence and construction of his letters; this from a man with minimal formal education. His knowledge of the hierarchical structure of the Catholic Church was thorough, and he was often called on to deal with various problems that arose at his council.

He was prominent in the Legion's Peregrinatio Pro Christo (PPC) movement from its inception in 1956 and volunteered for a project in the UK every year. He took part in the first ever PPC project to Sweden and was often delegated to lead the PPC team of which he was part. At the instigation of Frank Duff, the chief Legion council, Concilium, introduced the role of counselor; this group of people was composed of legionaries who had given, and continued to give, sterling service to the Legion. Tom Doyle became a counselor and as such had a major input into the deliberations governing the Legion worldwide.

All life was to be found in the Legion hostels, and Tom was often challenged in his work, but his gentle ways, his patience and charity managed to keep him grounded. The Capuchin, Brother Kevin Crowley, recalls on several occasions noticing cuts or abrasions on Tom's face, and on querying, the cause was told: "Ah, a little bother last night", or some similarly dismissive remark. On another occasion, Tom was struck by a man in the dining hall while the Rosary was being recited in the nearby oratory. Tom Foley, a formidable but affable man, marched into the oratory stripped to the waist shouting,

"I want the man who hit Brother Doyle NOW!" Needless to say, no one budged. Tom suffered many unprovoked attacks in the Morning Star, suffering a broken ankle on one occasion and a broken wrist in another attack. During the late 1960s and early 1970s, Tom was "dispensing" medication to mental patients who were residing in the hostel during the evening mealtime. An aggrieved man upended the tray containing the tablets, scattering the medication all over the floor of the dining hall. This incident precipitated the ending of Tom's brief medical career, and from then on tablets were issued to the men at their local dispensary. The many incidents that occurred during Tom's years in the Morning Star were so numerous as to warrant a book on their own, yet one can appreciate that looking after 150 men, many of them bedraggled and bitter, demanded courage, dedication, and, above all else, a prayerful attitude while looking after "the most wretched and dejected of the population". It was here that Tom's virtue emerged.

After fifty-three years of valiant service, Tom retired to a well-earned rest under the care of the Little Sisters of the Poor at the Sacred Heart Residence, Sybil Hill, Raheny, Dublin. I visited him almost weekly and kept him up to speed with news of the hostel and the Legion generally. He loved the tranquility of the place as it gave him all the time in the world for prayer. The Sisters knew that they had a very special person living with them as his holiness was obvious to all.

On October 30, 1992, Tom breathed his last. His mortal remains were brought to the Morning Star for veneration, but as the oratory was deemed too small for the expected congregation, the obsequies took place in his beloved Saint Mary of the Angels Capuchin Church, where a choir of legionaries sang the hymns and a group of Legion priests concelebrated the Requiem Mass. In accordance with his wishes, he was brought to Glasnevin Cemetery, where he was interred in the Morning Star plot, to rest with his beloved homeless men.

It is my earnest hope that the cause of Tom Doyle will be introduced and that I will live to see the day when he is raised to the altars as a Legion saint. Frank Duff once said to Sid Quinn, "You know, they speak a lot about Edel Quinn, but where do you leave Tom Doyle?"

Tom preached a sermon on love every day he lived. His life said all there was to say.

# 42

# Dame Judy Coyne

## (1904–2002)

## Layperson and founder

### *Mary Wilson*

Judy Coyne was one of the driving forces in the development of Knock Shrine. For seventy-three years she worked tirelessly to promote, enlarge, and enrich what was to become one of the major Marian Shrines of the world. She was a visionary woman ahead of her time.

Born in 1904, the youngest of eleven children, Judy's father was a well-to-do farmer, owning land outside Claremorris. She was educated at Taylor's Hill School in Galway and in 1923 married Liam Coyne, a District Justice for Mayo. Shortly after their marriage, they purchased Bridgemount House, some miles from Castlebar, which would be her beloved home until she died in 2002. They immediately set about modernizing it, and here they created a garden, entertained widely, hosted tennis parties, and lived a life of considerable privilege. Early in their married life, they helped found the "Mayo Industrial Development Organization" to promote Irish Industry across the county, an indication even at this stage of their commitment to charitable work.

Their initial interest in Knock was sparked following a visit in 1929 when the fiftieth anniversary of the apparition was commemorated. Shortly afterward, they visited Lourdes and were immediately struck by the contrast. At that time, Lourdes was a well-developed pilgrimage site, while the village of Knock was small, poor, and backward, with no facilities for visiting pilgrims. Judy and Liam realized that if the shrine were to grow, then the first task was to advertise it across Ireland. At that time, involvement by the laity in anything concerning the Church was discouraged, so it took considerable persuasive powers to obtain support from the Church authorities to proceed. However, the then Archbishop of Tuam, Thomas Gilmartin, was sympathetic and supportive of their ideas. Firstly, they commissioned over half a million leaflets explaining the apparition and requesting prayers for Knock's development. These they distributed widely, visiting and speaking in virtually every religious house in the country and organizing broadcasts on Radio Éireann. Archbishop Gilmartin asked Liam to write a history of Knock, and together he and Judy collected evidence from the remaining living witnesses and the pilgrims who ascribed their cures to visiting the shrine. Liam published *Cnoc Mhuire in Picture and Story*, the first history of Knock, in 1935.

In the same year, they founded the Knock Shrine Society—a group of lay volunteers who would work to promote and develop the shrine. The voluntary helpers that enlisted were called handmaids and stewards, and the society, which continues to this day, has played a huge role in the development of the shrine. Over the years, many thousands of men and women have selflessly devoted their time to volunteering to care for people with disabilities and to assist pilgrims. A large Sunday pilgrimage would often need around 500 volunteers to ensure the smooth running of the day. As the society grew, offices were established in Dublin, and for many years they ran an office in New York. In 1938, the first edition of the *Knock Shrine Annual* was published; Judy would edit it for fifty-eight years. The *Annual* provided a record of the Knock year, a list of the pilgrimages and important events, together with a number of reflective and religious articles. In more recent years, it has proved a huge resource for recording the history of the shrine.

For over forty years, all pilgrimages to Knock were organized by Judy from Bridgemount. This entailed managing bookings throughout the season, coordination of the volunteers to tend to the visiting disabled pilgrims, and liaising with public transport. Ireland's national transport provider, CIÉ, designed special train coaches for stretchers, and a huge fleet of buses would be arranged to bring the pilgrims from the nearest train station in Claremorris, a distance of eight miles. From dawn to dusk, the telephone rang to resolve last-minute changes to plans, and each day Judy tackled an enormous mail bag—often answering around a hundred letters. There was then the gargantuan task of catering to be considered as at that time there were no facilities in Knock to provide any food. Every Friday and Saturday, Bridgemount was transformed into one enormous factory, often cooking food for over 600 helpers and disabled pilgrims, which would then be transported to Knock on the Sunday morning.

Having established the handmaids and stewards, Judy and the society started to discuss with the Church the possibility of setting up a permanent house in Knock to provide residential respite care allowing people to visit for a few days or a week at a time. In 1959, a small house was purchased near the presbytery, and Saint Joseph's was founded. It was run by a group of dedicated volunteer handmaids who gave up their careers to come and work there, supported by nurses and other carers who would devote a week of their annual leave volunteering in Knock. Over the years, demand grew, and in 1968 a new Saint Joseph's was opened. The Knock Shrine Society has over the years provided retreats and holidays for people with disabilities free of charge. Those who came included residents of the county homes scattered throughout the country, and for many it would be their only outing in the year. The society raised funds through a network of promoters to support this work. Many thousands benefited, returning each year for the break to which they had looked forward from one year's end to the next.

In 1964, Pope Saint Paul VI made the first state visit undertaken by a pontiff since 1809. This was to the Holy Land; there he presented a golden rose to Bethlehem, describing it as the most significant Marian Shrine in the world. On hearing of this, Judy thought that if the pontiff could travel to Jerusalem, then why not to Knock, and so began a campaign to invite the pope for the 1979 centenary. From then on, she raised the idea of inviting the pope to Ireland for the Knock Centenary at every opportunity. Initially, the suggestion was met with derision by the clergy, but over time her ideas gained traction and eventually obtained support from the Church hierarchy leading to an invitation finally being issued to the newly elected Pope Saint John Paul II. He accepted. On that September day, when

Pope Saint John Paul stated that coming to Knock was the "Goal of my visit to Ireland", Judy clearly knew that Knock had finally achieved its rightful place on the global stage.

In 1935, when Judy and Liam founded the Knock Shrine Society, the gable end of the church was bare; they believed that a chapel should be erected to represent what the witnesses of the apparition had seen on that wet night on August 21, 1879. The society paid for the first enclosed shrine, which was erected in 1940, thus enabling services to be conducted in relative shelter from the elements. However, this was always a somewhat makeshift structure, and Judy believed that the statues within it did not properly represent what the witnesses had described. Both she and Liam had met and interviewed a number of those witnesses in the 1930s and 40s and had a firsthand account of their experiences. For many years, she had asked the archbishop to commission new statues, but the request had fallen on deaf ears. However, in 1960, the twenty-fifth anniversary of the society, she repeated the request and finally obtained permission to proceed. An international competition of sculptors was organized, and the winner was a Professor Lorenzo Ferri, who was based in Rome. Once started, work on the statues progressed rapidly, with Professor Ferri visiting Knock. In November 1960, Judy was asked to go to Rome to oversee their completion. She spent a number of eventful weeks in his studio, and the Carrara marble statuary now adorning the impressive apparition chapel is, in large part, due to her influence. The completed statues were finally shipped to Ireland in 1961 but were put in a hayshed beside the presbytery in Knock while discussions about a suitable building continued. It was not until the papal visit of 1979 was imminent that it was finally decided to erect a new shrine in which to house them, a somewhat temporary structure that was finally replaced in the early 1990s by the splendid chapel seen today.

Although Judy was the driving force behind so many of the developments at Knock, she always shunned the limelight. Her objective was to promote, expand, and publicize Knock Shrine, and she was always ready to let others take the credit for this so long as her goals were realized. On many occasions, she declined radio and television interviews, happy for others to have the public recognition. Over the years she received a number of awards from the Church, including two *Pro Ecclesia et Pontifice* medals. In 1997, she was awarded a papal damehood in the Order of Saint Sylvester. She was the first woman in Ireland to be given such an honor but with customary modesty was reluctant to receive it, only agreeing on condition she accepted on behalf of the Knock Shrine Society.

Judy had a deep spirituality and faith that influenced her whole life. She would wake at 5:30 each morning to pray, attending morning Mass and a contemplative holy hour within the local church in Belcarra. She would say all fifteen mysteries of the Rosary each day. She combined this with the most phenomenal work ethic, starting her correspondence on her return from Mass each morning and continuing late into the evening. She continued with this regime into her late nineties and would sometimes joke that a handmaid had written to her saying she was now sixty and would therefore have to retire from her work at Knock. Close family and friends who knew her well appreciated her excellent sense of humor and the great humanity with which she viewed the world. She especially loved the young and was always keen to engage with and encourage them.

Judy Coyne was a woman ahead of her time. Until the 1960s and Vatican II, the laity were expected to leave all Church matters to the clergy. For many years, she and Liam experienced significant prejudice from many within the Church's hierarchy, though from the beginning there was a small cohort of clergy who supported their aims. After Liam's death in 1953, it was especially hard for her to continue to take such a prominent role as a single woman, but it was a challenge to which she rose with great courage and tact. Many of her suggestions were initially ridiculed, but all of them have now been realized. In the minutes of the Knock Shrine Society meetings of the 1930s are proposals to build an airstrip, purchase land around the church for development, and build a suitable shrine at the gable end of the church. It was she who initially suggested inviting the pope to Ireland. As a result of her tireless efforts, her quiet influence has been massive in the development of the wonderful place Knock Shrine has become in the twenty-first century. An initial investigation into the life and virtues of Dame Judy Coyne is ongoing.

# 43

# Father Colm O'Brien

## *(1973–2009)*

## Priest

### *Father Michael Mullins*

The untimely death of Father Colm O'Brien from cancer at the age of thirty-six on September 16, 2009, sent waves of grief throughout the Diocese of Waterford and Lismore and beyond. That grief was felt not only in his home area in Waterford city and in the parishes in Clonmel and Tramore where he had served as curate, but it touched in a special way the hearts of the many friends he had made both in his college days in Waterford and Maynooth and in the Focolare Movement. Speaking at his funeral, Bishop William Lee, in referring to his untimely passing, stated that "Death played a dual role. It shortened his life, but it underlined its quality."

That quality of life made such an impact that nine years later on November 28, 2018, more than a hundred people gathered in the Hotel Minella in Clonmel in response to a call by Bishop Alphonsus Cullinan, who had been hearing of Father Colm even before he came to the diocese, and since coming had heard people talking about the possibility of his cause going forward. The people from Clonmel and the surrounding area were joined by members of the Focolare Movement. They gathered to share stories of Father Colm's life and the impact it had had on them and on their community. They spoke of his good humor, his deep devotion to the Eucharist, his exceptional but unostentatious piety and humility, how he attracted queues of people to his confessional, and above all how he bore his illness with great patience. Listening to the testimonies of so many people, one saw the huge impact he had made on their individual and communal lives in so short a time. After the meeting, which was overseen by Father Michael Toomey, the bishop said: "It was a wonderful meeting, celebrating holiness, goodness, simplicity and faith, and there was a beautiful sense of grace on the night." On April 9, 2019, a large group gathered in Saint Paul's Pastoral Center in his home parish in Waterford City for a similar sharing of testimonies to the impact he had had on their lives from his earliest days.

Colm O'Brien was born on January 20, 1973, son of Tom and Josie O'Brien in Belvedere Drive, Saint Paul's Parish, Waterford City. He attended the local primary and secondary schools in the parish. From his earliest years, Colm showed great spiritual depth, evident in his attention to personal prayer and in his interest in the Church and the liturgy, enriched through his experience as an altar server. He was a very good example to his young friends.

While still a young boy, he made known his wish to become a priest in order to serve God and God's people. He attended several "open days" in Saint John's College, the diocesan seminary, and those involved in organizing the open days saw in him great promise for a life of holiness and service in the priesthood. He looked forward eagerly to going to the seminary and beginning his spiritual and pastoral formation and his academic studies. However, he postponed his entry to the seminary for a year due to the terminal illness of his mother, in order to be with her and the family at a difficult time. During that year, he worked in a local supermarket. Being with his mother during her illness made a deep impression on him, and seven years later at his ordination, he spoke very movingly of his mother and of the experience of being with her during that very special time.

He became a seminarian for the Diocese of Waterford and Lismore and attended Saint John's College from 1994 until it closed in 1999, when he was transferred to Saint Patrick's College, Maynooth. He supported and inspired his fellow seminarians in Waterford and Maynooth and joyfully embraced the challenges of his spiritual, human, academic, and pastoral formation. He was a very positive presence and influence as he impacted on his fellow students with his prayerful words and ways and with his sense of the spiritual dimension of life in all its aspects. He showed a cheerful disposition to all around him. He was noted for his simple ways, his sense of humor, his warm friendship, and how he was always ready to put himself out for others.

During his student days, he came in contact with, and embraced wholeheartedly, the spirituality of the Focolare Movement with its great emphasis on Jesus' prayer "that they all may be one". He welcomed all who came to him or approached him on the street. The spirituality of the movement also places great emphasis on the prayer of "Jesus forsaken" with the cry of dereliction from the Cross, "My God, My God, why have you forsaken me?" This prayer of Jesus in his final hours would prove to be one of the greatest supports for Colm during his untimely illness and impending death.

Colm was ordained in his home parish of Saint Paul's in Waterford City on June 4, 2000. Among the many words of praise spoken on the occasion were those I delivered as a former president of Saint John's College and Colm's Scripture teacher in Waterford and Maynooth. I said that "time will show the quality of this man." Though that time was to be so short, his uncle recalled those words at his funeral and remarked how prophetic they had been.

Father Colm served as curate in the parish of Saints Peter and Paul in Clonmel from 2000 until 2008, when he was appointed to Tramore, where he served for the last period of his life. He immersed himself in parish life and was regarded as a man of warm personality and a priest of great generosity. His life of prayer gave him the grace to feel deeply for all the people he met. His pastoral touch grew, deepened, and was refined with experience and time. He was attentive to every person he met, seeing Jesus in each person and seeing himself as the servant of each one. If you walked on the street with Colm, you couldn't help but notice the many people who would greet him and stop to talk with him. He was so approachable that he regularly arrived late for appointments because of the many people who approached him in the street. He clearly made a deep impression on them and touched their lives in many different ways. Some ill people still keep his photo by their bed to experience his ongoing comforting presence. One woman who had never met him came to the meeting in the Minella Hotel because she felt so close to him and his protecting presence because of what she had heard about him.

Father Colm had a particular rapport with teenagers and young people. He was a member of the diocesan catechetical team for primary schools, where his kindness, approachability, and ready humor endeared him to many young people. His picture is in both primary schools in Clonmel where he served, and he is still cherished by the teachers though the pupils are long gone. At his funeral, parishioners from Clonmel were saying that Father Colm was the countersign to the bad publicity the Church and the priests had been experiencing and that people were holding him up to the younger generation as a shining example of priesthood and Christian living.

His unwavering faith and life of prayer gave him the grace to face his fatal illness and death so soon after his mother had traversed that same path. Very shortly before he died, a few of his friends, including myself, met him for an evening meal. His courage in the face of his fatal illness and imminent death was most edifying. "I cannot be selfish," he said, "as a priest I saw young mothers die leaving their children." Two weeks before his death, he met four of his priest friends and planned his funeral liturgy and gave specific instructions on the readings and liturgical music. Later that same day, Bishop William Lee visited him. He advised the bishop of his wishes and, true to form, told him not to worry about the homily.

On Wednesday, September 16, 2009, Colm was very ill, yet still fully aware of all who had gathered around him: his father, Tom, his aunt Lily, her husband Tony, his sister Lisa, his aunts and uncles, and his friends Father Michael Toomey and Father (now Bishop) Brendan Leahy. At 9 P.M., the hour of his death, those gathered around Colm sang the "Salve Regina"—and Colm's eyes began to open, and he mouthed along the words as he took his final breath.

Father Colm is a priest for our time. In the past, a vocation could be seen as an entry into a way of life that commanded respect and offered security, education, and social status. Families and friends boasted of members in the priesthood and religious life. Recent years have seen a significant change in family and peer support for vocations. The falloff in vocations to the priesthood and religious life had started with wider access to education and career opportunities. Then the dark age of abuse, scandal, failure, and cover-up on the part of Church authority resulted in a hardening of attitudes and even open hostility toward the vocation choice. Like the Little Flower,

Saint Thérèse of Lisieux, Colm did the ordinary things extraordinarily well. He would have blended seamlessly into the company of the carpenter from Nazareth and his fishermen disciples as they left all worldly attachments to become fishers of people and proclaimers of the Good News of the Kingdom.

As the Church struggles to emerge from a period of scandal and bad press, Colm's open simplicity and humility are a hallmark of what a priestly and religious vocation should be. He provides the headline—a model of priesthood for today, of total commitment to the Gospel. No show, no ambition for recognition or promotion, no cultivating of image, just straightforward Christian living of the Gospel characterized his life and priesthood. His impact on the community in the very teeth of the most difficult period of scandalous revelations provides a model of priesthood and hope for the future of the Gospel.

Perhaps if we were to pick a piece of Scripture to describe Colm's life, we would need go no farther than his favorite Scripture passage, which was read at his funeral, a passage that reflects his spiritual and human life. The passage from Micah 6:8 is like a summary of the main themes of Amos, Hosea, and Isaiah, and it sums up Colm's life and ministry:

> He has showed you, O man, what is good;
> And what does the Lord require of you
> but to do justice, and to love kindness,
> and to walk humbly with your God?

To reiterate the words of Bishop Lee at Colm's funeral: "death played a dual role. It shortened his life, but it underlined its quality", a sentiment so well expressed in the Book of Wisdom (4:7–9):

> But the righteous man, though he die early, will be at rest.
> For old age is not honored for length of time,
> Nor measured by number of years;
> but understanding is gray hair for men,
> and a blameless life is ripe old age.

# 44

# Mary Ann Gemma O'Driscoll

## (1990–2015)

### Layperson and missionary

*Megan McNulty Henderson*

Like her millennial peers, Mary Ann Gemma O'Driscoll seemed to be desperately searching for her calling amid the chaos of twenty-first-century life. The life of a wife and mother appealed to her, but so did the life of a religious, especially the idea of being a Missionary of Charity, working with the poorest of the poor. On the surface, it may have seemed as if her whims changed daily, that she had an immature or indecisive temperament. But beneath it all, Mary Ann strove to follow the promptings of the Holy Spirit, even when that led her to working as a missionary in Liberia in the midst of a deadly Ebola epidemic, and dying there at the premature age of twenty-four.

Named after her grandmother, she was born in 1990, the fifth of seven children in a humble North Dublin home, where she was influenced by both her mother's American roots and her father's pure Dublin sentimentalism. The house teemed with the predictable chaos of a large family, but also with the deep bonds of familial love. The entire family frequented the local parish, Our Lady of Dolours in Glasnevin, and the nearby Redemptoristine convent of Saint Alphonsus.

The O'Driscoll family were home-schooled, and most of Mary Ann's childhood was spent surrounded by her siblings in the familial warmth of the kitchen or near the fire in the small sitting room.

With few opportunities for private space or time, the children learned early from their parents that family, faith, and charity were the most important values of all. And with an instinctual moral compass, Mary Ann realized that love meant sacrifice and togetherness, not extra Christmas presents or luxurious amenities—a lesson that would produce much fruit throughout her life.

Renowned in later life for her infectious joy, this was not always evident in her youth. Growing up, she was moody, sensitive, and extremely stubborn. Her sisters recount that "nobody could glare or stare like she could." And though she had a natural attraction to the Faith, she was no stranger to bouts of vanity; her family distinctly remembers her choosing Saint Gemma Galgani as her Confirmation saint because she happened to be the prettiest saint in her book.

As Mary Ann stood at the edge of adulthood, she was excited about the unknown opportunities God would place in front of her. While she waited for clarity about her "calling", she would attend university and resolved to respond to God's love and grace in her life by sharing it with others in the small moments of her everyday life.

Mary Ann was not perfect in this period of her life. She was an average student but had a contagiously happy personality, making her a popular member of the frisbee team and the pro-life groups of which she was an enthusiastic member. Though she remained confident in God's Truth, she still wrestled with how to balance her faith and her relationship with her secular friends. College life had its distractions, and socializing and relationships tempted her periodically, but she already had a soft heart for those around her who seemed lost. This is evidenced in her compassion for millennial friends who did not know God; their lack of faith saddened her but also reinvigorated her personal faith and adherence to the Church's teachings.

After college and working hard to pay off her school debt to her parents, Mary Ann became more convinced that whatever path she chose in life must be oriented to the service of God's Kingdom. The more she encountered colleagues and friends who had no love for the Heavenly Father, the more determined she was to live her life for Jesus. By this time, she began signing all her documents and correspondence as Mary Ann Gemma as a reminder to herself of her decided service to God. The decision to save money to buy a plane ticket to Liberia was one of the easiest decisions of her life. She never planned on actually becoming a "missionary"; it was a term she would have been uncomfortable associating with herself. She simply identified a way to follow Jesus' command to take his Good News to the ends of the earth and went where she felt God called.

At the time of her first trip to Liberia in February of 2013, Mary Ann would never have guessed that a small rural village in one of the poorest, most war-ravaged countries in Africa would become the place she felt closest to God—or where her life would eventually end. Her new home became Liberia Mission, Inc., a Catholic charity closely associated with the Franciscans. Its work in Liberia included a Catholic school for about 300 local children, a residential home for over eighty of the "poorest of the poor" youth, a Catholic church and growing Catholic community, and a farm with year-round crops and animals.

Whether tutoring children in history, leading praise songs in morning and night prayer, or introducing and managing the after-school program for job training, Mary Ann became totally invested in the people around her. She had no farming experience, nor had she ever been interested in teaching, but that did not limit her—or the Holy Spirit working through her. By the end of her first three months in Liberia, she had fully embraced two fundamentally important truths: that her path to discipleship would be through self-sacrificing love to the Liberians (many of whom she realized had lost hope in themselves and in their circumstances) and that she would do everything she could to defend the dignity and worth inherent in each and every one there.

Over the course of the next two years, Mary Ann went back to Liberia three more times and was given greater and greater responsibility. She never liked the formality of becoming an "employee" of the mission, with a specific job title, but she was becoming increasingly central to the work of the mission. The mission leadership began to recognize that Mary Ann "gave herself freely, openly, and constantly to the Holy Spirit" and that broken generators, rebellious teenagers, or low funds could not derail the operation of God's grace working through her life.

Her first transition was into a House Mother role where she realized that to show the children their worth, she needed to introduce them personally to Christ in an ever more intimate and radical way. While other staffers and volunteers were burning out from exhaustion or discouraged by the everyday difficulties, she started a volunteer group called "Souldiers for Christ" and led youth and staff to live the Corporal Works of Mercy. Sometimes ten, sometimes twenty people would set out from the mission to visit the lonely, help the needy, console the sorrowful, or feed the hungry. They might walk ten minutes to help local families in their community or drive several hours to assist faraway parishes or the Missionaries of Charity in downtown Monrovia. Mary Ann showed the "Souldiers" that only by giving of themselves in love could they hope to live as members of Christ's body and share in his joy on earth—the same joy that she exuded in her own person. As Liberia Mission stated immediately following her death, "Mary Ann's most powerful impact on Liberia Mission was the faith she instilled in our students."

Mary Ann yearned to spread the Gospel on her breaks away from Liberia as well. Though she admitted it was more difficult due to the constant distractions of modern comforts back in Ireland, she never turned from Christ. She took the pro-life message across Ireland in 2013 as part of the Crossroads pro-life initiative and enthusiastically offered up long days, bed-less nights, and blistered feet for the sake of spreading the Gospel of Life. She also regularly volunteered for the Pro-Life Campaign, which recounted that anyone who ever knew Mary Ann would "reflect with joy and gratitude on Mary Ann's tremendous contribution, in her too-short life, to the great cause of promoting human dignity". She constantly gave her time and resources to her family as well, especially her nephew and niece whom she always appreciated as the epitome of God's love for their family.

Mary Ann's final job on the mission was the one she wanted least. In fact, she initially turned down the offer to take over as director. She could not believe that God wanted her—a twenty-four-year-old with no leadership experience or management training—to lead the mission through one of the worst crises they had seen yet: the Ebola outbreak of 2014–2015. Mary Ann had been in Liberia at the beginning of the outbreak but had returned to Ireland on the insistence of her family. But she was determined to return. She always trusted God would protect the mission from the worst of the outbreak and would say, "We'll be grand as long as we follow him." But she grappled with a lack of confidence in herself, and also with her family's deep attachment to her and their fear she would succumb to Ebola, a truly deadly virus that can kill up to 90 percent of those it infects.

In early 2015, however, Mary Ann realized that she had to let God use her as he wished. Accepting her new position as director of Liberia Mission, she wrote a letter to her parish in Glasnevin asking for prayers and support: "It is a huge challenge surrendering everything to God—your weaknesses, your strengths, your worries, your anxieties, and your ambitions. But there is incredible joy in giving it all to God." She felt completely at home in the simplicity and struggles of life at the mission, writing that "It was a home to me because it is the place I feel closest to God. I feel like I am best able to live as he intended when I am here."

Her last months in Liberia as the director were not easy. Mary Ann had to step back from her friendships with many of the children and staff as she balanced fundraising efforts, school management, and the spiritual development program for the entire mission. She recounted missing the chance to just spend time chatting on the school steps, but she knew it was her sacrifice to make. She had immense inner peace from listening to God's directions and was as outwardly joyous as she had ever been. And the fruits were plenty. As she predicted, the mission was largely spared the ravages of Ebola, and the church, school, and farm programs continued to grow under her leadership.

God unexpectedly called Mary Ann Gemma O'Driscoll to eternity on the morning of July 15, 2015, after a bus hit her on the side of the road. If she had known her fate, she surely would have laughed and told everyone, "I told you so"—God had protected the mission from Ebola, even if he had other plans for Mary Ann. She rejoiced in death, as she did in life. She knew she had seen the face of God in those she served and was confident that God had used her in innumerable ways, even if she did not always understand where that was leading.

Those who knew Mary Ann cannot deny the sense of having been touched by a "saint". She is a timely role model for a generation of millennials who seek meaning, but who will only ever find it in generous self-sacrifice.

# CONTRIBUTORS

**Sister Phyllis Behan, R.S.C.,** is a Religious Sister of Charity living in Dublin and is currently the Vice-Postulator for the Cause of Venerable Mary Aikenhead. Her background is in education, counseling, spiritual guidance, and retreat work. She can be contacted at: rsccause@rsccaritas.com.

**Brother Donal Blake, C.F.C.,** a native of Doneraile, Co. Cork, he joined the Christian Brothers in 1958. After studies at the Marino Institute of Education and UCC, he completed his Ph.D. at the University of Hull and Lateran University. He pursued many roles in primary and secondary education in Ireland and England, and as lecturer in Marino, TCD, and Newman University, Birmingham. Author of a dozen books on Church and social history, he also served as a missionary in the West Indies. He is Roman Postulator for the Cause of Blessed Edmund Rice.

**Patrick Corkery, S.J.,** a member of the Society of Jesus (Jesuits), is originally from Cork. Since 2015, he has been studying to become a priest; during this period, he has spent time in the United Kingdom, the United States, and Canada. He also worked at Gonzaga Jesuit College, Dublin.

**Father Seán Coyle, S.S.C.,** is a Columban priest from Dublin who spent most of the years between 1971 and 2017 in the Philippines.

**Father Terence Crotty, O.P.,** is a Dominican priest of the community of Saint Saviour's, Dublin.

**Professor Fergus A. D'Arcy** is Professor Emeritus, University College Dublin. He has lectured in modern history since 1970, was Dean of the UCD Faculty of Arts through 1992 to 2004, and has published extensively in the areas of British and Irish political, religious, and social history. He is the author of *Raising Dublin, Raising Ireland: A Friar's Campaigns—Father John Spratt, O.Carm. (1796–1871)* (Dublin: Carmelite Publications, 2018).

**Deacon Gaspar DeGaetano** was born in Brooklyn, New York, in 1948, of Sicilian heritage. Married with two children, he worked as an engineer until his retirement in 2006. In 2007, he was ordained to the permanent diaconate for the Diocese of Knoxville, Tennessee. Serving first in Hidden Harbor, he was coordinator of the parish RCIA program. Now based at the Basilica of Saints Peter and Paul, Chattanooga, in addition to his duties, he is active in pro-life and charity work and pilgrimage ministry. He is the Diocesan Postulator and Roman Vice-Postulator for the Cause of Father Patrick Ryan.

**Fiorella De Maria** is an Anglo-Maltese author based in England. She writes historical novels and is best known for her Father Gabriel Mysteries. Her book for younger readers *Hugh O'Flaherty: The Irish Priest Who Resisted the Nazis* is published by Ignatius Press.

**Sister Brenda Dolphin, R.S.M.,** is a member of the Congregation of the Sisters of Mercy, Ireland, and at present is the Postulator for the Cause of Venerable Catherine McAuley.

**John Donovan** has been an advocate of Nellie's cause for over twenty years. He has delivered many presentations on Little Nellie along with exhibitions of her relics and personal items. A native of Ballyporeen, Co. Tipperary, he lives in Dungarvan, Co. Waterford, with his wife, Audrey. They have one daughter and three sons.

**Dominic Dowling,** editor of *The Sheaf* and vice-president of Saint Joseph's Young Priests Society, is a retired Chartered Insurer. He has published some eighty articles on religious affairs in *Catholic Life*, Manchester. This work relates mainly to the lives of lesser-known Catholics, places, and customs in Ireland. Currently his interests include interdenominational discussion through the monthly meetings of the Pauline Circle in Dublin. He is a Knight Commander of the Equestrian Order of the Holy Sepulchre of Jerusalem.

Father Conor Harper, S.J., was Vice-Postulator of the Cause of Blessed John Sullivan, S.J.; he died on January 25, 2024.

Liam Hayden was a native of Coolock in Dublin. Educated at O'Connell's Schools, he initially worked with Aer Lingus and then spent a number of years as an insurance broker. A member of the Legion of Mary since 1964, he was an indoor Brother in the Morning Star Hostel from 1969 to 1970. He served in various roles within the Legion, including officership in its world council, the Concilium. He lived in Drumcondra and was married to Moria; they have six children, all of whom are involved in the Legion. He died on Holy Saturday, April 3, 2021.

Sister Maria Therese Healy, O.Carm., was born in Dalkey, Co. Dublin. Moving to the United States in 1979, she joined the Carmelite Sisters for the Aged and Infirm. She is a registered nurse and has worked with the elderly in various capacities for the past forty years. Caring for the frail elderly, especially the dying, is a ministry she finds both challenging and filled with blessings. Returning to Ireland in August 2015 to live closer to her elderly parents, she is currently acting Prioress for the Sisters living in Our Lady's Manor and working in Pastoral Ministry and Mission promotion. The most fulfilling aspect of her work "... is the opportunity to become a vessel of love, accompanying the elders in our care, [helping them] to live fully, as they make their final journey home to God".

Father John S. Hogan, O.C.D.S., is a priest of the Diocese of Meath. He has worked as a parish priest, chaplain, and teacher. Co-host of EWTN's series *Forgotten Heritage*, he is the author of a recent biography of Saint Thomas Becket. He is the Diocesan Postulator for the Cause of Father Willie Doyle, S.J.

Dr. Patrick Kenny is Head of Organisation Studies and Senior Lecturer in the Faculty of Business at the Technological University Dublin. He is the President of the Father Willie Doyle Association and editor of *To Raise the Fallen: A Collection of the War Letters, Prayers and Spiritual Writings of Father Willie Doyle, S.J.*, published by Veritas and Ignatius Press in 2017.

Dave Kindy is a freelance writer who has worked with Holy Cross Family Ministries for many years and is a great supporter of Father Patrick Peyton's mission and sainthood cause.

Father Brian Lawless is a priest of the Archdiocese of Dublin and Vice-Postulator for the Cause of the Venerable Matt Talbot.

Sister Beatriz Liaño, S.H.M., is from Santander, Spain, and entered the Servant Sisters of the Home of the Mother in 1992. She is in charge of the community's press office and media relations.

Father David S. Marcham is the Vice-Postulator for the Cause of Venerable Patrick Peyton and Director of the Father Peyton Prayer Guild, whose members pray for Father Peyton's beatification and spread his message on the importance of family prayer.

Sister Elizabeth Maxwell, P.B.V.M., was educated by the Presentation Sisters, UCD and Loyola University Chicago. Her primary ministry has been in education as a teacher and principal.

Father Columba McCann, O.S.B., was born in 1961. He was educated at Gonzaga College and, after completing a degree in music at UCD, trained for the priesthood at Holy Cross College, Clonliffe, Dublin. He was ordained in 1988. In 2004, he joined the Benedictine community at Glenstal Abbey, taking the name Columba in honor of his blessed co-diocesan.

Father Eamonn McCarthy is a priest of the Diocese of Cloyne, ordained in 1998. He is a Consultor on the Historical Commission on the Cause for the Beatification of the Servant of God Frank Duff. He is presently full-time Priest Director to Radio Maria Ireland.

Father John McEvoy is a priest of the Diocese of Kildare and Leighlin. He has worked at Carlow College and been parish priest successively of Tinryland, Paulstown, and his present parish of Rathvilly. He is interested in local and diocesan history. He compiled the bicentenary volume *Carlow College 1793–1993* (Carlow: Saint Patrick's College, 1993) and edited *The Churches of Kildare and Leighlin 2000 A.D.* (Strasbourg: Éditions du Signe, 2001).

Father Bernard McGuckian, S.J., currently ministers in the People's Church, Clongowes Wood College, Co. Kildare. Over several decades he was Central Director of the Pioneer Total Abstinence Association of the Sacred Heart and editor of the monthly magazine *Pioneer*.

Father Michael Mullins is a priest of the Diocese of Waterford and Lismore. Following studies at the National University of Ireland, he received the B.D. and S.T.L. in Biblical Studies from the Pontifical University, Maynooth and an LSS from the Pontifical Biblical Institute in Rome. He completed his doctorate at the Angelicum. Director of Studies at the Irish College in Rome and tutor at the Gregorian University, he was Professor of Scripture at Saint John's College, Waterford, where he also served as Dean and President, after which he was lecturer in Scripture and Associate Professor at Maynooth. Other appointments included Diocesan Director of Ecumenism and Vocations Director. He is currently the parish priest of Ballybricken Parish in Waterford City. He is a regular contributor to pastoral and liturgical journals and an author of and contributor to several books.

Megan McNulty Henderson served as the Chief Financial Officer at Liberian Mission, Inc., from 2013–2014. She earned an M.A. in International Development on the George Mitchell Scholarship in Dublin, where she was introduced to the beautiful faith of the O'Driscoll family. She subsequently served in the United States military for five years and currently lives with her husband, Warren, in Brookline, Massachusetts.

Tom Neary is a native of Knock Parish in Co. Mayo. A graduate of the National University of Ireland and Saint Patrick's Training College, Drumcondra, Dublin, he taught in both primary and secondary schools for over thirty years. He became a steward at Knock Shrine in 1960 and later Chief Steward, an office he held until 2015. He has gained much experience in radio broadcasting and television programs, and was recently featured in the award-winning EWTN film *HOPE—Our Lady of Knock*. He has written numerous books on Knock Shrine, was editor of the *Knock Shrine Annual* for twenty years, and has contributed many features to local and national newspapers. He has been a Knock Shrine delegate to the European Marian Network Conference of Major European Shrines for a number of years and has lectured at various conferences. He and his wife live near Claremorris Town, and they have a grown-up family of four.

Sister Louise O'Connell, D.C., entered the Daughters of Charity in 1960 in Blackrock, Co. Dublin. Missioned to teach in Dublin, she has also worked in Nigeria, Kenya, and China. She is now assigned to Cork. She has always had an interest in the missionary life of her congregation both in the past and in new developments today.

Father Philip O'Halloran, M.H.M., is a Mill Hill Missionary priest from Callan, Co. Kilkenny, and is currently involved with Mill Hill Society work in Ireland. He worked in East Africa from 1988 to 2016, mostly in Uganda, with three of these years spent running the Mill Hill Basic Formation Program in Kenya. He is presently serving as provincial in Ireland.

Father Joseph O'Reilly, I.C., comes from Kingscourt, Co. Cavan. He attended secondary school at Saint Michael's Omeath, Co. Louth, in the 1970s, where he first became acquainted with Luigi Gentili. Father O'Reilly is now Provincial of the Irish American Province of the Rosminians (Institute of Charity).

James Pinto is a leading authority on the life and legacy of Father James E. Coyle. He is the founder of the Father James E. Coyle Memorial Project, Father Coyle website, and author of *Killed in the Line of Duty*. The Coyle Project respectfully promotes the life, sacrificial death, and legacy of this holy priest and seeks to advance greater understanding, reconciliation, and peace among all of God's children. With his wife, Joy, Jim hosts the EWTN series *At Home with Jim and Joy*.

Sister Angela Ruddy, M.S.H.R., is a member of the Missionary Sisters of the Holy Rosary. She is a graduate of Mater Dei Institute, Dublin, and of the Pontifical Angelicum University, Rome, where she obtained an S.T.L. She has been on mission in Cameroon, Tanzania, and South Africa. She was Vice-Postulator for the Cause of Bishop Joseph Shanahan.

Father Oliver Skelly is parish priest of Coole (Mayne) in Westmeath. A native of Kells, Co. Meath, and an alumnus of the Pontifical

Irish College in Rome, he was ordained in 1991. He served as curate in Tullamore (1991–1999) and Batterstown (Kilcloon parish) before being appointed to Coole in 2001. He is Vice-Postulator for the Cause of Alfie Lambe.

Sister Isabelle Smyth, M.M.M., joined the Medical Missionaries of Mary in 1961. She obtained an M.A. in Philosophy at NUI Maynooth, a Ph.L. at the Pontifical University, and a diploma in Sociology and Social Research at UCD. Her overseas missionary assignments included an appointment as Hospital Administrator in Tanzania and later among the Basic Christian Communities in Brazil. She then took up the post of Communications Officer with the Irish Missionary Union, after which she became Director of MMM Communications for eighteen years. She continues to research different aspects of the life of Mother Mary Martin and her family in collaboration with various media.

Father Paul Francis Spencer, C.P., has written books on Saint Paul of the Cross, the Founder of the Passionists, and Saint Charles (Houben) of Mount Argus. He is currently Vocations Director for the Passionists and parish priest of Mount Argus.

Sister Cecilia Sweeney, F.M.S.A., was born and bred in Donegal. After secondary school at Loreto Convent, Letterkenny, she entered the Franciscan Missionary Sisters for Africa at Mt. Oliver, Dundalk, Co. Louth. After novitiate and professional training at UCC and London University, England, she was assigned to East Africa, first serving at Mount Saint Mary's Secondary School in Namagunga, Uganda, and afterward at Saint Francis Girls High School, Thika, Kenya. In 1998, she was appointed to the Franciscan Education Center in South Africa. In 2013, she was elected to the Leadership Team in Dublin, an appointment that was renewed in 2019.

Dr. Cecilia Gutierrez Venable is the director of archives for the Sisters of the Holy Spirit and Mary Immaculate. She received her Ph.D. from the University of Texas at El Paso and has worked in university, city, county, and private archives and has taught history classes. She has published several articles and books and is co-editing an anthology, *Centuries of Voices*, on Black women in Texas. She is also working on a biography of Mother Margaret Healy Murphy. She resides in Adkins, Texas.

Mary Wilson undertook medical training at Saint Bartholomew's Hospital in London and has worked for over thirty years as an NHS consultant in Manchester specializing in breast radiology. She is married with three children. She is a grandniece and goddaughter of Dame Judy Coyne, with whom she spent much time over the years.

Steven R. Wolf is president of the Father Flanagan League Society and Vice-Postulator for the Cause. An Omaha, Nebraska, native who was born out of wedlock and raised by a single mother, he arrived as a troubled youth at Boys Town at the age of fourteen, in 1977. Graduating from Boys Town High School in 1980, he earned a degree in journalism and M.S. in public administration. He held positions as a newspaper reporter and public affairs official for the Pentagon in Washington, D.C., and founded a national level consulting firm. He retired from his part-time military career in the U.S. Army Reserve as a sergeant major after thirty-eight years of service in 2018. Married for twenty-eight years, he has five daughters. Raised in the Protestant tradition, he attended Protestant services while a youth at Boys Town, and he attributes his journey and conversion to Catholicism in 2001 to the inspiration and intercession of Servant of God Edward J. Flanagan.